ENCOUNTERING THE LIVING WORD:
RELATIONAL INDUCTIVE BIBLE STUDY

Jackie David Johns

Cheryl Bridges Johns

Foreword
French L. Arrington

CPM PRESS | CLEVELAND, TN

ENCOUNTERING THE LIVING WORD: RELATIONAL INDUCTIVE
BIBLE STUDY

CPM Press (Permissions)
840 Hancock Road NE
Cleveland, TN 37323

Encountering the Living Word: Relational Inductive Bible Study by Jackie David Johns
and Cheryl Bridges Johns.

xviii + 372 p. Includes bibliographical references.
ISBN: 979-8-218-99471-6
I. Johns, Jackie David. II. Johns, Cheryl Bridges.
III. Encountering the Living Word: Relational Inductive Bible Study.

Manufactured in the U.S.A.   2025

Editorial Assistance by Lois E. Olena (Keystrokes: Lois.Olena.com)

Cover Design: Jackie David Johns
Cover Art: iStock.com/kevron2001

Dedication

To

French Arrington

J. Martin Baldree

James M. Beaty

&

R. Hollis Gause

True Gifts from God:
Our Professors who Became
Our Mentors,
Friends and Colleagues

And to

Lois and Mary LeBar

Master Teachers and Mentors
Who Taught Us
How to Live in and Minister Out of the Word

Acknowledgments

We give thanks to the Administration and Board of Directors of the Pentecostal Theological Seminary for granting Jackie a sabbatical leave during which time he was able to complete much of his portion of this project.

We thank David Han and Barry Callen of Aldersgate Press for their helpful suggestions.

We also thank our dear friend Lois Olena for her gifted labors assisting us in editing the manuscript.

Special thanks to French L. Arrington for his constant encouragement and for writing the foreword.

Contents

Table of Figures

Foreword

Should you hope for a book that will help in your study of the Bible, this one written by Drs. Jackie and Cheryl Johns is an excellent resource. In *Encountering the Living Word*, they will guide you in your efforts to understand the Scriptures and to grow spiritually in Christ. The authors (a husband-wife team) have each taught courses for years to college and seminary students on how to study the Bible. Now they have written this wonderful book which achieves a blending of scholarly and devotional elements that are ideal for fruitful Bible study.

Encountering the Living Word is remarkable for its clarity, simplicity, organization, and its reverence for the Bible. The book is written with two primary goals: *The first* is to help people develop a relational approach to the Bible, that is, to help them have an actual encounter with God as they study His living Word. *The second* is to help people gain some basic skills in direct Bible study, known as *inductive Bible study*.

The authors know the difference between the study *about* the Bible and the study *of* the Bible itself. As they emphasize, *inductive Bible study* requires students to engage carefully with the Scriptures and to allow the Scriptures to speak entirely for themselves. So, in the direct study of the Bible, we need to be open and sensitive to the voice of God and allow Him to speak to us in whatever manner that He chooses.

The inductive approach, explained by Drs. Jackie and Cheryl Johns, follows a fourfold pattern:

1) It begins with **prayer**—which prepares us to listen to the voice of God and to be open to the illuminating, transforming work of the Holy Spirit. Doing Bible study in the atmosphere of prayer opens us to the Holy Spirit, who inspired the Scriptures and who is vital to the genuine understanding of the Word of God. Spiritual truth is taught by the Holy Spirit to hearts that are open to Him (1 Corinthians 2:10-13). So as we study, prayer opens us to the Holy Spirit and gives us a teachable mind.

2) The second distinctive feature of inductive study is **observation**. At this point, students of the Bible are ready to read straight through a passage or a book of the Bible. As you *observe* the Scripture text, you may want to read more than one translation to get a broad, general perspective of the passage or book. As you do this, questions about meaning and interpretation may come to mind.

The objective of this *observation phase* is to begin getting comfortable with the text and to identify key words and phrases, along with any questions one might have. The goal is not to try to answer questions or concerns at this time, but to simply note them so that they can be explored later. For example, in a study of the book of Jonah, you might note words that relate to one another, such as: *anger, compassion, pity,* and *repentance.* If the study is on a passage in Paul's Letter to the Romans, some important key words you might note are *righteousness* and *flesh.* In a passage in John's Gospel, you might notice the key words *darkness, light,* and the *Holy Spirit.*

Since *observation* is the foundation to solid interpretation and application of the Scripture, the recording of one's observations has great value. For inductive study, the authors recommend that you use a Bible that you can write in, so that you can easily note your observations and the insights that you glean from your study.

3) The third feature of inductive study is **interpretation**. Often, Bible students have questions. To answer their questions, they often turn to experts (maybe to a commentary, a Bible dictionary, or a theological work). There is nothing wrong in consulting experts, but it is good for us to seek the answers to our questions *in the Bible itself.* Examining directly what the Scriptures teach will often provide the information we need for reaching the right interpretation and for ministering to our spiritual needs.

Jackie and Cheryl Johns offer us a number of guidelines that are helpful in interpreting the Bible:

- Accept *the Bible as fully truthful and absolutely authoritative* for faith and living. As God's Word, the Bible has all the doctrine that is needed.

- Interpret Scripture in light of the *immediate context* of the passage and the *larger context* of the whole book of which the passage is part.

- Use *Scripture to interpret Scripture.* The best commentary on Scripture is Scripture itself.

- Separate the *local meaning* from the *universal meaning.* For example, the account of deliverance of God's people from Egypt gives many historical details, but the essential truth that is taught is that salvation rests completely on God's grace.

- Take the *literal meaning as the primary meaning.* First and foremost, Scripture should be interpreted literally. Be sure to understand what the Word says before looking for deep, hidden meanings.

- Consider the *type of literature* you are studying in the Bible (*historical, poetical, proverbial, gospel,* or *epistle*). The dominant literary approach of the Bible is narrative, which provides the overarching framework of the Bible as a whole. More than anything else, the Bible tells the story of God's relationship with His people.

- Expect *the Holy Spirit to assist* in the study and interpretation of Scripture. From time to time, the Spirit may cause new light to break forth on the Word of God. Spirit-filled believers have rightly emphasized what is called *Pentecostal* or *Charismatic interpretation* of God's Word. The witness of the Spirit causes the Word of God to touch our hearts and transforms our lives.

4) The final feature in the process of Relational Inductive Bible Study is to **respond** holistically to the Word of God. Nowhere in the Bible do we find teachings in isolation from life. The Biblical writers consistently relate their teaching either to the world or specifically to worshipers of God (that is, to Jews, the church, or individual Christians).

Responding to the Scriptures should be done with beginning and ending with prayer. Seeking God is so crucial to the aim of good Bible study, which should always be *transformation* (through both the Word and the Spirit). The Holy Spirit will uncover things buried in our hearts and consciences and will help us correct wrong thoughts and unrighteous behaviors. Also, the Holy Spirit will use God's written Word to help us put on the fruit of Spirit (Galatians 5:22-23).

As we study and lovingly respond to the teachings of the Bible, we will discover that all aspects of the Biblical text have relevance for our lives. The historical accounts describe the virtues and noble acts of people, as well as their vices and failures. The lives of the ungodly can serve as warnings to us, and through the accounts of godly people, we can learn principles of godliness and apply those truths to our own life.

As you study, to ensure that the great truths of Scripture take form in your life, it is good for you to think in terms of specifics: your job, use of money, and relationships with persons, organizations, and possessions. Remember, that in the application of Scripture that every passage contains *doctrine*, *reproof*, *correction*, and *instruction*. Discern what is there and only apply what is there.

For those who are looking for a book that will explain to you in an easy-to-understand way how to study the Bible itself, you need to look no longer. Jackie and Cheryl Johns have written exactly what you need. *Encountering the Living Word* has grown out of their wide range of knowledge of the Bible and their experience of teaching hundreds and hundreds of students, who have experienced great joy and satisfaction as they have learned how to study God's Living Word. This great book will do the same for you.

French L. Arrington, PhD, DD
Professor of New Testament Greek and Exegesis and
of the Niko Njotorahardjo Chair of the Restoration of David
at the Pentecostal Theological Seminary

Preface

"I had perceived by experience, how that it was impossible to establish the
laypeople in any truth, except the scripture were plainly laid before
their eyes in their mother tongue, that they might see the
process, order, and meaning of the text."

—William Tyndale

The purpose of this book is to help you become a better student of
the Bible. The Bible is the Word of God continually being
"breathed" by the Holy Spirit. In its pages God is speaking to each
of us personally and to all of us collectively. We must discipline
ourselves to have "ears to hear" what he is saying.

We believe the Bible is studied best prayerfully and inductively. In
this book we will encourage you make your Bible study a time of
communion with God. And we will introduce you to an inductive
approach to Bible study. In brief, this book aims to guide you into
personal encounters with the Word of God through an inductive
approach to Bible study.

Inductive Bible study is a form of direct, book by book, study of the
Bible. The books of the Bible were written one at a time and they
were originally read and studied as individual books. This suggests
that we should give priority to studying them as individual books
that have been compiled into one unified Book of Books.

The inductive approach asks three main questions (1) what is actually
said in this book, (2) based on what it actually says, what is the
meaning of what it says, and (3) how does God want me to respond
to what it means? This approach helps guard against reading into the

Bible things it does not say. Thus, the mantra of the inductive approach might be "let the Bible speak for itself."

Inductive Bible study can be traced to Wilbert Webster White (1878-1945) who systematized and developed it as a methodological approach to direct Bible study. In the early 20th Century, White became a driving force for popularizing inductive study of the Bible, especially among conservative Christians. He always gave credit for the basics of his approach to his mentor, William Raines Harper, who as a pastor and professor had promoted the idea of direct, book-by-book, chapter-by-chapter study of the Bible.

White's name may not be familiar to you, but early part of the twentieth century he was one of the most well-known Bible teachers throughout the world. Tens of thousands of people in the United States, India, England, and other places gathered to hear him teach.

In 1900, White founded the Bible Teacher's College, shortly thereafter renamed the Bible Teacher's Training School, then The Biblical Seminary in New York—and finally, New York Theological Seminary. Under White, the seminary became the seedbed for inductive Bible study. From there the inductive approach was transported around the world, especially through conservative Bible colleges that hired White's students to teach the Bible.

We were taught the inductive method in our graduate studies at Wheaton College. Our instructor, Howard Newsom, had been influenced by the LeBar sisters, Drs. Lois and Mary, who were also our mentors at Wheaton. The sisters were introduced to the inductive approach as students at Moody Bible Institute where Wilbert White had once served as professor of biblical studies. Their instructor had studied the methods under White.

However, our first exposure to the approach had taken place in November of 1974 when we went to Wheaton to interview for admission into the graduate program. One of the LeBar sisters would have conducted the interview except they were both out of town. We were directed instead to the office of Merrill C. Tenney, noted New Testament scholar and former dean of the graduate school, who generously conducted the interview. We had a warm and gracious conversation.

During that session, Dr. Tenney made a comment that created an indelible impression on us: "Do not come to Wheaton for what you will learn; you will learn the same things here that you would learn at any other Evangelical school. Come to Wheaton for how you will learn. Our approach is different from others." He proceeded to give a brief description of the inductive approach, which he used in all his classes. We were privileged to take two of his courses, the Gospel of Luke and the Gospel of John.

We are profoundly indebted to the professors at Wheaton for their impact on us personally and professionally. Each served as a model of Christian character and scholarship. Our time with them transformed our lives. Their Evangelical spirituality and ethos resonated with our Pentecostal spirituality and ethos. They were what we later came to call "Evangelicals-at-large."

However, we did feel some dissonance. Inductive methods turned our Bible study into joy-filled treasure hunts with life-changing discoveries, but it also seemed to reduce the sense of awe and wonder that we knew as Pentecostals. The challenge for us was to hold on to our own spirituality in Bible study while also seriously engaging the Scriptures using methods grounded in inductive reasoning.

Later, under the influence of R. Hollis Gause at the Pentecostal Theological Seminary (formerly Church of God Theological Seminary), we realized that our dissonance was due to differing theologies of Scripture. Gause helped us see that our spirituality resonated with a more dynamic view of the Bible. The Bible is not merely the Word of God in the sense of being from God; it is the Word of God in its existence and its essence. God inhabits His Word, making it always a living and present revelation. Inspiration of the Bible is never ending. God remains always present in the Bible speaking to us. That is what makes the Bible holy Scripture.

Years later, we came to speak of the Bible as the Spirit-Word of God. The Holy Spirit and the Word of God are two persons existing with the Father as one eternal Being, the Holy Trinity. Just as Jesus Christ is the union of the Word of God with human existence—fully God, fully human—the Scriptures are the union of the Word of God with human language—fully Word of God and fully human literature. These books are not the Word of God merely because of their origin and infallibility but because of God's abiding presence in them.

It is our conviction that believers should view Bible study simultaneously as worshipful conversation with God and as diligent exploration of the Word that is of God. This book, *Encountering the Living Word,* is written as a guide into Bible study that takes seriously the presence of God in His Word and also takes seriously the nature of the Bible as inspired human literature. We also take the sincere student of the Scriptures seriously as one invited by God into honest dialogue with God about His written revelation. We call this approach to Bible study Relational Inductive Bible Study (RIBS).

On a special note, we are committed to using inclusive language when communicating though any medium. However, in this case, we recognize that the books of the Bible are traditionally understood to have been written by men. We therefore chose to use masculine pronouns when referring to the authors of the books of the Bible. Also, we are very comfortable with the ancient tradition of using feminine pronouns in reference to the Holy Spirit. However, we have opted to follow the centuries old tradition of using masculine pronouns for the Spirit.

---Jackie & Cheryl Johns

Chapter 1

Introduction

God himself has condescended to teach the way: For this very end he came from heaven. He hath written it down in a book. O give me that book! At any price, give me the book of God! I have it: Here is knowledge enough for me.

—John Wesley

The Bible is the most glorious book ever written. Full of captivating stories, words of wisdom, soul stirring songs, personal letters, visions of the future, and much, much more, it truly stands as the "Book of Books." Dozens of persons during a timespan that covered hundreds of years scribed it, yet it all fits together like a seamless garment to tell the greatest story ever told—the story of God's love for His creation, a story that unfolds as the good news of Jesus Christ.

The Book of Books

Few who have read the Bible in its entirety would not readily attest to its beauty and complexity. It contains passages young children can easily grasp, yet other passages confound the most learned of persons.

No other book in human history has inspired such levels of devotion to others and insights into the self. On one hand, it has the most practical messages that speak to every aspect of human existence. On the other, it lifts the human spirit into the realm of the eternal.

It is a mystery filled with mysteries—truth for every nation and generation.

The Bible is both the most cherished and the least read of books in many modern Christian homes. The typical Christian reads the Bible only a few minutes a week or less and never takes the time to sit down and study it. Many, if not most, would say that beyond what they learned during childhood, the rest just takes too much effort to understand. They are content to let others study for them and feed them secondhand interpretations of the Scriptures.

But that is not what God intended. He desires for us to go beyond the 'milk' and eat the 'meat' of His Word (Heb 5: 11-14). He gave us the Bible so we might discover His will for our lives and—more importantly—so that we might know him personally. The Bible is the voice of God speaking to us so that we might live in fellowship him, not just know about Him.

A Living Word

This book, *Encountering the Living Word*, has been written to help you develop confidence in your ability to study the Bible and to get out of your study all that God wants you to receive. It is a book on how to study the Bible inductively—but not just a book on inductive Bible study methods. Good study methods are essential for a proper understanding of the Bible, but methods alone will not guarantee that we will hear what God is saying to us through the Scriptures.

For our study to prove most fruitful, we must approach the Bible in a way that honors the nature of the Bible as the inspired Word of God. It is more than human literature. It is a spiritual book that can only truly be understood if we are in touch with our own spirituality. We are spiritual beings who are by grace capable of communion with God.

There is no distance between God and His Word. The Bible is more than a record of words that God spoke long ago to special people.

It is the Word <u>of</u> God and not just words <u>from</u> God. The Scriptures are always being breathed by the Holy Spirit. When we approach the Bible as being <u>of</u> God, we come "face to face" with Him, and the discipline of Bible study becomes a worship-filled encounter—a sacred time of communion with God.

Meditate on this: the Bible is infused with God's presence, making it sacred space where we can meet with him. The Holy Spirit is always speaking through the Scriptures, and the Spirit is always working within us, to bring us into intimate fellowship with God (1 Cor 2:10-16). We should then study the Bible from the vantage point of seeing it as God speaking to us now and that on a personal level.

In the space of these ancient books, the Spirit of God seeks to teach us and renew us in the life of God. When we open ourselves to these things, studying the Bible will provide us with the nourishment needed for our journey into the fullness of knowing God (Eph 4:11-16).

Bible study should serve as a form of worship, as an event of full surrender to God.

Foundation Stones

The chief foundation stone of *Encountering the Living Word*, then, is that one should approach Bible study as a response to God's invitation to know Him more fully. We go to the Bible to encounter God because He has invited us to meet with Him there.

---

1. One should approach Bible study as a response to God's invitation to know Him more fully.

3

Another foundation stone of this book is that Bible study should serve as a form of worship, as an event of full surrender to God. We must come to the Scriptures with ears to hear the voice of God. We must hunger to go through and beyond the interpretation of the Bible into a place of communion with our Creator, a place where the Scriptures interpret us more than we interpret them. In that place, we come to know God better, and we come to know ourselves better. Through this kind of study, God works with us to make us better: better human beings, better followers of Christ, and better sons and daughters of His Kingdom.

2. Bible study should serve as a form of worship, as an event of full surrender to God.

A third foundation stone of this book is that the Bible must also be studied as human literature. The Bible is the eternal Word of God, but also the words of humans recorded in a variety of literary forms and styles. It is a book of divine origin, while at the same time fully a book of human origins. It is the Word of God wed to the thoughts of human beings, words conceived by the Holy Spirit within the hearts and minds of selected apostles and prophets. In it, God has joined himself to human language and works of human literature.

3. The Bible must also be studied as human literature.

Two Natures—One Book

As stated above, the Bible is both the living Word of God and divinely inspired human literature. It has two natures, and we must consider both natures when studying the Bible. It is a spiritual book to be approached as God's ongoing revelation and it is also human literature to be read and studied like all other literature. We should experience it as the voice of God to be heard, celebrated, and obeyed, and we should experience it as books to read and studied. *Relational Inductive Bible Study* (RIBS), the approach we describe in this book, attempts to guide the Bible student through the process of engaging both natures of the Bible at the same time.

We can best understand this approach as being like the growth of an intimate relationship. For this reason, we sometimes refer to it simply as "relational Bible study." Intimacy with someone requires that each person be both a subject who acts and an object that volunteers to be acted upon. We know someone more intimately only as we allow them to know us more intimately. The person we love is the object of our affections while at the same time we surrender ourselves to be the object of her or his affections.

We can best understand this approach as being like the growth of an intimate relationship.

Human relationships require an element of study. It may be informal study but it is study nonetheless; we diligently 'research' the person with whom we are entering an intimate relationship. We observe their appearance, behavior, and moods. We gather data, learning the names of their family members and friends, their birthdate, and their hobbies. We want to know their likes and dislikes. The deeper we move into knowing someone, the more we apply ourselves to knowing and remembering these things.

In Bible study, we should know that we are being loved just as we know that we love God and His Word. We should view the Bible as a great gift from God, a gift we are privileged to have and to hold. It is a gift of God's loving presence. The Bible is a treasure containing many treasures, and the greatest treasure of all is God himself. But never forget that you are also a treasure to God. In your Bible study, know that He is valuing you as you are valuing Him.

One of our cherished professors, Dr. Merrill C. Tenney, stated in class that we should study each book of the Bible as if it is a love letter from God. We do not read a love letter one paragraph at the time with long spaces of time between the readings. Neither do we skip around in the letter, reading one or two sentences and then jumping to another page to read a sentence there. No, we read it from beginning to end as soon as we receive it. Only then do we go back and analyze what our beloved has written. Why did he or she use that word? Why did he or she begin with that salutation and close the way he or she did? Did "love" mean friendly love or the kind I have for her or him?

We should study each book of the Bible as
if it were a love letter from God.

None of this implies that Bible study should be easy. Serious Bible study is hard work. It requires a disciplined mind, a devoted heart, and a humble spirit. We must bring to this task our best reasoning, good study skills, and sustained effort. We must work to maintain a determined desire for God and His Kingdom. We must apply ourselves to achieve a deeper understanding of God as we seek a better relationship with Him.

In one sense, this book is an introduction to a set of Bible study methods that are collectively known as inductive Bible study (a type of direct Bible study that requires students to carefully engage the Scriptures for themselves). In the past, these methods were sometimes referred to as "scientific Bible study."

The inductive approach takes great care to let the Bible speak for itself. It follows a set pattern. First, the student makes careful observations about what a passage of Scripture literally says and how those observations connect with the rest of the book being studied—**observe**. Second, the student interprets the meaning of those observations—**interpret**. Then the student considers how he or she should act in response to those interpretations—**apply**. At the heart of this approach is a firm commitment to limit our interpretations of the Bible to those drawn from observable facts within the text and the relationships that exist between the various facts, i.e., the factual.

This book, then, is written with two primary goals. First, we want to help you develop a relational approach to Bible study. Second, we want to help you gain some basic skills in inductive Bible study. Ultimately, these are the same goal. We want to help you strengthen your relationship with God by practicing *Relational Inductive Bible Study* (RIBS), Bible study filled with hope for the life changing presence of God.

How to Use this Book

Encountering the Living Word is in part a training manual on how to "rightly divide the Word of truth" (2 Tim 2:15). Because of its nature as a training manual, you should plan to not read it straight through like a novel. The first division of the book, "Foundations for Relational Inductive Bible Study," is comprised of nine chapters addressing some foundational issues for doing Relational Inductive Bible Study. The second division, "Methods of Relational Inductive Bible Study," is comprised of nine chapters intended to guide the student through the methods of an inductive approach to Bible study, including a chapter on how to lead a group in RIBS.

You should slowly work your way through Chapters 11 through 18; they include exercises in the various study methods. Each exercise builds on the ones that came before it. You should not go from one to the next until you have gained the basic skills each requires. Plan to spend some extended time practicing each of the methods as directed.

Like most exercise programs, you will need a few things to make this process work well: a Bible, a good place to study for extended periods of time, a good set of pencils or pens, some writing paper, and we highly recommend a regular schedule for study. You might also use a concordance, Bible atlas, and a Bible dictionary. That's all you need—besides this book of course!

You may find it helpful to substitute a computer-based word processing program for the pencil and paper. However, if you have a computer-based Bible study program, plan to not use it while studying this book. Such programs can prove very beneficial for Bible students, but they will prove to be a distraction as you work through this book. You are learning how to do direct Bible study, and you should concentrate on making your own discoveries. Also, plan not to consult Bible commentaries or Bible encyclopedias. You can and should return to these secondary tools after mastering the methods needed for direct study of the Bible.

Bible Translations

The Bible translation you choose for study is important. It should be one that you find easy to read with understanding. Each of us has our own level of reading skill and our own working vocabulary. Choose a translation that challenges you without getting you bogged down looking up a lot of words in a dictionary.

It is very important that you choose a Bible translation with clear paragraph indentions or markings. Chapter and verse numberings in the Bible were added long after it was written. They do not always match the literary structure of a text and can steer you in the wrong direction. Paragraph divisions are much more helpful for studying the Bible as literature.

For purposes of Bible study, we encourage you to not use a paraphrase version of the Bible such as *The Message* or *The Living Bible*. One of the problems with using paraphrased translations for Bible study is that in their effort to communicate the big ideas of a passage, the translators often gloss over many of the literary clues found in the original text. Another problem with using a paraphrased translation is that they are more highly influenced by the theological commitments of the translators. By their very nature, they tend to be skewed toward preexisting doctrinal convictions, at least more so than the other types of translations.

Also, as you work through *Encountering the Living Word*, do not use a study Bible regardless of the translation you are using. Study Bibles can be helpful, providing notes on the translation of passages, internal dictionaries, helpful background information, useful maps, and more. But, to get the most out of this book, you must concentrate on what is actually written in the Bible. Study Bibles provide too many temptations to follow rabbit trails and lose focus, especially as you are learning a new set of study skills. Bibles that include references to parallel passages and brief translator's notes are acceptable.

Many good translations exist today from which to choose. Each has a different set of strengths and weaknesses. The methods presented in this book will work with all of them. However, we recommend that you consider choosing one from the following list:

New International Version (NIV – 2011 edition)

New English Translation Bible (NET)

Christian Standard Bible (CSB – 2017/2020 editions)

New Revised Standard Version (NRSV – 1989 edition)

New American Standard Version (NASV – 2020 edition)

English Standard Version (ESV)[1]

---

[1] The ESV is a good translation except for a small set of theological biases. For example, the translators openly admit their commitment to a

New American Standard Bible (NASB – 1995 edition).

Each of these translations was completed by a team of scholars who had strong commitments to remaining faithful to the original texts of the Scriptures. We present the list above in order from easiest reading level (NIV) to most challenging reading level (NASB – 1995 edition), according to our own assessments.

Correspondingly, the translations in this list are given in the reverse order of how formal the translations are. Formal translations are sometimes called "word for word" translations; they follow the original wording and grammar closely even if that makes the English translation awkward for most people to read. The NASB – 1995 edition follows this approach.

Less formal translations are sometimes called "thought for thought" translations. While the translators were also concerned about the original wording and grammar, they had a heightened concern that the original thoughts behind the words and grammar be communicated in the style of everyday English. In the list given above, the NIV is the best example of this approach.

In this book, we will primarily use the Christian Standard Bible (CSB – 2017). The New Revised Standard Bible (NRSB) and others are also occasionally used for the sake of adding clarity. The CSB is considered slightly easier to read than the NRSB, but both are consistently reliable translations. It is recommended, but not necessary, that you use the CSB. It is available for reading online at https://read.csbible.com, but a hard copy is preferable.

---

complementarian view of male and female gender roles. They are decidedly biased against gender inclusive language. For example, the Greek word for "man" often refers to humanity, i.e., male and female. When the text might legitimately be translated as referring to both men and women, the ESV opts for "man" except when the context demands otherwise.

Primary Bible Texts

As you work through this book, you will find many examples taken from various books of the Bible. The two primary books are Mark's Gospel and Paul's Epistle to the Ephesians. Ephesians will serve as the text for the learning exercises in the second half of the Book. We chose to take many examples from Mark because it is often used as the primary text for learning inductive methods of Bible study. We recommend that you read through Mark before you move into the exercises in this book and that you complete a study of Mark after completing the exercises in this book.

Summation

This book is designed to help you gain skills and confidence in an approach to Bible study that focuses on direct engagement with the books of the Bible. We call this approach *Relational Inductive Bible Study*. This approach understands the Bible to be the Word of God in the sense that it carries His personal presence and not just His ideas. It aims at building a more intimate relationship with God both during and after the study itself.

This book is also built around the belief that the Bible is human literature. It should be read and studied like all other literature is read and studied. As such, understanding the Bible requires a basic understanding of the types, styles, and forms of literature that exist within the Bible. These concepts will be surveyed within this book.

Furthermore, this book is grounded in the belief that Bible study is for everyone. Anyone who actively seeks can indeed hear the voice of God reverberating through this ancient Book of Books. God gave the Scriptures to all of us. The Bible is an open invitation to a lifetime of communion with God in His Word. You only need a discerning and adventurous spirit, a disciplined mind, a humble heart, and a good set of study skills.

When you have completed working through the contents of this book, you should have the basic skills needed to be a good student of the Bible. If you apply yourself to this goal, you will gain confidence that you are growing in your knowledge of what the Bible says; more importantly, you will have fresh, life-altering encounters with God through the process. We hope you will want to share these skills with others so they too can discover that Bible study can be a dynamic discipline that results in deep, personal encounters with God.

Before moving into the body of this book, we invite you to meditate on what the Bible means to you. What role does it play in your life? In what sense is it the "Word of God" for you? Do you encounter God when reading and studying the Bible? What follows is a prayer in poetic form. It represents what we have personally known the Bible to be and what we hunger for it to always be in our lives. It is a testimony and a desire for ongoing renewal. Please read it prayerfully asking God to renew your own love for His Word.

<u>*Into Your Presence*</u>

In the cool of the day
I run into Your presence
In the garden of Your Word
Hungry for Your touch, Your face
Your will, Your warm embrace
There I quiet my spirit
And listen for Your voice
Echoing through those ancient books
Scribed by human hands
Both eternal and created
Word of God born in thoughts of men

More than a window into the heavens
Or a relic of the past
The Spirit hums across the pages
Grace and Truth for all the ages
Love beyond imagination
Wed to human communication
Mysteries hidden from the angels
Written in the lyrics of mere mortals
In the whole and in each part
Intoning Your very heart
Every syllable a revelation
Alpha and Omega within creation[2]

---

[2] Jackie David Johns, "Into Your Presence" in *I Am Not a Poet: Journeys in Faith and Self-Discovery* (Cleveland, TN: CPM Press, 2011), 49.

PART I.
Foundations for Relational Inductive Bible Study

Relational Inductive Bible Study is a distinct approach to Bible study. The key difference is found in the approach to the Bible more than in the methods. The Bible is a living book and should be approached as the living Word of God. It should be cherished as if God is in it speaking to us personally—because He is. It should also be read, studied, and enjoyed like great literature, because it is.

The second half of *Encountering the Living Word* is intended to help the reader gain skills in inductive Bible study methods. Anyone can develop these skills and become a better student of the Holy Scriptures, but this book is written to help the reader gain much, much more than skills in Bible study methods. It is written to help people encounter God as they study the Bible.

Encountering God in Bible study requires that we approach the Bible as a meeting place with Him and that we have a corresponding openness to spiritual transformation through Bible study. However, we must simultaneously approach the Bible as literature to be studied. The Bible is God speaking through human literature. In the first half of this book, we lay a foundation for how the Bible should be approached as both a living book and as human literature—as God's personal presence and as the ancient words of apostles and prophets.

Chapter 2

Bible Study for a New Generation

"It is by the Spirit alone that the true knowledge of God hath been,
is, and can be, revealed. And these revelations, which are absolutely
necessary for the building up of true faith, neither do, nor can,
ever contradict right reason or the testimony of the Scriptures."

—John Wesley

Most Christians have a list of things they know they should do on a regular basis but don't. Bible study is typically at, or near, the top of that list. We all know it is something we should do. From time to time, we commit ourselves to be more faithful to this basic Christian discipline, but we just don't seem to follow through.

Most of us are extremely busy trying to survive and get ahead in our modern world. In families, it is typical for both parents to have at least one job and sometimes more. Singles have the same drive to get ahead, and youth are pressured to participate in all kinds of extracurricular activities. On top of these time-consuming 'necessities' are our impulses for entertainment and recreation. This faulty sense that we just don't have enough time for Bible study robs us of the wonder and joy of regular meetings with God in His Word.

Many other excuses exist for our inconsistencies in Bible study. "The Bible is too confusing." "What if I misinterpret what I read?" "I don't like all the new translations, and I don't understand the King James Version." "Isn't that what we pay our pastor to do?" "I've tried and tried, and I just don't get much out of it." "It seems disconnected from my everyday life." If any of these have been your thoughts, do not be discouraged; you are not alone. We promise you, there is a solution. Have hope.

> This faulty sense that we just don't have
> enough time for Bible study robs us of the
> wonder and joy of regular meetings with
> God in His Word.

We believe there is a new generation of Bible students emerging—one that sees Bible study as an opportunity for a vibrant connection with God. This generation takes seriously the presence and work of the Holy Spirit. It is not content with limiting the Holy Spirit to the role of a mild-mannered, whispering coach who gently nudges the believer toward truth. Rather, this growing group of people hungers for the real presence of the living God, and they know deep down that the Bible is linked to His real presence. They may not be able to explain or even describe the connection, but they know by experience that the Bible can be a place of wonder, transformation, and communion with God. You can join them in this quest to encounter God in the Scriptures.

This book is written for all who want to encounter God in His Word—those who know that the Scriptures come from God and who believe that the Bible will help us know God better. This book for those who know that the Bible points toward a fuller life and that principles for godly living can be drawn out of it but who want more. It is for those who want to encounter God when they study His Word, who want the awe of God's presence and the peace that comes from ongoing transformation and communion with Him, and who want their Bible study done with and through the Holy Spirit.

The Spirit and the Word

In this book you will frequently see the Bible referred to as "Spirit-Word." We will explain why we use this term in a later chapter, but for now, just accept that we believe that as Spirit-Word, the Bible brings the reader into the actual presence of our living God. As Spirit-Word, the Bible is more than some perfect document that God dictated and signed. It is more than a holy relic handed down from the past. The Holy Spirit was active in the writing of the books of the Bible, and the Spirit continues to inhabit the Scriptures, making them a sacred vessel of the presence of God. The Spirit and the Word are inseparable, so that the Bible exists as an ever-current revelation of God.

As Spirit-Word, the Bible brings the reader
into the actual presence of our living God.

In the present, the Holy Spirit is doing much more than quickening our minds to better understand ancient texts. Don't make the mistake of thinking of the Holy Spirit as some sort of personal assistant for your Bible study, a light switch for your understanding. Rather, believe that the Holy Spirit is God's active and willed presence, revealing God and drawing us to His Son, Jesus Christ, who is after all the Word of God. In Bible study, the Spirit is always pulling us toward a deeper personal knowledge of Jesus.

As Spirit-Word, the Bible is filled with the power of God's personal presence. Meditate on this—the Bible brings us into the actual presence of our triune God. When Christians read the Bible as God's Word, they are ushered into the very life of God. How wondrous to know that reading the Bible can bring us into a place of fellowship with God, a place where we hear the very thoughts of God. In that place of fellowship, we find comfort in God, become more conscious of what pleases and displeases Him, are renewed in His mercy, and experience ongoing transformation into the image and likeness of Christ.

Too many Christians live far below this wondrous reality. In our modern era, still dominated by rationalism, we have lost awareness that the Bible is a sacred vessel of God's presence. It is treated like a lifeless specimen to be studied, a static text that is more an artifact from the past than a present and living word. Even those who profess faith that the Bible is the Word of God may treat it as a book from God detached from His actual presence.

For many, the Bible serves as a rulebook on moral living, a map that points to heaven, a resource for proof-texting what they already believe, and/or a repository of stories and teachings from which to discover principles for living—but not an actual link to the voice of God.

People are told to read the Bible in order to "think like Jesus" or to have a "Christian worldview." These are good objectives, but beyond these, we should read the Bible in order to come into the very presence of God, who desires to speak with us directly and to know us intimately. Only by knowing God can we be transformed into His image. Just trying to think like He thinks is not enough.

This kind of Bible study requires that we do our part—the looking, digging, searching, and questioning. We must remain intentional about believing that God's Spirit is active and present in our study. We must expect transformation to take place during Bible study. We must transition from seeing Bible study only as a means of gaining knowledge about God and His will to seeing it as occasions for direct and intimate knowledge of God and His will. We must change our posture from one of seeing the Bible as a book from God to a posture for experiencing the Bible as current and living Word of God for us.

All of this is possible because Jesus sent us the Holy Spirit to lead us into truth. Consider the words of Jesus about the Holy Spirit:

"If you love me, you will keep my commands. And I will ask the Father, and he will give you another Counselor to be with you forever. He is the Spirit of truth. The world is unable to receive him because it doesn't see him or know him. But you do know him, because he remains with you and will be in you" (John 14:15-17, CSB).

The Holy Spirit is an active and personal helper who is the very presence of God. The Spirit, who knows the deep things of God, knows our deep things as well and will commune between our spirit and God if we desire the Spirit to do so (1 Cor 2:10). This makes the Spirit-Word of God not a heavy hand from the past but a living and helping hand for the now. The same Spirit who brooded over the waters in creation and who breathed upon the prophets and apostles to write the Scriptures is our personal guide in our quest to know God and His Word more fully. The Spirit is more than able to quicken our minds to understand, our hearts to surrender, and our wills to obey. The Spirit will give us ears to hear and hearts to conform to the voice of God.

Let God's Word Speak

There are many reasons why people fail to hear the voice of God when they study the Bible. One of the greatest reasons is that we all tend to set limits on how God speaks. We may expect an audible voice that sounds something like the King James Version of the Bible with all the *thees* and *thous*. We may think the voice of God will always come as a thunderous theophany. On the other hand, we may limit God to Elijah's "still, small voice" or to an inner feeling about what to do.

We must let go of any artificial restraints on God and invite Him to speak for himself in the way He wants to speak. Stated more precisely, we must remove our self-imposed limits on how we are willing to hear God speak. At the same time, we must recognize any patterns in how we hear God speak and follow those patterns. For most of us, the voice of God is very seldom, if ever, a thunderous experience. Most often it comes as an unfolding of our understanding, new thoughts formed in our heads and our hearts with an undeniable sense that God is speaking to us personally. We must have a hunger to hear from God and an openness to what He might say and how He might say it.

We must let go of any artificial restraints on God and invite Him to speak for himself in the way He wants to speak. ... we must remove our self-imposed limits on how we are willing to hear God speak.

How we value and approach the Scriptures will largely determine what we can hear from them. If we think of the Bible as a textbook on how to live, that is what it will be for us. If we think of it as a history book, it will primarily serve as a book of history for us. If we think of it as great literature, it will be great literature. Believe that it is nourishment and a light for the Christian journey, and it will be that. But if we have faith that the Bible is God speaking to us, it will be all of these and so much more. It will serve as a place of communion with our Creator.

Knowing what the Bible *is not* is also important. The Bible is not a magic book with secrete formulas for getting what we want out of life nor a modern mystery book full of secret codes that only a select few can unravel to find truth. It is not a philosophy book pointing to higher levels of reality or a self-help book intended to assist us in our quest for "self-actualization." In short, the Bible is not a tool we can use to get what we want out of life.

The Bible is God speaking to us, about us, and about our relationship with Him. It is given to show us what we really need to live a full life in Christ. It is an open book for everyone who will dare pay the price of serious Bible study—open to the uneducated and the educated, the young and the old, the wealthy and the poor, the minister and the layperson. It is God speaking to all of us, and it demands that we let it speak for itself.

How can we let the Bible speak for itself? Above all, the voice of God in the Scriptures must be prayerfully discerned. Bible study must always be a spiritual task. We must engage the Bible with our whole being: our body, soul, spirit, intellect, emotions, and affections. All we are must be brought into the presence of God and laid bare before Him.

We must come desiring to hear what He wants to say and hungering to be what He wants us to be. Searching the Scriptures should not just be about learning how to walk with Jesus; it should be an experience of walking with Jesus.

Searching the Scriptures should not just be about learning how to walk with Jesus; it should be an experience of walking with Jesus.

This does not diminish the role of the intellect—our ability to think and reason. On the contrary, it demands that we bring to the Word of God our best efforts to rationally understand what God is saying through what has been written. The Bible is the present and eternal Word of God but also an ancient collection of human literature. It is divine revelation in human language, given to us to be read and studied.

Studying the Bible as present revelation wed to human literature requires that we study it as literature. As we have said before, and will say again, this kind of Bible study requires effort and time as well as the application of some basic learning skills. Much of this book is given to help you develop those skills.

Always remember this: God's Word and God's holy presence are married. They should never be divorced in our minds. By the power of the Holy Spirit, God lives in and speaks through His Word. The Bible is a sanctified vessel for the Word of God to come to us as the divine presence of God.

The Bible can be read like any other book but should be read as *more* than a book. When people being made alive by the Spirit of God read the Word of God, they enter into a world entirely "of God." They enter the realm of the reign of God where His plan for creation is now being fulfilled. To read and study the Bible as Spirit-Word of God is to be in the place where God reigns!

Three Faulty Approaches to the Bible

How we approach the Bible will largely determine the limits of how well we understand what the Bible says and the extent to which we encounter God in our studies. We have identified three common approaches to the Bible that result in faulty understandings of the Scriptures and that tend to hinder a person from encountering God in their Bible study: the pre-packaged approach, the heart-warming approach, and the deductive approach. Let's have a look at them. As you read, check yourself to see whether your Bible study falls into one or more of these categories.

The Pre-Packaged Approach

It is much easier to depend on others to read and study the Bible for us than to read and study it for ourselves. We say again, Bible study is *hard work*. Another person's hard work can be drawn upon to aid our understanding; however, if we depend primarily on others to interpret the Bible for us, we may know their opinions about life in the kingdom of God without experiencing the Kingdom for ourselves. Many times, Christians only meditate on what others think about living a life pleasing to God. These believers spend more time in devotional books than they spend in the Bible.

God has given us guides to help equip us for works of ministry (Eph 4:11-12), persons who help us mark the pathways of true Christian living. To fulfill this task, these guides must be dedicated students of the Word. This is not to say, however, that they should replace our own diligent search of the Scriptures. If done well, their ministries will lead us more deeply into our own study, not replace it.

We must not allow our knowledge of God to be reduced to pre-digested pablum. When we settle for secondhand Bible study, we settle for a "secondhand God," and we miss the great joy of our own fellowship with Him in the garden of His holy Word.

This secondhand knowledge of God is everywhere: Sunday Schools, Bible study groups, sermons, and Bible conferences, to name a few. People follow popular teachers, listening to their sermons and podcasts, buying their books, and reading what they believe. It is all too easy to let this become spiritual entertainment that distracts us from real contact with the Word of God.

Even persons serious about understanding the Bible can slip into the pre-packaged approach. They may skip the devotional books to spend time in commentaries and other scholarly writings. Commentaries written by scholars can serve as powerful tools to assist us in our Bible study, but we must not allow them to substitute for our own direct engagement with the Scriptures. We must not be like the children of Israel at Mount Sinai who out of fear withdrew from the presence of God and begged Moses to be their go-between with God (Exod 20:18-21).

The pre-packaged approach to Bible study has provided 'processed food' for generations of Christians. The healthy meat of the Word is cast aside, resulting in spiritually weak believers who have lost the sense of a personal relationship with God and who easily get led away from sound doctrine. Let the hard work of others inspire you to study more and delve more deeply into the Scriptures. Learn from them. Let them challenge you. But always hold their work up against the light shining through your own disciplined study of God's Word.

The Heart-Warming Approach

The heart-warming approach to Bible study uses the Bible for emotional comfort with the purpose of feeling better about oneself or one's current situation in life. Feel unloved? Find a passage that speaks about God's love. Feel lonely? Find a passage that says that you are not alone.

We all use this approach from time to time as we seek consolation or encouragement. There is nothing wrong with turning to relevant Scripture texts in times of need. The problem arises when we only, or primarily, study those portions of Scripture that speak to our momentary felt needs—the verses that tell us what we want to hear. If that is our primary approach, we leave most of the Bible unexplored, and our lives remain largely unchanged by it.

People who limit their study to the heart-warming approach will typically have Bibles with their favorite passages marked for handy reference. This may lead to a 'top ten' view of God's Word. The list may be short or long, but it contains those verses that are read over and over to the neglect of the rest of the Bible. In a similar manner, some people have a favorite book of the Bible to the neglect of other books. Most often it is the Psalms or possibly Proverbs, but seldom Leviticus or any of the prophets.

When we only approach the Bible to make ourselves feel better, we distort the scope and magnitude of the kingdom of God. This approach may reduce the gospel to platitudes like, "Cheer up—all things work together for good" or "Be encouraged—I've never seen the righteous forsaken," or "God is merciful; He will forgive me if I confess after I do this." There is a scriptural reference that lies behind each of these statements, but the statements stretch the Word of God far beyond what God intends.

Life in the kingdom of God entails more than simplified connections between a few Bible verses and the difficult challenges we face as Christians. Life in the Kingdom involves the totality of God's plans for us. His Word must not be limited to making us feel better. This holy book must not be forced to fit our narrow vision and our limited range of emotions. We must conform to its message. It will not be made to fit our wishes.

The heart-warming approach denies us the thrill of God breaking into our lives in new ways. It blinds us to the awe and wonder of experiencing new insights drawn from previously uncharted territories. It robs us of the pleasure of discovery and replaces it with a faulty sense of assurance. It confuses happiness with the joy that comes from steadfastness in the face of tribulations. Without our realizing it, the heart-warming approach places the reader in control, forcing the Bible to say what he or she wants it to say. When we make the heartwarming approach to the Scriptures our primary method of Bible study, we make the Bible little more than a magical feel-good drug.

The Deductive Approach

Another common faulty approach to Bible study is the deductive approach. It involves going to the Scriptures with ideas and beliefs that we already hold in order to find support for those concepts. In many ways this approach is like the heart-warming approach except that it replaces emotions with intellect and more systematic and logical methods. Both approaches involve bringing to the Bible our preconceptions to find scriptural support for what we already think we know. The difference is that the deductive approach is often a distorted form of serious Bible study.

Deductive Bible study is an outgrowth of deductive thinking, or logic, that involves moving from a general, accepted truth to specific expressions of that truth or specific applications of that truth. This may be illustrated by the following syllogism:

- All humans have a heart. (a general, accepted truth)

- I am a human. (another accepted truth)

- I, therefore, have a heart. (a truth claim deduced from the others)

Notice that the above statements begin with a general idea (all humans have a heart) and finally make a specific conclusion (I, therefore, have a heart). That is an accurate and reasonable line of thinking.

When used properly, deductive reasoning is helpful and even necessary. It is good for fitting things into categories and for moving quickly into new insights (I have a heart) and applications. For instance, learned persons worked out of the assumptions of Newton's "laws of thermo-dynamics" (accepted truths) to invent (through deductive reasoning) most of our modern conveniences.

Deductive thinking is helpful for connecting scriptural teachings with our lives. It is needed for making decisions about how we should respond to new challenges. For example, if we begin with the general principle taught by Jesus that we are to love our neighbor as we love ourselves and move to another verifiable truth, "John is my neighbor," we then must deductively conclude, "Jesus expects me to love John as I love myself."

However, deductive reasoning has its limits and can easily lead to faulty conclusions. For example, during the Middle Ages, deductive logic was used to develop and refine Church dogma. The result was that there was a given body of 'truth' that could be defended with point-by-point deductive reasoning. For most Christians, this body of doctrines was made to stand in the place of the Scriptures as the primary source of truth. Truth became locked into a rigid system of deductive reasoning, and the Bible was made to serve that system.

When Galileo (1564-1642) discovered that there were spots on the sun, he was greatly opposed by the Church and threatened with being put on trial for heresy. (Later, he was tried and convicted of "vehement suspicion of heresy" for the publication of his belief that the earth revolved around the sun, and he was placed under house arrest for the remainder of his life!) Why did the Church object to his announcement about the existence of sunspots? Well, Galileo's findings did not fit into the Church's system of doctrines about the nature of the universe. The accepted reasoning went something like this:

- The sun is a heavenly body.

- Being close to God, who is perfect, heavenly bodies do not have blemishes.

- Therefore, the sun cannot have blemishes (spots).

Galileo was told that if anything had spots, it was his telescope—but certainly not the sun!

This type of deductive thinking closed the door on the search for truth through science, and only the brave would dare push through that door. It was also closing the door on serious Bible study. A century before Galileo, Martin Luther through his own direct Bible study, came to believe that salvation is by faith without the aid of our works. This contradicted established, deductively derived, doctrines of the Church. Luther insisted that the Bible is a higher authority than Church doctrine, and for this he was excommunicated. Deductive reasoning often serves as a powerful tool for resisting needed change.

Deductive Bible study begins with an accepted truth claim and moves to finding specific support for, or expressions of, or applications of, that truth claim. In other words, deductive Bible study primarily looks to prove, or expand on, what we already believe. When this happens, it becomes sophisticated proof-texting. The beginning point is the conclusion. A general principle, law, premise, or doctrine is assumed to be true, and then specifics are deductively connected to it in support the original truth claim.

Deductive thinking is helpful for developing standard procedures needed to work out systems of thought. In Bible study, one might work from the general assertion that "God is almighty," and move from there to find instances in the Bible that demonstrate the power of God. Similarly, deductive thinking is needed to identify ways to apply the truths of Scripture. See Figure 2.1 below.

Figure 2.1 -- "Deductive Thinking"

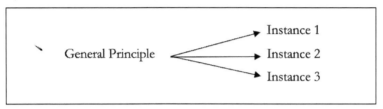

Applying the deductive approach to Bible study can also help us systemize our beliefs into doctrinal statements. Systems of belief begin with a general idea or faith statement and then find those particulars in Scripture that support and/or clarify that general idea. Then, from the established general idea, we can deduce sub-doctrines that can be further supported by particulars within the Scriptures. It is an ongoing cycle of logic and discovery that can help us organize our thoughts about God and life in a healthy way.

When the general ideas and the particulars match and correspond with the whole of Scripture, the deductive approach serves to help Bible students clarify for themselves what they believe. If, however, one begins with a faulty general premise or inserts a faulty premise at any step in the process, the conclusion is made invalid. The whole argument collapses, and Scripture texts are then used to support faulty doctrines or applications. For example, someone might reason, "(A) Jesus said I must love my neighbor as I love myself. (B) I don't really love myself. (C) Therefore, I don't really have to love my neighbor."

Satan used faulty deductive reasoning when he tempted Jesus:

> Then the devil took him to the holy city and placed him on the pinnacle of the temple, saying to him, "If you are the Son of God, throw yourself down; for it is written, 'He will command his angels concerning you,' and 'On their hands they will bear you up, so that you will not dash your foot against a stone'" (Matt 4:5-6, NRS).

He used deductive reasoning:

- <u>If</u> you are the Son of God, and

- <u>if</u> the Scriptures say that God will command the angels to bear you up,

- <u>then</u>, fulfill the prophecy, and throw yourself down.

Notice Satan's logic. The initial truth claim is the statement about Jesus being the Son of God, and the two other truth claims were composites of quotations from the Old Testament. Jesus could not deny that any of this was true. The faulty element in Satan's logic is the implication he deduced—that Jesus should fulfill the prophecy and demonstrate that He is the Son of God by throwing himself down. Jesus was not obligated to prove that He is the Son of God, especially not to Satan.

There is a tendency with the deductive approach to make Scripture speak what we want it to say and not to allow the Holy Spirit to lead in our study. When we use biblical passages as support for faulty beliefs, we reduce the Bible to being a tool for defending our personal opinions. The Bible student may gain extensive knowledge of facts within the Bible—especially those related to his or her favored topics—but those facts may be wrongly interpreted and disjoined from the true meaning of what the Bible says.

Another major problem with the deductive approach is that, like the heart-warming approach, it often ignores the vastness of Scripture. It may be hard for us to accept, but much of the Bible exists to address issues we may not have ever considered. God is right there speaking to us about life in His Kingdom, and we turn a deaf ear to Him.

We need deductive reasoning to faithfully apply the Scriptures to our lives. It can help us arrange our discoveries and interpretations into usable concepts. We can also use it to point us toward other passages that support and amplify what we have learned. It can shed light on faults in our interpretations of Bible passages and thereby help us refine our understandings.

Later, we will see more on the importance of good deductive reasoning for inductive Bible study. Good inductive study is incomplete without a deductive component, one that asks, "What must we do with the truths we have discovered?"

The Relational Inductive Approach

The pre-packaged, heart-warming, and deductive approaches to Bible study are not wrong in and of themselves. We need teachers to help us understand the truths found in the Bible. We need to know that whenever we have a need, we can find it addressed in the Bible. We also need to articulate and defend our doctrinal beliefs. However, when any one of these is relied upon as the primary method of our Bible study, we are in danger of dictating to Scripture our ideas rather than approaching the Bible to hear God's message.

There is no purely unbiased approach to Bible study. We all have preconceived ideas that we bring with us to our studies.

There is no purely unbiased approach to Bible study. We all have preconceived ideas that we bring with us to our studies. However, we believe the approach, which we call *Relational Inductive Bible Study*, allows the message of the Bible to break in upon our lives in new and challenging ways.

This approach holds together two guiding concepts. First, it is committed to studying the Bible as a present word from God for us. Second, it is committed to carefully studying the details of Scripture passages in their literary context before making any general conclusions about what those passages mean. It is a relationship-based, inductive, orderly, systematic, and often time-consuming approach—but a rewarding one!

Inductive thinking is a form of logic defined as moving from the specifics to the general. It requires that we study the facts and the factual within a text before interpreting the meaning of the text. It is a way of thinking that is open and not closed, holding off on conclusions until sufficient evidence is gathered. In inductive study, we do not begin with an established assumption or general principle. We end the process there. See Figure 2.2 below.

Figure 2.2 -- "Inductive Thinking"

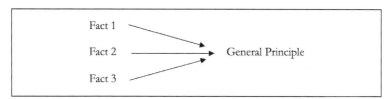

A direct-inductive approach to Bible study uses a variety of methods for moving from observable facts to general principles. This book will introduce you to several of those methods. Inductive methods follow a set pattern: observe the facts (specifics), then interpret the meaning of the facts (make general conclusions), and then apply the interpretations to life (a deductive component). See Figure 2.3 below.

Inductive thinking requires a spirit of openness. You cannot be defensive and be inductive at the same time. RIBS is a discovery process in which the student carefully observes what the text says

Figure 2.3 -- "Inductive Bible Study"

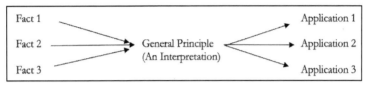

and how it says it. It involves looking closely at the text to see the patterns, relationships, and structures of the text to discover the true meaning. The student does not begin with pre-conceived ideas but rather presents himself or herself as a living vessel fully surrendered to the Spirit-Word of God to be formed by and filled with truth. In a truly inductive approach, we enter the Scriptures open to have our beliefs refined and corrected however they need to be.

Almost everyone we know who has learned the inductive approach has found it to make Bible study fun. Using this approach to search deep into the Word of God unearths one hidden treasure after another. When we find one, it is ours to keep—not a hand-me-down truth. It is a great gift from God's hand to our hearts, as if it belonged just to us. Oh, the joy of getting a private tour led by the Holy Spirit into God's reign of truth.

Oh, the joy of getting a private tour led by the Holy Spirit into God's reign of truth.

No one need fear that they will lose their faith by fully surrendering themselves and their belief system to God in Bible study. You can trust God and His Word to correct your faulty understandings and to perfect your faith. You can also trust yourself to hear what God is saying through His Word, provided you really want to hear. Only, make certain that you stay within the boundaries established in the ancient Christian creeds, and do not take the journey alone. Share what you discover and listen to the responses of others you trust. The journey into the fulness of God is a shared journey.

Openness, surrender, a spirit of humility, and a sense of awe characterize RIBS when done well. These traits fit perfectly with approaching the Bible as the Spirit-Word of God. They call for a posture in which we submit ourselves to the Holy Spirit as the ultimate guide for our journey into knowing God more fully. As we surrender to the Spirit as our teacher and guide, we find ourselves "seeing what we are looking at." The Spirit unveils the text and opens the world found therein. In Spirit-led inductive Bible study, the literary patterns and connections between events and characters come into sharper focus. These patterns begin to converge into a force of meaning that further reveals the living God in the text.

You Can Join the New Generation

Having read through this chapter, you are now at a crossroad. Will you lay this book aside and continue to pay little attention to the Bible? Will you continue doing Bible study using your existing patterns? Will you look elsewhere for an approach that works better for you. Or will you venture further down this road into relational inductive Bible study? Will you join the new generation of Bible students in their quest to encounter God in the Scriptures?

Having read through this chapter,
you are now at a crossroad.

Many of us struggle to understand this new generation of Bible students. We are products of modernity, and the individuals in this new generation are the children of what has been called post-modernity. Their approach to truth and reality is more open than ours, which has both positive and negative aspects for Bible study. They are right when they reject the idea that reason is the only route to truth. They believe there is truth beyond our abilities to comprehend—truth best attained by faith, truth that should sit at the center of our lives. This does not mean they have rejected reason or that they necessarily believe reason is at odds with other forms of truth. For most of them, reason and all other forms of knowing must exist in harmony with each other.

This new generation of Bible students also rejects the idea that objectivity can be fully attained outside of God. We all have blinders that limit and shape our perceptions of reality. Recognizing the delusion of objectivity demands a posture of humility when looking for truth, a posture that must permeate all of life. They want more than a truth system that makes sense; they want one they can fully own as their own and that adds meaning and purpose to their lives. They want more than principles to live by; they want truths to live in. They long for authentic Christianity, and they believe that authentic Christianity can be found in the Scriptures.

Most importantly, this new generation of Bible students believes that Truth is the person Jesus Christ and that the truth that really matters is the truth that flows out of a relationship with him. This truth is relational and experiential. For them, the Bible serves as a place for having those experiences and serves to define and govern those experiences.

You can become a part of this new generation. It really is not a long leap from where you are. All it requires is that you begin to truly believe those things you learned in your childhood. Jesus has risen from the dead. He is alive. He is with us by the presence of the Holy Spirit. He is the Way, the Truth, and the Life. He is the Word of God. The Bible also is the Word of God inspired by the Spirit of God. The Holy Spirit has come to lead us into the truth. Holding tightly to these old truths will empower us to read and study the Bible in ways faithful to the One who permeates the Bible.

Chapter 3

The Spirit-Word of Truth

"The Spirit of God not only once inspired those who wrote it,
but continually inspires, supernaturally assists, those that
read it with earnest prayer."

—John Wesley

In this book we uplift a model for a direct, inductive approach to Bible study, one also committed to the spiritual and personal nature of the Scriptures. The inductive component of this approach includes a set of powerful methods for analyzing the written text, for understanding what the passage says and means. The inductive approach does not, however, guarantee that one will discover the great truths of the Scriptures or encounter God in them. The approach has some shortcomings.

Perhaps the greatest flaw in the inductive approach is that it tends to reduce the Bible to a lifeless object to be studied, a collection of books to be mastered. As mentioned earlier, the inductive approach was at one time known as the "scientific method of Bible study." A common metaphor used to describe the method was that of dissecting a specimen in a lab. This made Bible study largely an exercise in deconstructing the Word of God and subtly reduced the Bible to a corpse that no longer exhales the life-giving breath of God.

On one level, the metaphor of dissection can provide a helpful "quick look" at the first step in the inductive approach. Observing the parts of a book and how they fit together, however, is only one component of the approach. Students must also make interpretations and plan for applications. When all the steps are taken together, they nudge the student toward a posture of control over a lifeless relic. The living nature of the Bible is suppressed, and the voice of God is muffled.

We can overcome these shortcomings if we remember that the Bible is more than a record of past revelations that hold implications for the present. It is not a dead specimen to place under a microscope. The Bible is the Word of God continually breathed outward by the Spirit of God. It is not just spiritual in that the Holy Spirit inspired it and the words speak to the human spirit. It is spiritual in its essence in that the Holy Spirit is always actively present in it.

God has given us His Word in literary form with the expectation that we will read and study it. However, we must never forget that it is of God. Through the Scriptures, God is reaching out to touch us. As we study the Bible, we are objects of God's affection as well as students of his intentions. If we are open to the Word, the Spirit of God will embrace us as we study. At its best, then, Bible study is a dialog, an interpersonal conversation between our hearts and the heart of God.

The Teacher Come from God

During His life and ministry on earth, Jesus was given many titles: Son of God, Son of Man, Lamb of God, Messiah, and others, but He was best known as rabbi, the teacher come from God. We need to think of that title as much as possible in the way it was understood in first century Judaism. In modern times we tend to associate the word "teacher" with classrooms and formal instruction with an emphasis on information and skills. This was not how Jews of the first century pictured their teachers.

In ancient Judaism, the term "teacher" was holistically connected with life. Rabbis were concerned with knowledge of the Scriptures and the traditions of Israel, but they were ultimately concerned with how those things were integrated into life. They were more concerned with the question, "How should we live in order to please God" than with the question, "What should we understand about God?".

In the time of Christ, knowledge about God, the Scriptures, and life was like the threads in a tapestry woven together to nurture lives pleasing to God. Jesus was not a mere lecturer; He was (and is) the Way, the Truth, and the Life. In Him, these three remain inseparable. He taught as He traveled from place to place, and his 'lessons' most often arose out of the needs and questions of those who came to him. Through the Scriptures, he continues to call us unto himself and invites us to bring our concerns as we journey with him in the Way, the Truth, and the Life.

It makes perfect sense that the one who is the Word of God (John 1:1-18) would be the Teacher come from God (3:2). Imagine with us Jesus standing up in the synagogue, as was His custom, taking the scroll of the Book of Isaiah and reading from it:

> The Spirit of the Lord is on me,
> because he has anointed me
> to preach good news to the poor.
> He has sent me
> to proclaim release to the captives
> and recovery of sight to the blind,
> to set free the oppressed,
> to proclaim the year of the Lord's favor
> (Luke 4:18-19, CSB).

The Word of God incarnated was holding and reading the Word of God inscripturated. Reflect on that a moment. Jesus is the Word of God wed to human existence, and the Scriptures are the Word of God wed to intangible human language in the form of literature. The two Truths are one and the same; the Truth was reading and speaking the Truth. In Christ, truth abounds without limit.

When we study the Bible, we stand in the place of Christ the Word of God, holding the Word of God, and reading the Word of God. Only, we are also being read by the Word of God. Bible study should not just entail a conscious effort to focus on Jesus; it must be done in and with Him. Bible study is an opportunity to wrap our hearts and minds around our Savior's feet and there be lifted and embraced by Him. This beautiful image is made real by the presence and work of the Holy Spirit who will come upon us as He did Jesus. To handle and truly know the Word of God, we must, like Jesus, allow ourselves to be handled and known by the Spirit of God.

Another Teacher[1]

Before his departure to heaven, Jesus promised he would send someone to take his place—the Holy Spirit. We find this promise in John's Gospel, between the Last Super and the betrayal of Christ by Judas (John 13:31-17:26). In this section, Jesus gives some final instructions to the Eleven to prepare them for his death and departure. At the heart of this "final discourse" was a promise that in his absence he would send another teacher, a Paraclete, who would be in them and make Christ's presence real to them. In those instructions, Jesus firmly links His ministry with the coming ministry of the Holy Spirit.

The word "Paraclete" has been translated into English in several different ways, such as Helper, Comforter, Counselor, Advocate, and even Friend. The root meaning of the word is simply "one called alongside." Jesus promised to send someone to be with His followers, but that leaves the question as to why the Paraclete was going to come alongside them. What was the Holy Spirit going to do? What role would the Spirit have in their lives? Some scholars have concluded that the answer to the question of who the Paraclete

---

[1] This section and the one following draw heavily from: Jackie Johns, *The Pedagogy of the Holy Spirit: According to Early Christian Tradition* (Cleveland, Tennessee: CPM Press, 2012) 42-48.

is rests in what the Paraclete does; the Paraclete is what the Paraclete does.[2]

In these final instructions, Jesus refers to the Holy Spirit as the Paraclete five times, with each reference shedding some light on what the Holy Spirit would do with and for His followers. The first reference (14: 15-21) has a clear overtone of comfort. Jesus tells them He is going away but would not leave them as orphans. He would no longer be with them, at least not in the flesh, but the Paraclete would be with them forever. With the arrival of the Paraclete, Jesus would also be with them forever. Jesus had been their Paraclete, and this new Paraclete would be with them in the place of Jesus, making the presence of Jesus real to them.

This first reference to the Paraclete lays the foundation for the ones that follow. Significantly, Jesus made this promise to the disciples in conjunction with his instruction that they must keep his commandments—with an emphasis on His commandment that they love one another (John 13:34-35; 14:15-21). The Christian life is a life of love. There seems to be an implication that the Holy Spirit will help us love others even when it is difficult.

Also, in these verses, he identifies the Paraclete as being the "Spirit of Truth." He uses that phrase in reference to the Paraclete in two more of the five sayings. Jesus is the Truth, and Truth is of the Spirit; they are one. The Spirit will be a true connection between Jesus and His followers. The Spirit will not come just to console them. The Spirit will come to faithfully continue the teaching ministry of Jesus; the Spirit of Truth will lead them into Truth.

The other four references to the Paraclete expand on the role of the Spirit as teacher. In the second Paraclete reference (John 14:25-31), Jesus states that the Spirit/Paraclete will teach them "all things" and

---

[2] Eskil Franck, *Revelation Taught: The Paraclete in the Gospel of John* (Chicago: C.W.K., 1985), 21.

remind them of everything he (Jesus) had said (v. 26). The point is that the Spirit will teach them everything they need to know and do this in part by making the words of Jesus freshly relevant to everything they would face. The message is vibrant: the Holy Spirit will keep the Word of God alive, fresh, and relevant for the followers of Jesus.

Jesus makes the third reference to the Paraclete (John 15:20-27) in connection with the coming hatred of the world for the disciples. Jesus links their future with the world's rejection of Him and of His Father. He had been rejected because of His words and His works. When the Paraclete comes, He will speak on behalf of Jesus, and the words of the Paraclete on behalf of Christ will be accompanied by the words of the disciples (v. 27). In the face of great opposition, they will be partners with the Holy Spirit in bearing witness to Christ.

The last two Paraclete sayings are even more closely linked. Taken together, they offer complementary pictures of the work of the Spirit. The Spirit will expose sin, righteousness, and judgment, and on the other hand, the Spirit will bring glory to Christ by instructing believers. The Spirit will cause people to know the ugliness of evil and to know the beauty of Christ.

More specifically, in the fourth saying (John 16:7-8) the Spirit is portrayed as the agent who makes known what sin and righteousness are, and the Spirit also ensures God's judgment on the "ruler of this world." These are further references to the Paraclete acting in the role of a teacher. The Spirit will help people recognize the differences between sin and righteousness.

The final saying (John 16:12-15) again places the Spirit/Paraclete in the role of a teacher. In this instance, the Spirit is promised as a guide into "all the truth" and as one who will announce things yet to come (v. 13). He will speak only that which He hears from Christ and the Father. In this role, the Paraclete will fulfill the great task of glorifying Christ by "taking" what belongs to Christ and "declaring" it to His followers.

From these five sayings, we can draw several conclusions that should aid us in our Bible studies. First, the work of the Spirit/Paraclete is an extension of the teaching ministry of Jesus. The Spirit is "another" Paraclete but only in the sense that He is of the same kind as Jesus. Jesus and the Spirit are one in nature, purpose, and message. The Holy Spirit is present with us, connecting us to Christ who is teaching us the way of life.

Second, the Spirit/Paraclete centers his teachings on the recorded commandments of Christ and on other words coming from Jesus and the Father, all of which is Word of God. The Spirit will help us know what God wants us to know. The Spirit will do this by making the life and teachings of Christ fresh and relevant to our lives. It is evident that the Spirit will make meaningful the things Jesus taught while on earth and that the Spirit will communicate things not yet recorded in the Scriptures, i.e., timely prophecies.

Third, the Spirit/Paraclete will actively participate in the mission of the Church to make Jesus known. The Spirit will testify about Jesus and assist us as we testify about Jesus. There is a strong and important implication here—truly hearing the Word of God leads to speaking the Word of God. Coming to know the Scriptures results in living the Scriptures and fulfilling the Scriptures. By the Spirit, Bible study will not just change who we are, it will also change what we do—making us agents of the Kingdom of God. Our Bible study must always be toward those ends.

Taught by the Spirit

The Book of Acts offers a narrative of how the Holy Spirit continued the teaching ministry of Christ. In the introduction of the book, Luke states that his first book, the Gospel of Luke, was about all that Jesus "began to do and teach" (Acts 1:1). By implication, the second book was about what Jesus continued to do and teach after His ascension into the heavens. Acts, then, is the story of how Jesus and the Spirit taught and directed the first Christians.

While it is impossible to say exactly how the early followers of the resurrected Christ experienced the Spirit on a day-to-day basis, there are within Acts multiple accounts of the Spirit speaking to and otherwise directing the Church. From the Day of Pentecost forward, the Spirit is referred to in concrete terms as an active presence in the life of the Church.

On the Day of Pentecost, the Holy Spirit was experienced aurally as a powerful sound and visually as flames of fire with the flames settling on each of the gathered followers of Christ. When the Spirit filled the believers, they began to speak in languages they had not learned and were heard speaking of the mighty deeds of God in those languages. Being filled with the Spirit, Peter drew upon the Old Testament to proclaim the gospel. The Old Testament Scriptures were being made fresh and relevant as the Church bore witness to Christ. God was offering salvation and the promised Spirit to all who believed in Jesus Christ, God's Son, crucified and resurrected (Acts 2).

As the Book of Acts unfolds, the Spirit is seen fulfilling the roles of the Paraclete described in John's Gospel. When Peter and John were brought before the Sadducees, rulers, priests, and high priest (Acts 4:1-22) for preaching Jesus, Peter "being filled with the Spirit" responded. When Peter and John were released, the gathered Church "with one voice" spoke out of the Old Testament Scriptures words appropriate to the situation and attributed those words to the Holy Spirit speaking through David (v. 25). The story climaxes with the statement that they were all "filled with the Holy Spirit and began to speak the word of God with boldness" (v. 31).

Likewise, when some Jews from regions outside of Israel challenged Stephen, they could not "resist the Spirit" by which Stephen spoke (Acts 6:10). Elsewhere in Acts, the Spirit revealed future events (11:27-28; 21:11), guided the Church in decisions (13:2; 15:28), identified evil and righteousness (13:9-10) and gave specific instructions for ministry (8:29; 10:19-20; 11:12; 13:2-4; 16:6-8; 20:22-23).

The teaching role of the Spirit is further seen in the Pauline epistles of the New Testament. The Spirit knows everything, including the depths of God (1 Cor 2:10). The Spirit reveals the things of God and gives understanding as to their meaning (vv. 11-12). The Spirit teaches things that cannot be learned by human wisdom (vv. 13-14). The Spirit teaches through charismatic gifts at work in church gatherings, including words of wisdom, words of knowledge, prophesies, tongues, and interpretation of tongues (12: 8-10). The Spirit is an immanent guide and aide in righteous Christian living (Gal 4:16-25). The Spirit has revealed the mystery of the gospel to Paul, to the Apostles, and to the prophets (Eph 3:1-5). The Holy Spirit works through the Word of God (6:17).

The General Epistles paint a similar picture of the Spirit. The Spirit sanctifies so that believers might be obedient to Jesus (1 Pet 1:2). The Spirit is an active agent in the preaching of the good news of Christ (v. 12). The prophets who wrote the Scriptures prophesied under the unction of the Spirit so there should be no private interpretation of the Scriptures (2 Pet 1:20-21). There is a link between knowing the Spirit and obeying the commandments of Christ (1 John 3:24). Only by the Spirit do we know that we abide in Christ (4:13). The Spirit testifies of Jesus, for the Spirit is the truth (5:6-8). It should be noted as well that in the Book of Revelation, it is the Spirit with Christ who instructs the churches (Rev 2:1-3:22).

For the Christians in the New Testament, the Word of God came to them through the life, ministry, and words of Jesus and through the Old Testament Scriptures, the believer's experiences with the Spirit, and prophetic revelations. The Holy Spirit was the agent communicating God's Word to the Church. One can deduce from the experiences and beliefs of the early church that it was the Spirit who gave the Scriptures, and only the Spirit can guide believers into the proper understanding of the Scriptures. The Spirit communicates the Word of God in all its forms.

In the 21st Century, it is clear that the Spirit continues to teach those who hunger to know God. The Spirit speaks through the Bible to transform lives and make the Bible relevant to our daily lives. The Spirit emboldens us to proclaim the message of the Bible. With the active assistance of the Holy Spirit we can understand the Word of God and conform to the Word of God. We can have the Holy Spirit's help to know God and His Word. By the Spirit, the Word of God continues to flow into and through the lives of believers.

Knowing What We Study

If we seriously consider what the Bible says about the Holy Spirit, our Bible study will be transformed from an intellectual struggle to understand into a personal and relational event of knowing. Knowing requires understanding, but understanding does not always lead to knowing, at least not in the biblical sense of knowing.

In the Western world, we think of knowledge as a measurable thing. How much do you know about cars, computers, chemistry, or anything else? Like the ancient Greeks and Romans, we think of knowing as something that requires observing, measuring, and categorizing. Like them, we also think of wisdom as knowing what to do with that knowledge. In the Bible, knowledge and wisdom are more experiential and relational concepts.

The ancient Hebrews did not perceive of knowing something as the product of standing back, looking at it and analyzing what it is. They knew someone or something not by objective analysis but by encountering the person or thing. Knowledge comes through engagement. They might say, "You don't know a cake by studying the recipe; you know it by the taste and texture." This is why in the Bible sexual intimacy is referred to as *knowing* a person. Knowledge arises out of a shared experience.

The ancient Hebrews were also less inclined to know the contents of a book than to know the author of the book as revealed by the contents of the book. They did not meditate on the law of God just for self-improvement; they studied the Scriptures so they might know and please God. Wisdom for them was less about knowing what to do in various circumstances than about knowing how to exist before God and with others in all the circumstances of life.

This is the great promise of the gospel. In Christ, God came and dwelt among us so humanity might see and touch Him, i.e., know Him. Because of Jesus, we can know God and stand face to face before Him. If we know Jesus, we know the Father. This, then, is also the central promise of the Spirit's arrival on Pentecost. The Holy Spirit has come so we might know Jesus and the Father. Knowing the Spirit is the means of knowing the Father and the Son. The Spirit, the Son, and the Father can be known by knowing the Spirit-Word of God.

Similarly, we in the Western world tend to think of words as abstract concepts detached both from what they represent and from the person speaking the words. The word *ball* is not a ball, and the word *ball* is the same no matter who speaks it. In the Bible, words are expressions of the person speaking the words. "Out of the abundance of heart the mouth speaks" (Matt 12:34). A person is known by his or her words; by words a person expresses himself or herself. When we speak, we do not just reveal what we think, we also reveal something of who we are.

In the Scriptures, words can be expressed as thoughts or actions, but they are never completely detached from the person who offers them. This is one of the reasons we say that God is always present in the Bible; it is His Word. It is also one of the reasons we say the Spirit and the Word cannot be separated. They are one; they completely know each other. Therefore, to know one is to know the other.

It is important that we keep in mind, however, that God is only known by faith. Knowing the presence of God does not require a palpable experience. It requires faith that God is speaking even when we are not hearing. The presence of God does not depend on our ability to sense His presence. Even powerful manifestations of the Spirit of God require faith to know that it is indeed God at work. Faith that God is speaking through the Scriptures then nurtures faith that the Spirit will help us hear all we need to hear. RIBS must be faith-filled Bible study.

God is not speaking at us; He is speaking to us with a desire to speak with us.

Take a moment to reflect on what we have been saying. The Bible is an ancient book of books that is also the present Word of God. It is literature but it is also a living book. It is more than a Word from God; it is the Word of God. The Spirit of God and the Word of God are bound together making the Bible the Spirit-Word of God. The goal of Bible study should be to know God and not just know about him. Knowing God is not through reason alone; we know God through encounters with Him by faith. When we study the Bible believing it is the Word of God, we are encountering our triune God: Father, Son, and Holy Spirit. God is not speaking at us; He is speaking to us with a desire to speak with us. The Holy Spirit has come to us to teach us everything God wants us to know.

Bible Study as Consecrated Worship

When we worship in the Spirit and in truth we have entered deep fellowship with God. In those times, we discover our worship in the Spirit unites us with the Father, the Spirit, and the Word. Jesus alluded to this connection between the Father, the Spirit, the Word, and our worship when He was talking with the Samaritan woman at the well:

> But an hour is coming, and is now here, when the true worshipers will worship the Father in Spirit and in truth. Yes, the Father wants such people to worship him. God is spirit, and those who worship him must worship in Spirit and in truth (John 4:23-24, CSB).

This exhortation takes on fuller meaning later in John's Gospel when Jesus says,

> I am the way, the truth, and the life. No one comes to the Father except through me. If you know me, you will also know my Father. From now on you do know him and have seen him (John 14:6-7, CSB).

A few verses later in His first reference to the Holy Spirit as "the Paraclete" (translated "Counselor" in the CSB), Jesus speaks about the Spirit with words very close to what He had just said about himself and the Father:

> If you love me, you will keep my commands. And I will ask the Father, and he will give you another Counselor to be with you forever. He is the Spirit of truth. The world is unable to receive him because it doesn't see him or know him. But you do know him, because he remains with you and will be in you (John 14:15-17, CSB).

In summation, God desires that we worship Him in Spirit and in truth. Jesus is the Word of God in human flesh. He is the truth. The Paraclete is the Spirit of truth. Just as Jesus and the Spirit are inseparable, the Word and the truth are inseperable. To know Jesus is to know the truth. To know Jesus is also to know the Father. The Spirit of truth is a gift from Jesus and the Father, given that we might know all three of them, given that we might worship them in truth.

In light of these observations, Bible study should be thought of as an event of worship. Consciousness of God's presence should circumscribe our Bible reading and study, demands an attitude of worship. As worship, attending to God's Word becomes more than a Christian duty meant to prepare us for life; it becomes an opportunity to present ourselves before God as living sacrifices. We are priests in the kingdom of God who offer ourselves before the fire of God's Word to be judged, taught, transformed, commissioned, and empowered. These are our "reasonable acts of worship" (Rom 12:1-2).

When we enter the Scriptures, we enter into consecrated time, space, and service; we enter the world of the kingdom of God.

In Bible study then, we are (or should be) priests serving before God in the holy Temple of His Word. This requires that we recognize that when we enter the Scriptures, we enter into consecrated time, space, and service; we enter the world of the Kingdom of God. Our study then belongs to God. We apply ourselves to understanding the Bible because the process of Bible study is ministry to our heavenly Father; it is worship. By our study, we then conform more and more to the image of our Creator and that brings Him glory.

We live in a time when few things are held as sacred and when few people see a need for the consecration of anything. For many, God has become an option, and the things of God are treated like tools for self-fulfillment. If we are to hear God speaking in the Scriptures, the Bible must be for us a sacred vessel of his presence. Our times of reading and studying the Bible must be consecrated to Him— seen as holy, belonging to God, and set aside by us for His service.

Acts of consecration bridge the ordinary world in which we live and the world that is coming through Christ, that is, his reign. The ordinary and the sacred are fused as the temporary is enfolded into the eternal. Time and space exist in two worlds that are merging. Heaven comes to earth, and we enter the presence of God. That which is passing away fades into the brilliance of that which can never fade.

Let us never forget that the presence of God is a fearful thing. He is to be revered. Time in his presence requires withdrawal from everything that might distract us, everything that does not belong with us in his presence. Communion with him in Bible study demands that we focus on him and ignore things that might sidetrack our studies. This suggests that we be intentional about when and where we study God's Word. If possible, we should have designated times for study and a dedicated place for study. It helps if the place is one set aside just for meeting with God. The ordinary patterns of our lives must be set aside to the extent possible. It takes effort to alienate ourselves from distractions.

Consecration further requires that we be intentional about preparing ourselves to study God's Word. We must spiritually prepare by quieting our hearts and minds, setting aside things that might be pressing in on us so we can renew the consecration of ourselves. We should examine ourselves to see whether there is anything that might deafen our ears to the voice of God.

It helps to review that which qualifies us for the kingdom of God, our adoption into God's family through Jesus Christ our Lord and this by grace alone. We can then enter God's presence with confidence, reverence, and humility, having made certain that everything about our Bible study is dedicated to the glory and purposes of God.

Through these preparations, Bible study becomes a form of prayer. By this we mean something more than just praying about our study. Yes, we should pray before, during, and after studying the Bible, asking God to open our eyes to see, our ears to hear, and our hearts to obey. Beyond this, the study itself should be seen and experienced as prayer.

We are inclined to think of prayer as talking to God when we should view it as talking with God. That is, our prayer times should be laced with active listening to hear from God. Much like the rhythm of our breathing, Bible study should be peppered with pauses to meditate on what we are studying. Since the Bible is God speaking to us, Bible study itself should be seen as listening to the voice of God. The question is, will we hear clearly what God is saying?

Approaching the Bible as an opportunity to talk with God requires that our study be marked by both reasoned research and spiritual discernment. We must hone our readiness for communion between God's Spirit and our spirit. We are seeking both meaning and personal transformation. In the presence of God, the questions of what we should think and believe, what we should be and feel, and what we should do are all bound together in the one question, what does God want to speak into my life?

In the presence of God, the questions of what we should think and believe, what we should be and feel, and what we should do are all bound together in the one question, what does God want to speak into my life?

Bible study should not just lead one to understanding followed by Christ-like actions; it should itself be approached as a Spirit-led activity. It should do more than prepare us for an unseen future; it should bring God's promised future into our present lives. Bible study should not just point toward godly affections; godly affections should be birthed and renewed within us as we study. Bible study should bring our whole being into the presence of God where we bow before Him with praise and thanksgiving.

No set of skills can be learned that will cause this kind of Bible study to happen. It happens when persons who have been made alive by the Spirit of God enter the garden of God's Word in faith. It happens when sincere hearts hunger to hear from God. It happens when our spirits know and discern the Holy Spirit. It happens when we are filled with faith and are fully committed to disciplined study of the

Scriptures. Faith and reason are then united with worship and study in a single effort to know and please God.

Summary

Relational Inductive Bible Study begins with a heart that desires to know and please God and a mind dedicated to hearing and understanding the Word of God. It must then be carried out with faith that God desires to communicate with us personally through our Bible study. We must believe that God is in his Word and will reward all who diligently seek him in his Word. We must have confidence that the Holy Spirit is by our side and within us as we search the Bible to know God better. We must believe the Spirit-Word is the agent that links our hearts with the heart of God.

Chapter 4

Literature That is of God

Did you know the word *bible* comes from the Greek word for "books?" We think of it as one book, but historically it was thought of as a collection of books. It is an anthology of sacred literature. The word *scripture* is derived from a Latin word for "writing," or what might be called a "document." There are sixty-six documents in the Bible. Each is a piece of literature breathed by the Spirit of God through the hearts and minds of human authors. Together, they tell the story of God's personal involvement with humanity and his ongoing plans for reconciliation with all of creation.

Books of Literature

God gave the Bible one book at a time. For generations, the books of the Bible were distributed and read as individual pieces of literature. In time they were gathered into small libraries along with other books considered sacred. Before the time of Christ, the Hebrew scrolls of biblical texts were being gathered in the synagogues of the Jewish people. Although it has been recently challenged, tradition holds that the Old Testament canon of thirty-nine books was established at the Jewish councils of Jamnia (Yavneh) in 90 and 118 A.D.

Decades after Christ's life on earth, the Church began collecting the writings of the apostles and in time united them with the Old Testament Scriptures. These early collections of scrolls and manuscripts included some Jewish and Christian writings not believed by all to be the inspired Word of God. The Christian Bible with Old and New Testament books took its lasting form during early Christian history as the Church began segregating the books that did not measure up to being divinely inspired Word of God. In 397 A.D., the Council of Bishops at Carthage formally recognized the canon of Scripture as including the sixty-six books of the Bible. The Council also included some apocryphal books from the time between the Old and New Testaments, but these were given lesser status and were later removed by most Protestant Christians.

When we say the Bible is the Book of Books, we are making two assertions. First, we are affirming the unity of the books of the Bible and declaring it to be one great book inspired by God. In this we are exalting the Bible above all other books; in its essence, it is beyond comparison with any other literature. Of all the books in the world, it alone is Word of God.

Second, we are stating that the Bible contains multiple books authored by dozens of different human beings. Each book was originally written to stand on its own. Different authors wrote in different times, under different circumstances, and each had different persons in mind as they wrote. The Bible is an anthology of Judeo-Christian literature.

For most of us, it is a challenge to hold both these truths together, but it is a challenge we must take. We cannot accurately hear what God is saying to us if we do not accept that the Bible is both fully the Word of God and fully the words of humans. The Bible is one book of divine authorship, and it is many books of divinely inspired

Judeo-Christian literature. God inspired people to write the books of the Bible without the loss of any aspect of their human existence.

Inspired Human Literature

When we say the Bible is human literature inspired by God, we have three realities in mind: historicity, objectivity, and practicality. First, when and under what circumstances were the books of the Bible inspired? Second, who/what is inspired, the authors or the text? Third, what does inspiration mean in practical terms?

In one sense, inspiration was a series of events that took place in history—something that happened to the apostles and prophets as they wrote the books. Unfortunately, many people think that inspiration ended when ink touched paper (or parchment, as may have been the case). They see inspiration as the experience of the writers of the Scriptures. Yes, inspiration was something that happened to the writers, but it is important that we recognize that inspiration did not end there.

The writers <u>were</u> inspired, but the Bible <u>is</u> inspired. Focusing on inspiration as something that happened to the human authors overshadows the nature of the Scriptures as Word of God in literary form. The persons and events that birthed the Scriptures are important, but we should never think of inspiration as something that merely happened in the past. Rather, we must place more emphasis on the divine side of the Word of God as inspired literature. The Bible is the eternal and living Word of God existing within creation. It has a history of becoming inspired literature, but the inspiration of the Scriptures is not limited to that history. The Bible exists as literature continually being breathed by God. As such, it continues in history, making history.

As noted in earlier chapters, we believe the Bible is the Spirit-Word of God. The Holy Spirit continues to dwell in the books of the Bible, making them holy space where God is continually present. God can be found in His Word. Inspiration of the Bible is never ending. In brief, it is not events of inspiration that make the Bible the Word of God. It is being the Word of God that makes the Bible inspired.

It is not inspiration that makes the Bible the Word of God. It is being the Word of God that makes the Bible inspired.

The inspiration of the Bible began with the experiences of persons knowing God's presence. By the Holy Spirit, human authors had some type of immediate contact with God. We don't know the exact nature of that contact, that is, how each one experienced divine inspiration. For some, clearly, they knew they were speaking and writing the Word of God. For others, the level of their awareness remains unclear. But it is clear from many of the texts themselves that the writers were conscious of what they were writing and wrote with their own volition. Sometimes, as with Jeremiah, God would dictate specific prophecies to write down, but for the most part the exact words seem to have been jointly those of God and the human authors.

Because it is Spirit-Word of God, the Bible was written both for specific times and for all times. That is, the books of the Bible were written in certain historic contexts to address unique sets of human issues. At the same time, the Bible was inspired so as to address issues for all generations. Whenever we read and study the Bible, God is speaking directly to us. What He says to us, though, can never be disconnected from what He was saying to the first readers.

Some have concluded that the meaning of biblical texts changes with every generation. In this view, the Spirit speaks through the Bible words appropriate to changing realities without any clear link to the realities of the first readers. In this view, there is no need to understand what the Bible meant when originally written. What is important for those who hold this view is that God is speaking through the Bible words meaningful for the current reader. They hold that the Bible contains the Word of God or is a channel for the Word, but it is not itself the Word of God. This approach reduces the Bible to an ahistorical looking glass through which different people find different meanings.

Our understanding that God is always present in the Bible does not imply that there is discontinuity between what He is saying to modern readers and what He was saying when the books were first written. It is quite the opposite. God's presence establishes continuity. There is only one true message in every text of the Bible. Every generation, however, must discover that message and discern its meaning for their situation.

Many will challenge what we just stated. They insist that there can only be one message and one meaning for each text of the Bible—the original ones. Their approach to Bible study then is a quest to discover the one, true, and original meaning of each text of the Bible. Because they limit inspiration to the moment the text was being written, they can only allow for one meaning—the one in the human author's mind at the time he wrote. Subsequent readers must discover that original meaning and then try with God's help to apply it to their situation.

Our view is that the Bible is Word of God wed to human language continually being inspired by God. Through inspired persons and literature (the Bible) God was and is speaking to all generations in His eternal now. This demands that we understand a dynamic link to exist between the meaning for the original readers and the meaning for all other readers. For every biblical text, there is but one eternal message enveloped within the limits of human language, a message that speaks to all generations and contexts. God's continuing presence makes limited human literature to be unlimited and therefore applicable to all regardless of the situations in which they live.

Our quest is to understand God's message that lies behind as well as within the words. It was not what the human author or the original readers understood that was the eternal Word of God. It is what God was and is saying that is eternal and life giving. Our task is the same as theirs, and that is to answer these questions: What is God saying through the biblical text, and what does that message mean for us?

Our quest is to understand God's message that lies behind as well as within the words.

Our answers to those questions cannot be separated from the contexts of the author and the original recipients, but neither should our answers be limited to their understandings of the text. In biblical interpretation, we have the benefit of knowing some things about their contexts and knowing many things about our own. We can also bring with us to our interpretations the long history of how believers received the text.

The essential nature of the Bible is that it is a continuing gift of God's presence. It is revelation from God about God and revelation from God about creation—about us. Recognizing that there are limits to analogies, we risk offering one; the Scriptures are a light shining on us so we might see. They are both what God wants us to see and the means whereby we can see. They are the windows through which we can see and the ray of light that makes it possible to see.

The Scriptures are ... both what God wants us to see and the means whereby we can see.

With that understanding, the Scriptures are like a beam of light; the one beam has many shades of color within it which are only seen when the beam is refracted. The same beam of light has differing effects on things it might shine upon. With one ray of light, things are seen as red, yellow, blue or some other hue. Likewise, the light that shone on the original receivers of the Scriptures in their context is the same beam that shines on us in our context; it is the colors of our contexts that differ.

The beam does not change even if its effects do. To see clearly what God is showing us about our lives, we need to consider both what He was revealing in the original context (the beam touching them) and what He is highlighting in our own (the same beam touching us). The two must flow together as one direct revelation given to many contexts so that all may see and be seen. We should view the Bible as both revelation of and about the past and as revelation upon, about, and to us.

Human reality does not vary greatly from generation to generation. There is nothing new under the sun. Our immediate circumstances vary but as humans we have common life experiences. Loneliness is loneliness. Joy is joy, Sorrow is sorrow. Fear is fear. Faith is faith. Evil is evil.

Furthermore, we should keep in mind that the message of the Bible is more than the words it contains. One might think of it this way: God purposefully chose the author, the context, who the initial recipients were, and what the subject matter was to be. All these elements, combined with the type and style of literature, contributed to the messages of the books. They are bonded to the message so that the whole is greater than the sum of its parts. In other words, how something is said and the context in which it is said are elements of what is being said. For example, the words, "I love you," spoken to a close friend who is dying and the words, "I love you," spoken romantically to one's spouse on a wedding anniversary have very different meanings. Context matters.

This raises a complex question as to how the original contexts of the books of the Bible contribute to the message of the book for us. Knowing about the context helps us understand the author's intended meaning, but what does it contribute to our understanding? As previously stated, the message of a book of the Bible for our generation is linked to the message for the original recipients. Our interpretation should not stray far from theirs. Our task, however, has only just begun when we determine its meaning for the original recipients; we must journey further to inquire as to the eternal meaning for all generations and how that speaks to us in our context.

We are not saying that we must uncover the principles beneath the text. Principles are constructs two steps removed from the voice of God. They are impersonal, abstract, and lack the force of the particular. Looking for principles to live by gives more authority to our constructed opinions than to the text from which we derive them. Our goal must be to hear God speak to us directly out of His Word. He may through the Scriptures give us principles to live by, but we must never reduce the Bible to principles.

Finally, if the persons and events surrounding the origins of the books of the Bible are indeed aspects of the message of the Bible, in what sense was God active in all those things? Did God orchestrate all the events within and surrounding the origins of the Bible? These are deep theological questions about the sovereignty of God that have been greatly debated. In our view, we should read the Bible as an accurate record of how God interacted with His creation and not a record of how God controlled His creation. God did not sanction everything recorded in the Scriptures. The fact that God spoke in history and continues to speak through the events of history does not mean that God acted to make all those events take place. God used the events of history to speak into creation, incorporating history into His written word. In brief, the events within the Bible are accurate records of how God has interacted with humanity and not records of how he controls human history.

Characteristics of Human Literature

As human literature, the books of the Bible share some common traits. For one thing, each of the books of the Bible has a central theme or message around which the book revolves. The author had a primary reason for writing. The themes are developed using a variety of methods. The methods may include stories, poems, argumentation, or declarations, etc., but each book has a primary purpose and theme revealed through the content, type and form of the literature.

In most cases, secondary themes support the main theme and may be concentrated in one section of the book or woven throughout the book. For example, John's Gospel has been called the "Gospel of Belief." This main theme is stated near the end of the book: "But these are written so that you may come to believe that Jesus is the Messiah, the Son of God, and that through believing you may have life in his name" (John 20:31, NRSV). But the theme of belief is developed throughout John's Gospel and only reaches its climax in chapter 20.

There are two secondary themes reflected in verse 31 of chapter 20. One secondary theme addresses the question of what it means that "Jesus is the Messiah, the Son of God." The other secondary theme addresses the question of what is "life in his name." These two sub-themes are also woven throughout the book.

Another characteristic of literature is that each book has a structural design that contributes to the development of the theme of the book. The structure marks how the theme is developed through units and sub-units of text. Each of the books can be divided into large and small units just like modern books are divided into chapters, chapters are typically divided into sections, sections are divided into paragraphs, etc.

For several centuries, Bible translations have been marked with chapter and verse divisions. These can mislead readers. Yes, they can serve as helpful aids for quickly locating portions of Scripture, and, to a lesser degree, for Scripture memorization, but they are not part of the biblical text. Through the centuries a variety of systems for dividing and numbering the books of the Bible into chapters and verses have been used. Our current chapter divisions were arranged in the thirteenth century, and our verse divisions are from the sixteenth century.

The verse numerals are especially problematic when it comes to reading and studying the Bible. Quite often they simply are in the wrong place. Sentences are sometimes split between verses, and in some cases two sentences appear in the same verse; sometimes one verse contains parts of two different sentences.

Another problem with the verse markings is that they chop the Scriptures into little bits and pieces misconstrued as freestanding nuggets of truth. This leads to faulty readings of the text. The markings all too often lead to interruptions in the author's flow of thought, making it easy to blur the big picture and misinterpret what is written. When studying the Bible as literature, it is best to try to ignore these artificial divisions, especially the verse numberings, except to use them as reference points. Do your best to read sentences and not verses.

Modern translations of the Bible do a better job of marking the literary structure of the books and providing titles that describe the content of each of the smaller sections of a book. Still, these divisions and titles were not in the original books of the Bible; they are not inspired Word of God. They are helpful, but they may not be the best representations of the contents of the unit they describe. Different translations divide books at different locations and give titles that vary as well.[1] As we will see, the inductive approach to Bible study encourages the student to make his or her own determination of where divisions in a book exist and how they might best be titled.

---

[1] See Appendix A, which provides a chart comparing the divisions and titles of Ephesians according to the CSB, NRSV, and NET translations.

Parts and the Whole

In good literature, every part of the book contributes something to the whole, but not every part is of equal significance. Some sentences just seem to encapsulate large portions of a literary piece and might even be pulled out to stand on their own. They carry a heavier weight of meaning than other portions of the work. This is true for the Bible. Consider John 3:16, "For God so loved the world that he gave his only Son, so that everyone who believes in him may not perish but may have eternal life" (NRS). This beautiful and powerful sentence in many ways carries the full weight of the gospel. Yet even this beloved verse loses most of its meaning for those who do not know who God or His Son are.

This does not make any portion of the Bible less than the eternal Word of God. Every sentence is of great significance to the whole. It merely means that some portions of the books of the Bible have more supporting roles than others. God still speaks through every word.

Likewise, some sections of a book might be plucked out to stand on their own as statements of God's truth. For example, the Parable of the Prodigal Son (Luke 15:11-32) is a story with deep meaning that could be published and read as a separate tract. If that were done, it would continue to be the eternal Word of God with a powerful message, but some of its meaning would be lost. The connection between the father in the story and God our Father would be missing without the image of God contained in the rest of the Gospel. The parable draws much from its place in Luke's Gospel, and the Gospel draws much from it. The full meaning of any biblical text can only be gained by considering its place within the book from which it comes.

One of the major tasks of Bible book studies involves discovering how the various parts of a book fit together to convey the central theme of the book. This task requires the student to identify the major theme, discover the structure of the book, and describe how the various sections fit together to communicate the theme.

Whether poetry or prose, narrative or epistle, books have points of transition, places where the author shifts emphasis, or topic, or literary style. Those places of change mark the structure of the book, and the structure reveals how the author developed the theme of the book. In other words, the message of a book is woven into the structure of the book. Each part of a book contributes to the message. The author's purpose for writing is most clearly seen by recognizing how its various parts fit together.

Varieties of
Biblical Literature

When studying the Bible, it is helpful to keep in mind how the book relates to other books in the Bible. Where and how does it fit with the whole. We noted above that the messages of the various books of the Bible are contained in more than the words in the book. The genre, or general type, of literature and the style of writing do not just help communicate the message; the message is within them, and they are within the message.

There are reasons why much of the books of the prophets is written as poetry; the rhythm, cadence, and word patterns tap into different dimensions of the human psyche, adding meaning beyond the limits of prose. The personal and informal character of the prose of the epistles has a different impact from the prose of the narratives. Those reasons may be difficult to identify, but that does not make them unimportant.

We typically group the books of the Bible according to the order in which they appear. The two testaments are commonly grouped as follows in Figure 4.1.

Figure 4.1: "Classification of Bible Books"

Old Testament

The Books of Moses (also known as the Pentateuch, the Law, or the Torah): Genesis, Exodus, Leviticus, Numbers, Deuteronomy

Historical Books: Joshua, Judges, Ruth, 1 and 2 Samuel, 1 and 2 Kings, Ezra, Nehemiah, Esther

Wisdom Literature: Job, Psalms, Proverbs, Ecclesiastes, Song of Solomon

Major Prophets: Isaiah, Jeremiah, Lamentations, Ezekiel, Daniel

Minor Prophets: Hosea, Joel, Amos, Obadiah, Jonah, Micah, Nahum, Habakkuk, Zephaniah, Haggai, Zachariah, Malachi

New Testament

Gospels and Acts (or New Testament Narratives): Matthew, Mark, Luke, John, Acts

Pauline Epistles: Romans, 1 and 2 Corinthians, Galatians, Ephesians, Philippians, Colossians, 1 and 2 Thessalonians, 1 and 2 Timothy, Titus, Philemon

General Epistles: Hebrews; James; 1 and 2 Peter; 1, 2 and 3 John; Jude

Apocalypse: Revelation

Because we are accustomed to it, the traditional order and grouping is perhaps the easiest with which to work, but it may not prove the most helpful for studying the Bible as literature. This is especially true when it comes to the wisdom literature and the prophets. It can be helpful to categorize the books of the Bible according to literary genre.

Grouping according to genre requires re-classifying some of the books in the Old Testament. The Psalms and the Song of Solomon would not be listed as Wisdom Literature. They would be set alongside Lamentations and labeled as what they are—Books of Songs. Thinking of them as lyrics originally set to music adds depth to their meaning. Job, Proverbs, and Ecclesiastes would then be grouped as Wisdom Literature.

Except for Daniel, the major and minor prophets would all be identified simply as Books of the Prophets with the option of subdividing the set according to literary sub-types or length (long and short). Daniel in the Old Testament might be joined with Revelation in the New Testament to form the genre of Apocalyptic Literature. The remainder of the Old Testament could be collected as Narrative Literature.

The four Gospels would typically be recognized as existing in a genre of their own. Each contains narratives from the life of Christ, but they are distinct from narrative literature in that the sequence of events are not entirely chronological. They are doing more than telling a story. They use events in the life of Christ to reveal the person of Jesus Christ. They are more commentaries on who Jesus is that biographies of his earthly life.

In terms of genre, the Acts of the Apostles could be grouped with the Old Testament narrative literature, or because of its unique traits, it could stand on its own.

We cannot stress enough that the Bible must be approached as being both the Spirit-Word of God's presence and as human literature— the eternal Word of God wed to human language. If we are to receive from our Bible study all that God desires for us, both natures must be honored. Being mindful of genre is one way of honoring the Bible as human literature. As will be seen in Chapter 10, this calls for careful preparation before we take up the Bible to study it.

Chapter 5

Literary Types and Structures

"I then search after and consider parallel passages of Scripture, 'comparing spiritual things with spiritual.' I meditate thereon with all the attention and earnestness of which my mind is capable.

—John Wesley

The Bible is the Word of God and a literary treasure. Good inductive study takes careful note of the literary types and structure of each book. Bible study must always seek the meaning that lies behind the text. Just what is God saying? The human author's choice of literary tools holds significant clues for the meaning of the texts.

In Chapter 4, we introduced the concepts of literary types and structures (structural design). Literary type refers to the genre of literature the author has chosen to write her or his book: prose or poetry. Literary structure refers to the way the author develops the theme of the book in progressive sections of text, i.e., how it is divided into parts. Observing literary types and structures helps the reader make discoveries within the text at a deeper level. When you see how the elements of a book connect at this level, you can begin to see some deeper meanings.

Literary Types

The Bible is written in the two basic types of literature: prose and poetry. Prose is literature written in the general pattern in which people speak. It may be formal in style, conforming to all the rules of grammar, or it mày be informal, written in the style of everyday conversation.

Poetry is a type of literature not strictly bound by rules of grammar. Many of us think of it as using rhymes, but that definition is way too narrow. Poetry uses the interplay of words and rhythms (and sometimes rhyme) to create a multidimensional message that connects more holistically with the human psyche. Observing the literary type(s) of a book or passage within a book helps us get a more complete picture of the author's frame of mind. It sheds light on the scope of the meaning being shared.

Prose Literature

In general, the sections of the Bible written in prose are the historical books of the Old Testament, the Gospels, Acts, the epistles, and the apocalyptic books. Sections of the prophetic writings also contain prose. There are two categories, or sub-types, of prose literature. The first may be called discursive prose, a written discourse or speech presenting the direct communication of a message. Paul's epistles are good examples of this style of literature.

Narrative is prose that tells a story. Narratives are written stories created to convey a message or theme. Stories are told for a reason. The elements of the story are fitted together to have a primary effect on the reader. The story form avoids the dull rehashing of mere facts and concepts by embedding the facts and concepts in a narrative that exposes a larger meaning.

In biblical narratives, there is always truth that is larger than the story being conveyed as history. Every book of the Bible is written to communicate theological truth. Study of the Bible as literature is a quest to excavate those truths. This is not to say that the events described in the stories of the Bible are not accurate or important. It merely says that the truth of God often comes into and through the messiness of human history.

The Bible chronicles how God came to be known, how He reaches out to touch His creation, and how people have responded to His self-revelation. God inspired narratives to be written that speak of what He has done (past) in a manner that reveals what He is saying and doing (present). These stories teach sound doctrine when properly interpreted.

Poetic Literature

Prose is not always adequate to plumb the depths of the human soul. Poetry takes up where prose leaves off. It is an unbounded artistry well suited for tapping into affections, feelings, and the mysteries of life. It makes use of elements of sound such as rhyme, rhythm, and cadence. In poetic literature, joy, love, grief, anger, and other emotions can be expressed in profound and beautiful ways. Poetry can delve deeply into the human soul as the soul struggles to survive and thrive. It speaks to the human spirit in ways prose cannot.

Scholars type poetry in different ways, using many labels. For our purposes, we may view poetry in the Scriptures primarily through the lens of three sub-types. The first, epic poetry, is narrative; it tells a story in poetic form. There are many examples of epic poetry embedded in books of the Bible. For example, the "Song of Moses" in Exodus 15:1-19 recounts Israel's deliverance from Egypt, and the "Song of Deborah" in Judges 5:1-31 recounts the story of Jael, the woman who drove a tent peg through the head of Sisera, the commander of the Canaanite army.

A second sub-type of poetic literature in the Bible may be called lyric poetry, which is reflective in nature. It involves sharing one's thoughts and feelings concerning relationships, events, situations, and concepts. Lyric poetry has the benefit of exposing the internal life of the poet and by that generating a real sense of personal connection with the person behind the poem, inviting the reader to be open to her or his own inner realities. The Book of Psalms is full of beautiful lyric poems. There are also lyric poems embedded in books primarily written in prose.

A third sub-type may be called didactic poetry, poems that communicate practical wisdom. Predominantly, they are moral lessons communicated by parents to their children. The Book of Proverbs is a collection of this type of poetry.

When making observations on a text, note the literary types and sub-types of the text. Noting these things will aid in clarifying the author's purpose for writing, which will in turn aid your interpretation of the text.

Structural Design

One of the early tasks in inductive Bible study is to determine the structural design of the book. The books of the Bible were not written like disjointed streams of consciousness pouring out one unrelated idea after another. All the authors composed their works around themes presented in creative and logical ways. Each book has a recognizable structure on which its message is framed.

When we write about structural design, we are referring to how a book divides into sections. Structural design reveals how the author developed his or her message from beginning to end. How does the book unfold before the reader as marked by points of transition in the author's thoughts? How is the book logically divided into units and sub-units that work together in progression to reveal the author's message? How does the book proceed from the first sentence to the last to fulfill the author's purpose for writing?

Identifying the structural design of a book begins with discerning the author's main message and the main themes supporting that message. Structure exists to support the main message. Identifying the message and themes first will guide a student in discovering the major divisions and subdivisions of the book. Depending on the size and complexity of a book, subdivisions may be further divided into sub-subdivisions, etc., but for our purposes we will primarily deal with divisions and subdivisions.

There are no universal rules for what the various levels of book divisions are to be called. We will use the following labels: books are divided into "divisions," and divisions are divided into "subdivisions." Larger books require further subdividing. Subdivisions would then be divided into "sub-subdivisions," followed by "sub-sub-subdivisions." We will not, however, be working with large books in *Encountering the Living Word.*

Regardless of how many levels of divisions, for our purposes we call the smallest literary units of books "segments." Segments are comprised of one or more paragraphs that when taken together constitute a single literary unit. Each is set in its own immediate context. At this level we look most closely for the significant facts we need to study and analyze. We will more closely consider structural design of books in later chapters. For now, hold onto the idea that books by their author's design can be divided into meaningful units that work together to convey the author's message.

Meaning Behind the Words

Before looking closer at how the books of the Bible are structurally designed, it will be helpful to back up and consider the basic building blocks of communication. The Bible is, after all, written to create events of communication. What is happening when a person attempts to share his or her thoughts with another? In this section we offer a model for understanding the basic elements of communication. How does language work?

The model presented here begins with trying to understand the human thought processes that must exist before one can attempt communication. How are thoughts formed in one person to be communicated to another person?[1]

In its most basic form, communication is an attempt by one being to share with another being elements of his or her perceptions of reality. All perceptions of reality are ultimately based in experience. In essence, communication is the sharing of perceptions of reality grounded in personal experiences. This definition holds true even when the communicator is intentionally attempting to deceive.

The internal construction of our personal perceptions of reality is a dynamic process that requires both logic and imagination to "make sense" of the experiences of life. Imagination is necessary for problem solving. Without imagination, we could not 'connect the dots' of our reality or apply logic to the interpretation of experience. We could not "name our world." Communication requires creativity, both to express our perceptions and to interpret the expressions of others.

Experience teaches us that there are many things we know before we know that we know them, that is, before we can organize thoughts about an experience. Experience begs for words to help us place the experience within our ever-developing construct of reality. There is a progression of experience-based thought from wordless knowledge to worded knowledge. We may think of this as levels of meaning that move from concrete experiences of knowing to symbolized ideations of those experiences of knowing—or moving from concrete meaning to symbolic representations of meaning.

Concrete meaning may be thought of as experiences remembered but without words with which to understand or express them. Symbolic meaning may be thought of as concepts one can share with

---

[1] The following thoughts on the meaning behind the words are adapted from Robert Traina's work. Robert A. Traina, *Methodical Bible Study* (Grand Rapids, MI: Zondervan, 2002), 49-52.

others using symbols that represent concrete meaning. Concrete meaning exists only in the internal world of an individual. Symbolic meaning can be externalized as communication with others. Words are symbols for concrete meaning.

Concrete Meanings

Concrete meanings are the most fundamental units of meaning. Grounded in experience, they are root perceptions that can exist before the individual has words by which to label them. They are the foundation stones on which humans construct meaningful thought. They are "pre-words" that lack the form needed for communication between persons. A person knows the reality exists but lacks the means to label it. For example, the base concepts of "hot" and "cold" exist in a child's life before he or she knows the words needed to express them.

Concrete meanings are the subliminal blocks upon which people build language. Common human experiences create common concrete meanings ("hot" and "cold") that then give rise to the possibility of communicating through language. One may think of concrete meanings as existing with levels or stages of complexity: primary concepts, secondary concepts, primary units of thought, and expanded units of thought. Concrete thought is progressively more complex.

Primary Concepts. The most basic form of concrete meaning is a primary concept we may think of as a preconception. Primary concepts exist in one dimension of reality or truth. Psychologically, they are the "other" moving around us and acting on us. They are root conceptions that exist before they can be named: mother, father, man, woman, brother, sister, food, dog, cat, tree, flower, sit, stand, run, etc. When primary concepts come to be expressed as words, they are subjects who act, objects acted upon, or verbs that express action.

Secondary Concepts. Secondary concepts are those that descriptively enhance a primary concept or a primary unit of thought. They are a second, descriptive dimension of concrete thought. They are added texture to that which is "other." These are concepts such as red, blue, large, small, bright, dark, good, bad, fast, slow, old, young, etc. When people express secondary concepts as words, these concepts are adjectives describing subjects or objects, or adverbs that describe actions. Prepositional phrases describing objects in motion are also a type of secondary concept.

Primary Units of Thought. A primary unit of concrete thought is one that links an object with an action; it is an object-in-motion or object-in-position. When primary units of concrete thought are expressed as words, they constitute a clause, that is, a complete, understandable thought. Every primary unit of thought is an image of two primary concepts working together. If expressed in words, it is a subject acting, such as, "Joe ran."

Expanded Units of Thought. Expanded units of concrete thought are primary units with additional descriptive concepts added which provide more precision in meaning. An expanded unit of thought is a primary unit of thought descriptively enhanced. Secondary concepts add texture and a sense of completion to a primary unit of thought. The thinker is imagining more than the basic concept that "Joe ran." He or she concretely knows things like how Joe ran. When the secondary concept is added to the primary unit of thought and is expressed with words, "Joe ran" becomes something like "Joe ran fast" or "Joe ran to the store."

Keep in mind that concrete thought is wordless. A concrete thought exists within an individual as an experiential reality for which the individual may not have words to express it, at least not yet. Concrete thoughts are thus basic units of meaning that lie behind words and phrases. Whether we think about it or not, we use words to try to communicate deeper realities. There is always experiential meaning behind a worded message.

Symbolized Meanings

Language requires the use of symbols to communicate concrete meanings. Words are symbols for concrete meanings; they are not the meanings themselves. On top of that, words are fluid; a word may represent multiple meanings and shades of meaning, and words evolve over time. As symbols, words serve to help persons express concrete concepts to others in a form that can be broadly understood. Words on a page have meaning only because readers connect the written symbol(s) with the concrete concepts being represented.

The most basic word-symbols are artistic representations of concrete meanings. For example, a drawing of a bird in flight symbolizes a real bird in flight. This is the basic concept behind ancient hieroglyphic writing. Emojis (🌐) are modern examples of this most basic form of symbolized communication.

In complex languages, there are layers of symbolic representation. For example, letters from an alphabet (which are actually symbols for sounds) are combined to create word-symbols that represent concrete meanings. The letters of an alphabet have no rational meaning in and of themselves. Yet, letters of an alphabet can be combined in established patterns to represent words that then represent concrete realities. In complex languages, symbols are used to create complex symbols that convey meaning. The letters "b," "i," "r," and "d" are combined to form a complex symbol, the word "bird," which in turn represents the concrete concept of an actual bird.

It is important to understand that symbols are not the concrete meaning they represent. Symbols are necessary to give expression to inner thoughts and to understand the expressed thoughts of others, but they are not exact representations of the thoughts of others. At best, we can only come close to understanding what someone means by their symbolic words given as expressions of their concrete thoughts. "Run fast" does not mean precisely the same thing to everyone.

If you pause to think about it, interpreting any written document is a complex endeavor, demanding that we put forth great effort to understand what the author had in mind. There is no simple "plain reading" of any text. We must try to step outside ourselves and attempt to see reality through the eyes of the author. Finding the meaning behind the words inspired by God is the critical goal of inductive Bible study. This complexity is why we have said that humility and skill are both essential for proper interpretation of the Word of God.

Structural Elements of Literature

One skill needed for good interpretation of the Bible is the ability to identify the basic structural elements of language and literature, and to know how the author connected them in efforts to convey his or her meaning. It will be helpful from time to time to remind ourselves of these basic elements of language and literature. We know what they are, but we often neglect their significance when studying the Bible.

Word

A word is the most basic unit of language and literature. It helps to always keep in mind that words are just symbolic representations of primary or secondary concepts. Words are the building blocks of language, but there always is a reality that lies behind a word, both in the mind of the speaker and in the hearer. Both bring their own meaning to each symbolic word. The use of words is always an attempt to convey to others the concrete realities that lie behind the words.

Prepositional Phrase

A prepositional phrase is a group of two or more words that work together to express a secondary concept. Using the example from above, we can add a prepositional phrase to the primary unit of thought, "Joe ran," that gives further meaning to Joe running. Joe ran "to the store." Prepositional phrases are incomplete thoughts that have no real meaning except when attached to primary or expanded units of thought to provide descriptive details. In this case, the prepositional phrase "to the store" has meaning only as a descriptor of Joe running.

Clause

A clause is a group of words that expresses a complete thought; it includes a subject and a verb. It is a thought that symbolically represents either a primary ("Joe ran") or an expanded unit of meaning ("Joe ran to the store"). There are two types of clauses: independent clauses and dependent clauses. Independent clauses are complete thoughts that can stand on their own. Dependent clauses, also known as subordinate clauses, have the elements of a complete thought but for full clarity in meaning are dependent on an independent clause to which they are attached. Dependent clauses complement the meaning of an independent clause. In the sentence, "Joe ran to the store because it was about to close" "Joe ran to the store" is an independent clause and "it was about to close" is a dependent clause. The second clause is dependent on the first for meaning. "It" has no meaning if it is not attached to something, i.e., "the store."

Sentence

A sentence is an independent clause with any attached complements. It symbolically represents either a primary or an expanded unit of thought plus any attached secondary concepts included to enrich the thought. That is, a sentence/clause may include words and phrases that amplify the basic unit of meaning. Complex sentences are attempts to more precisely use symbols to communicate concrete units of meaning.

As noted, a sentence may be built with two clauses. Both clauses may be independent in that they both could stand on their own, in which case the two clauses are known as "coordinated" clauses. When two independent clauses are linked together as one sentence, they form one unit of thought slightly different from the meaning of the two clauses appearing as separate sentences. As noted, it is also possible for one of the clauses to depend on the other for meaning; as expressed, it could not stand on its on as a meaningful statement.

Paragraph

A paragraph is a group of sentences that center around one sentence or concept. Typically, in prose literature, a paragraph has one sentence at the heart of the paragraph; it is sometimes called the thesis sentence. The other sentences support and/or complement the thesis sentence. It is normal, but not necessary, for this central sentence to be placed either at the beginning or the end of the paragraph.

However, paragraphs do not always come in such neat packages. For example, consider dialogues; one person speaks using one or more sentences, and the other person responds in kind. It is helpful to think of such exchanges as a single paragraph as long as the verbal exchanges connect as one topic. Long dialogues may have more than one paragraph.

The Segment

For our purposes, a segment is a group of sequential paragraphs that together form a small coherent unit of a book. It is a unit of literature that conveys a coherent story or message. As such, it constitutes an immediate literary context which should be studied and interpreted as a unit and must also be studied for its contribution to the book as a whole. It is possible for a segment to be made up of only one paragraph, but that is not typical.

One might think of a segment as a scene in a play or a room in a house. Like a room, it has its own unique reason for existence, but it is joined to at least one other room and may even have a dual purpose as a passageway between rooms.

Inductive Bible study gives special attention to how the author constructed a segment. Working upward from words, phrases, sentences, and paragraphs, a segment may be thought of as a literary structural unit built to convey a message within a more complex message. Or, as we will see below, working downward from the book as a whole, a segment may be thought of as the smallest literary division of a book. Segments will be discussed more thoroughly in Chapters 14-16.

Every sentence adds to the meaning of the central thought of a segment. Inversely, each sentence draws its more precise meaning from the central thought of the segment. The meaning of a text is found in the interplay between sentences and their context within a segment. Every sentence in the Bible draws its fuller meaning from how it connects with the other sentences. Look for these connections; they will guide your interpretations.

Structural Divisions

Above, we looked at how the elements of language are combined to construct a segment of text. That information is needed to observe how an author used the elements of language to construct a primary unit of the book as literature—the segment. We saw how words are combined to form phrases and clauses, how phrases and clauses are combined to form sentences, how sentences are combined to form paragraphs, and how paragraphs are combined to form segments as primary units of literature.

Another question needs to be answered: how do the segments of a book combine to give the book meaningful structure? To answer that question, it is best to begin with the book as a whole and look at how it naturally divides down to the level of segments. Books have points of transition. Some transitions mark dividing points between major sections of the book and other transitions mark divisions within major sections of the book. In other words, major divisions may have subdivisions, which in turn may have their own subdivisions and so forth. The structure of a book is determined by how the various levels of subdivisions are joined within the book. Observing the structure is critical for understanding the context and meaning of the segments of the book.

There are several ways to present the structural design of a book. One method is to develop a traditional outline of the book that would look something like Figure 5.1 below.

The outline approach creates some challenges. First, there seems to be a near universal drive to force an outline to fit our preconceptions of how the content of the book should be divided. There is a tendency to force our theological convictions onto the text instead of letting the text speak for itself. This is especially true for preachers and teachers who study to prepare sermons and lessons.

Second, when using the outline method, most people have a predisposition toward symmetry and balance, an inclination to make each division mirror the others. From the example in Figure 5.1, for many people it just doesn't look right for II b and III b to not have sub-subdivisions like the others at their level. The result may be that important sections of the text are dropped from the outline. We highly recommend that the outline method of dividing a book not be used until a thorough study of the book is completed.

Figure 17.1 in Chapter 17 provides a method for illustrating how a book is structured. That method follows the linear flow of the book in a way that also makes it easy to see the divisions. At this point, just reflect on the important task of observing how the author of a book structured the book. The structure is an important component in the development of the main message.

Figure 5.1 -- "Outline Method for Book Structure"

Book Title

I.   Introduction

II.   First Division

    A. First Subdivision
        a. Sub-Subdivision 1
        b. Sub-Subdivision 2
        c. Sub-Subdivision 3

    B. Second Subdivision

III.   Second Division

    A. First Subdivision
        a. Sub-Subdivision 1
        b. Sub-Subdivision 2

    B. Second Subdivision

    C. Third Subdivision
        a. Sub-Subdivision 1
        b. Sub-Subdivision 2
           1. Sub-sub-subdivision 1
           2. Sub-sub-subdivision 2
        c. Sub-subdivision 3

IV.   Concluding Remarks

In summary, books may be seen to have one or more divisions. Divisions may be seen to exist as a whole without subdivisions or divided into two or more subdivisions. Subdivisions may be seen to exist as a whole or to be divided into two or more smaller units of book divided and subdivided it into units of text.

Always keep in mind that books are seldom symmetrically divided. One division may not have any subdivisions while the next may have subdivisions and even sub-subdivisions. Always let the text determine where the divisions are. Your job is to discover how the author structured the book.

Conclusions

In this chapter we have offered a model for how human literature is structurally designed to be a form of communication. Authors of the Scriptures designed their works to communicate big ideas. Written communication may begin with a single word, but that word has limited meaning outside its relationship with other words, sentences, paragraphs, and the larger units of the book. Inversely, meaning does not actually reside in the word; meaning resides in the reality inside the person entertaining the word, whether the speaker or the hearer.

Biblical interpretation must aim to understand the meaning behind the words of the Bible. What was in God's mind and the human author's mind as they together wrote?

Biblical interpretation must aim to understand the meaning behind the words of the Bible. What was in God's mind and the human author's mind as they together wrote? Words matter; they are an essential link to the intended meaning of the authors. They are the doorway, and we must go through them if we are to know what God is saying. But words are only symbolic representations of meaning. Like the proverbial snowflake, no two people hold to the exact meaning for any given word.

The distance between the author's meaning and the reader's meaning can be narrowed by looking closely at how a word is used in relationship to other words. The meaning of words can be refined by the context in which the words are used. An author's statement that "Joe ran" becomes more precise in meaning both for the author and the reader with the addition of the one word "fast." The meaning of "Joe ran" would become even more precisely received if the author added more information about Joe. He is "young" gives way to "he is a young teenager," etc. Even more precision is added by the context as it radiates outward from the words "Joe, the young teenager, ran fast" to include the context around the sentence.

The context of meaning for a single word begins with the phrase and clause in which the word rests and moves outward to its paragraph, its segment, subdivision, division, the book, and even beyond to the language, culture, and experiences of the author and intended readers. In inductive Bible study, we remain especially concerned with the structural context of the book because that is the primary, and most certain, context for discovering the author's meanings.

Because meaning lies behind the words, we must move beyond thinking that there is one obvious, plain, and simple meaning for a Bible text. There never is a straight line to someone else's thoughts; the author's meaning is woven into the literary context of the words he or she chose to use. Finding an author's true meaning requires effort.

The author's meaning must be filtered through our own complex set of meanings that are built on our individual experiences. Bible study must be a process of progressively moving closer and closer to certainty about what God has said and is saying through the Scriptures. Knowledge of the original languages can be a valuable aid in this process. But reading Greek and Hebrew does not create a direct link between our understanding and Scripture's meaning.

For example, one of the most recognized and universally honored statements in the Bible is simply, "You shall not murder" (Exod

20:13; Deut 5:17, NRS). This is one of *the* Ten Commandments. But what does it mean? What is murder? In our time, there is a general impression that "murder" means something like "to intentionally take the life of another person without legally just cause." However, the Hebrew word also appears in Deuteronomy 4:41; 19:3-6; and Joshua 20:3 where it refers to unintentional manslaughter. In other places it is used with different shades of meaning. Some early Christians understood it to refer to intentionally ending a human life under any circumstance, including war. They considered it essentially an unforgivable sin when done by a baptized Christian. What do you think "murder" means? Inductive study can help you better understand the meaning of the word in the various contexts in which the word is used.

In the next chapter we look at some literary devices that authors use to help readers better understand the meaning behind their words. There is more to great literature than simply combining words into phrases, clauses, and sentences and then stringing sentences into paragraphs. Literary devises such as figures of speech, illustrative stories, relational patterns, and other literary techniques help clarify the author's meaning.

We should think of our times in Scripture as events in which we sit face to face with God for him to communicate his reality (the only true reality) to us so that our perceptions of reality (our minds and hearts) are changed to conform to his. After all, his perception of reality is truth. Our perceptions of reality are distortions of his. We can know truth only if we desire to be made true, only if we desire to fully conform to him, to be what he created us to be.

God's Word is Truth and truth is greater than perceived meaning. The quest for meaning is a poor substitute for hunger for God. The Spirit-Word is powerful and effective to transform and form us into the image and likeness of Christ, if only we will be joined to it and let it accomplish what it wills in our lives. We can live by and out of the Scriptures if we commit ourselves to live with and in them as the

Word of God. Then we will find the true meaning of life, God's meaning.

None of this implies that the Word of God is not a reliable revelation from God. The words of the Bible are the words God chose. We must cling to them as we cling to life itself. They are the primary medium through which the Spirit of God is speaking to us. We are merely saying that our ability to understand what God means by the words he chose is fallible. We can get it wrong.

We will get it wrong when we fail to recognize the literary contexts in which the words are planted. Literary types and structures must be considered as we study. But as we do that, we must remember that we will never get it right if we divorce the presence of God from the Word of God.

Chapter 6

Literary Devices

"Every truth which is revealed in the oracles of God is undoubtedly of great importance. Yet it may be allowed that some of those which are revealed therein are of greater importance than others as being more immediately conducive to the grand end of all, the eternal salvation of [humanity]. And we may judge of their importance, even from this circumstance, that they are not mentioned only once in the sacred writings, but are repeated over and over."

—John Wesley

Throughout the ages, authors have made use of literary devices to enhance their writings. Authors could write with concise, sequential statements avoiding repetition and unnecessary embellishments. The resulting product would undoubtedly read something like a spreadsheet: artless, dull, and difficult to remember. Literary devices are employed to strengthen the author's main ideas, to add tone and depth, to concretize abstract concepts, and to better connect with the reader.

For our purposes, literary devices can be grouped in five categories: figures of speech, illustrative stories, literary techniques, structural patterns, and relational connections. Each of these categories has multiple devices, with each of the devices having defining characteristics as described below. Inductive Bible study is greatly aided by familiarity with the most common of these literary devices. Knowing them and how they are used will make it much easier to identify the main points being made by the author and how those points are developed. Each of the devises exists to provide clarity to the author's meaning.

Figures of Speech

Figures of speech are used in place of straightforward statements. They provide variety that keeps literature from becoming dull and dry. They also create mental images that help the reader connect with the author's message. They are intended to provide clarity and to help the reader better understand the author's meaning. In other words, they can help create more direct links to the concrete meanings that lie behind the words.

Misconceptions about God's Word often come from not recognizing the use of a figure of speech. We may tend to interpret something literally which was not meant to be interpreted literally. Or, on the other hand, we may not interpret a passage literally when the passage requires a literal interpretation. Below are descriptions of some of the most common types oof figures of speech found in the Scriptures. These have been adapted and expanded upon from *Direct Bible Study* by Ronald W. Leigh.[1]

Litotes

Litotes are when an author uses a negative statement to make a positive point. For instance, Jesus's statement in John's Gospel, "Everyone the Father gives me will come to me, and the one who comes to me I will never cast out" (John 6:37, CSB). Christ is saying that He will accept all who come to him. By expressing a positive outcome using the negative assertion, "I will never cast out," He in effect strengthens His promise to accept all who come to Him. Litotes often serve to provide absolute certainty to a statement.

---

[1] Ronald Leigh, *Direct Bible Discovery: A Practical Guidebook for Personal Bible Study* (Nashville: Broadman Press, 1982).

Verbal Irony

Verbal irony is a figure of speech in which the author intentionally writes the opposite of what the author intends the reader to understand. The Apostle Paul made use of irony that sometimes bordered on sarcasm. Consider how he compares himself with the Corinthians:

> You are already full! You are already rich! You have begun to reign as kings without us — and I wish you did reign, so that we could also reign with you! For I think God has displayed us, the apostles, in last place, like men condemned to die: We have become a spectacle to the world, both to angels and to people. We are fools for Christ, but you are wise in Christ! We are weak, but you are strong! You are distinguished, but we are dishonored! (1 Cor 4:8-11, CSB).

Irony is sometimes difficult to recognize. Distanced by culture and time, it is often easy to mistake an ironic statement for a straightforward one. Be very careful to discern the presence of irony.

Simile

When a person compares two things not directly associated with each other, he or she is using a simile. Usually the words "like" or "as" are used to make the comparison. For instance, the Apostle Peter writes, "Your adversary the devil is prowling around like a roaring lion, looking for anyone he can devour" (1 Pet 5:8, CSB). The use of this simile creates a visual image far more intense than a straightforward assertion such as "Satan is after you to destroy you."

Metaphor

When a person symbolically speaks of one thing as if it were another, he or she is using a metaphor. For instance, Jesus uses a metaphor when He says, "I am the bread of life. Whoever comes to me will never be hungry, and whoever believes in me will never be thirsty"

(John 6:35, NRSV). Notice that a metaphor is like a simile in that both involve descriptively linking one thing with another, but a metaphor establishes the link on a much stronger level.

Personification

Personification is a type of metaphor that speaks of an object as if it were a person, as in Psalm 98:8— "Let the floods clap their hands; let the hills sing together for joy" (NRSV). The author certainly has no expectation that trees will clap hands or that mountains will sing songs, at least not literally. It is strictly a figurative expression.

Anthropomorphism

Anthropomorphism is like personification. Both project human qualities onto something not human. Anthropomorphism is when a human trait is projected onto a non-human entity as a means of describing a corresponding non-human trait that exists in the non-human. Both the human trait and the non-human trait are realities. The difference between anthropomorphism and personification is correspondence. A personification merely figuratively projects human attributes onto non-human entities; that is, the non-human has no attribute that corresponds to a human attribute. Trees have no hands to clap, and they have nothing that corresponds to clapping hands. On the other hand, anthropomorphism uses an actual human trait to describe an actual non-human trait.

The Scriptures contain many anthropomorphisms to describe God. For example, "See, the LORD's hand is not too short to save, nor his ear too dull to hear" (Isa 59:1, NRSV).

God acts as one who has hands and ears, even if He is a Spirit who does not have or need literal hands or ears in order to touch and hear. The easiest way for us to think about God as a personal being is for us to project onto his non-material existence human traits that correspond with aspects of his spiritual existence.

Hyperbole

When a person makes a deliberate over-statement for the sake of emphasis, she or he is using hyperbole. One example is Jesus's statement, "If your right eye causes you to sin, gouge it out and throw it away" (Matt 5:29, CSB). Hyperboles are effective in stressing the importance of a point one wishes to make. When reading the Bible, it is critical that we recognize hyperboles as figures of speech not to be taken literally.

Symbol

A symbol is any object used to represent something other than itself. The object used as a symbol may be chosen because it shares some innate traits with that which it figuratively represents. For instance, the bald eagle is used as a symbol for the United States of America. The eagle is considered by many to exemplify some of the characteristics of the United States: strength, majesty, independence, etc.

Some symbols, such as a stop sign on the highway or the written words on this page, have no connection with the thing they represent. An example from the Scriptures would be the rainbow; when it rains and a rainbow appears, it symbolically reminds humanity that God has promised that the earth will not be destroyed by flood again. The rainbow is a symbol of God's promise; while it has a direct connection with rain, it has no direct connection with God's promise.

A Special Note: In common usage, the words *sign* and *symbol* are synonyms, but the scriptural use of "sign" is not the same as a symbol. A symbol represents something from which it is disconnected. It may share some traits, but it is in its essence very different. On the other hand, in the Bible, signs have a direct link with or are of the same essence as that to which they point. Jesus performed many signs pointing to His messiahship and the presence of His Kingdom. Miracles and healings did not just point toward a coming reality—they were expressions of that reality.

Illustrative Stories

Sometimes an author will use a story to illustrate a point. These are typically placed inside the larger narrative and are told by one of the characters of the larger story. There are two major types of illustrative stories in the Bible: parables and allegories. While these are in some ways similar to each other, each is distinct in some ways. Both are also sometimes classified as figures of speech.

Parable

A parable is a story about everyday things that is used to illustrate a truth or a principle. Parables abound in the life and ministry of Jesus. They were for Him a favored form of teaching. Through them, He provided His followers with tangible illustrations of Kingdom truths while often at the same time hiding those truths from those who did not have "ears to hear" (Matt 13:13; Mark 4:11-13). A parable is a straightforward story told to illustrate a truth or principle. In a parable, all the characters and events work together to communicate a truth.

Allegory

An allegory is a story with layers of symbolic meaning. Like metaphors, allegories use symbolism to help express a message, but allegories embed the symbols in a story. Typically, in an allegory each of the main characters and events are symbols representing elements from real life, and the story illustrates the author's perceived spiritual or social realities. Allegories are often written as critiques on society.

One of the most memorable allegories in the Bible is the story the prophet Nathan told King David after the king had committed adultery with Bathsheba and subsequently sent her husband to the front lines of battle to be killed. The story the prophet told was about a poor man who only owned one little lamb, which was like a daughter to the man. In the story, a rich man who owned many sheep stole the poor man's lamb to feed a guest. After David heard the story, he responded in anger about the mistreatment of the poor man. Then the prophet revealed to the king that he was that (rich) man (2 Sam 11-12). The rich man was a symbolic representation of David, and the lamb represented Bathsheba.

There is not always a clear distinction between a parable and an allegory; they sometimes overlap. Jesus explained His parable about the sower's seed in a way that makes it read more like an allegory. He identified the types of soil onto which the seed fell as representing different groups of people and as representing the different effects of the Word on the lives of group members. Notice that it is identified in Scripture as a parable, but it has multiple layers of symbolic meanings. It goes far beyond illustrating a single principle.

A Word on Historicity — The existence of parables and allegories in the Bible might give rise to questions about the reliability of the Scriptures as it relates to science and history. Many people struggle with whether the entire Bible is historically accurate and/or scientifically reliable. This struggle is very real for them and should not be taken lightly. But it is not a necessary struggle. The Bible and true science are not in competition with each other. God has chosen to reveal himself both in the Scriptures and in His creation.

How we respond to questions about history and science as they relate to the Bible will largely be determined by where we begin to find our answers. Simply put, what do we truly consider to be the higher authority: science/history or the Bible? It is one thing to look at the Bible through the lens of science and another to look at science through the lens of the Bible. It is still another to look at each through the lens of the other, holding them in dialectic tension.

The nature of the Bible as God's Word requires that we consider it to be reliable and our highest authority for Christian living.

Questions about the historical realities associated with a literary device are secondary if not totally irrelevant. The question is not whether a parable or allegory are historic events. The question is what does the story contribute to the author's message?

There are instances in the Bible when a previously recorded event is included inside a literary device. When that happens, the historic reality should be treated primarily as part of the literary device. The author has placed the historic event inside the literary device to communicate a greater message and not to provide commentary on the historic event. The author is saying, "let me use an event from history to illustrate my point." In sum, those things reported in the Bible as historical facts should be considered factual, and those things used as literary devices should be approached as literary devices.

Always keep in mind that we are looking for the meaning behind the words and not the science behind the words. When it comes to Bible study, the bottom line is, do we truly believe that God is speaking to us through the Scriptures, and do we have ears to hear what He is saying? These are issues of faith and not questions of scientific reasoning.

We are not by any of this saying that questions about science and the Bible are wrong or to be avoided. Those questions can be valuable tools to inform our reading of the Scriptures. We are saying that we should never allow secondary questions to interfere with the serious work of uncovering what the Bible says and means. Secondary questions should never be allowed to determine what we believe the Bible is saying.

Literary Techniques

Literary techniques are tools authors uses to emphasize prominent concepts and/or strengthen the presentation of their themes. Such techniques serve as patterns of thought development that contribute to the author's style of writing. When an author uses a common literary technique, it is as if he or she is saying "Look here, look here, this is important." The following list of literary techniques is adapted from David R. Bauer and Robert A. Traina; they refer to their list as "Structural Relationships."[2]

Recurrence

Perhaps the most important technique for providing emphasis is simple repetition. Sometimes authors will repeat terms, phrases, events and/or concepts to add emphasis to a main point. Watch for repetition when studying a book. It probably means something important! Observing the recurrences of words and phrases can be a relatively simple exercise for connecting dots the author wants to be connected. But those are not the only types of recurrence; look for recurrence in character presence, geography, event types, topics, and more. Bauer and Traina identify three major functions of recurrence:

- To indicate emphasis—the author is attempting to show what is important.

- To develop a theme or concept—the author uses recurring people, ideas, places, images, etc. to develop a theme.

- To develop richness of presentation—the author may repeat images, words, etc. for artistic reasons.[3]

There is a fourth function for recurring words or phrases, which is to help identify distinct sections of a book. For example, the subdivisions of the second half of Ephesians are marked by the use of the word *walk* (4:1, 17; 5:2, 8, 15) within each of the subdivisions. In our opinion, most modern translations give insufficient attention

---

[2] David R. Bauer and Robert A. Traina, *Inductive Bible Study* (Ada, MI: Baker Academic, 2011), 94-122.

[3] Ibid., 96-97.

to Paul's use of this technique in Ephesians. They translate the Greek word for "walk" (*peripateo*) as some form of the word "live" because "live" better fits the idioms of modern English.

However, it might be argued that the use of "walk" creates a more dynamic and richer image for Paul's message. The use of "live" also loses the significance of the wording of the last subdivision where Paul transitions from "walk" to "stand." A literal translation makes clear Paul is bringing his theme to a climax, that is, walking faithfully culminates in standing strong in the faith.

A suggestion: in your study of a book of the Bible you may want to highlight or color-code recurring characters, words, phrases, concepts, or locations, etc.. This may help you see the emphasis being made and better see how the theme is being developed.

Flow of Intensity

Some level of ebb and flow of intensity characterizes virtually all literature. A section with little movement may be followed by a section of rapid-fire activity. Transitions from reflection to action, from calm to crises, from peace to conflict, etc. vary the intensity of a book. This may be seen in the Gospels as they shift from Jesus ministering without opposition to Jesus being challenged by His enemies.

Climax

Good stories and good arguments reach a climax—the high point of the author's thesis or narrative that most often comes near the end of the argument or story. Narratives weave characters, themes, ideas, and the plot toward the climax. Didactic literature, such as Paul's letters, build layer upon layer of argumentation to reach the pinnacle of the author's thesis. Observing the move toward the climax of a book yields rich insight into the major themes/messages being conveyed and how they fit together. For instance, in each of the Synoptic Gospels, the passion, crucifixion, and resurrection of

Christ bring the reader to the climax not just of the plot of his life, but of everything he taught and did leading up to those events.

Generalization

A generalization is a technique that encapsulates details into a general idea or message. We might call it "painting with a big stroke." Generalizations may appear without the support of any details. In that case, the author did not feel the need to bog the readers down with minutia that the readers already knew or that would serve only to distract. For instance, in Ephesians, Paul generalizes the sinful behavior of the Gentiles in cryptic terms:

> Therefore, I say this and testify in the Lord: You should no longer walk as the Gentiles do, in the futility of their thoughts. They are darkened in their understanding, excluded from the life of God, because of the ignorance that is in them and because of the hardness of their hearts. They became callous and gave themselves over to promiscuity for the practice of every kind of impurity with a desire for more and more (Eph 4:17-19, CSB).

These generalized descriptions stand in stark contrast with Paul's ensuing practical instructions for the believers:

> Therefore, putting away lying, speak the truth, each one to his neighbor, because we are members of one another. Be angry and do not sin. Don't let the sun go down on your anger, and don't give the devil an opportunity. Let the thief no longer steal. Instead, he is to do honest work with his own hands, so that he has something to share with anyone in need. No foul language should come from your mouth, but only what is good for building up someone in need, so that it gives grace to those who hear. And don't grieve God's Holy Spirit. You were sealed by him for the day of redemption. Let all bitterness, anger and wrath, shouting and slander be removed from you, along with all malice. And be kind and compassionate to one another, forgiving

> one another, just as God also forgave you in Christ. --
> Ephesians 4:25-32 (CSB).

In the Bible, generalizations often include references to information that would have been familiar to the original readers but would not be common knowledge for modern readers. This may require the Bible student to look to extra-Biblical sources for clarification, but most often the needed information can be deduced from the text of the book. Always look first to the book before turning to outside sources.

Summarization

When an author provides an abbreviated review of a section of a book, he or she is using summarization. This literary technique allows writers to highlight what they consider important by recounting the main points or events in their argument or story. The summary statement can indicate how the particulars come together, uplifting the important ones. They also help the reader remember important things that are needed to understand that which follows.

Summation

A summation is a type of generalization, one that serves to draw a conclusion or name the implications of what went before. A summation is not a summary statement that merely recounts what has already been written. It offers something more that builds on what went before. These summative generalizations can bring about closure to a section of a book or to the book as a whole. One example of this is in the second chapter of Luke's Gospel: "When they had completed everything according to the law of the Lord, they returned to Galilee, to their own town of Nazareth" (Luke 2:39-40, CSB). The later portion of this sentence introduces that which follows as "they returned to Galilee," but the first portion of the sentence is a summation of the events that came before, that is, they "completed everything according to the law of the Lord."

Structural Patterns

The authors of the books of the Bible made use of structural patterns in their writings. Earlier we discussed the structural design of a book in reference to how it unfolds from beginning to end with recognizable points of transition. In this section, we discuss structural patterns embedded within a text as literary devices.

These patterns add a creative flare to the texts. They follow set formulas that need to be understood before interpreting a text. These structural patterns in the Bible are grounded in Hebrew poetry, but over time they came to be applied to prose literature as well. They appear in both the Old and New Testaments.

Parallelism

A very common structural pattern used in Hebrew poetry is that of parallelism. In poetry, parallelism is a technique in which two or more lines of a poem complement each other. The second and/or following line(s) exist in parallel with the thought expressed in the first. There are several forms of parallelism. We offer here some of the most common.

Synonymous Parallelism

In synonymous parallelism, the second and any subsequent lines serve essentially to restate the first line. In some cases, the second line appears as a simple restatement of the first just using different words. In other cases, the second line is a restatement that is more emphatic than the first. Consider the opening verse of the Book of Psalms:

> How blessed is the man who does not
> walk in the counsel of the wicked,
> Nor stand in the path of sinners,
> Nor sit in the seat of scoffers (Ps 1:1, CSB)!

Notice how each of the three parallel lines carries the same basic message: blessed is the person who doesn't follow the ways of sinners.

Examples of synonymous parallelism can be found in the prose of Paul's epistles. For instance, "For the Jews ask for signs and the Greeks seek wisdom, but we preach Christ crucified, a stumbling block to the Jews and foolishness to the Gentiles (1 Cor 1:22-23, CSB). In this text, Paul parallels Jewish and Greek responses to Christ crucified. Jews ask for signs and find the crucified Christ a stumbling block. Greeks seek wisdom and react to Christ as nothing but foolishness.

Antithetical Parallelism

In antithetical parallelism, the second line serves as a contrast to the first line. Typically, the second is an inverse of the first. An example may be found in the last verse of the first Psalm: "For the Lord watches over the way of the righteous, but the way of the wicked leads to ruin" (Ps 1:6, CSB).

Paul uses antithetical parallelism in his prose. For example, in 2 Corinthians, he offers a description of his ministry that includes the following list of antithetical parallel thoughts:

> … through glory and dishonor, through slander and good report; regarded as deceivers, yet true; as unknown, yet recognized; as dying, yet see—we live; as being disciplined, yet not killed; as grieving, yet always rejoicing; as poor, yet enriching many; as having nothing, yet possessing everything (2 Cor 6:8-11, CSB).

Notice that even in Paul's prose, antithetical parallels have a poetic rhythm. When you discover these sections, slow down and reflect on the author's message within and behind the parallels.

Synthetic Parallelism

In synthetic parallelism, the second part completes or expands the idea expressed in the first part. A prime example is from the 23rd Psalm.

> *The LORD is my shepherd,*
> *I shall not want* (Ps 23:1, NRSV).

Notice that the second line brings completion to the more general first line. "The Lord is my shepherd" could have many implications. In this case the psalmist is reflecting on the Lord as his provider.

Emblematic Parallelism

Emblematic parallelism is when the first line includes a figure of speech (an emblem) that illustrates the second line. In other words, the second line makes plain the meaning of the figure of speech found in the first line. Sometimes the lines are reversed with the figure of speech appearing in the second line instead of the first. These are common in Hebrew poetry, especially in the Psalms and Proverbs.

> As a deer longs for flowing streams,
> so I long for you, God (Ps 42:1, CSB).
>
> Iron sharpens iron,
> and one person sharpens another (Prov 27:17, CSB).

Notice how the second line makes concrete the metaphorical first line.

Alternate Parallelism

Alternate parallelism alternates the parallels in the pattern of A-B-A-B. For example:

> *You hide them in the protection of your presence;*
> *you conceal them in a shelter from human schemes, from quarrelsome*
> *tongues* (Ps 31:20, CSB).

The parallels:

    A. You hide them
    B. In the protection of your presence;
    A. You conceal them
    B. In a shelter
          B.a.   From human schemes,
          B.b.   From quarrelsome tongues

Notice that the second (alternate) line includes a synonymous parallelism: "from quarrelsome tongues" parallels "from human schemes."

Chiasm

A chiasm is a special type of structural pattern that originated in Old Testament poetry but may also be found in Old and New Testament prose. The name is taken from the Greek letter *chi*, which resembles the letter "X." Basically, a chiastic structure is a parallelism that structurally resembles the left half of an "X." Thinking of it as an outline, a point "A" is made, followed by a sub-point "B," followed by a sub-sub-point "C." The outline is then repeated in reverse order using parallel wording or concepts. The parallel lines may be synonymous, antithetic, synthetic, or some other form of parallelism.

The basic structure of a chiasm looks like this.

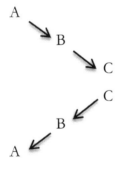

An example of a chiasm may be found in Isaiah 6.

A. *Make the **minds** of these people dull;*

    B. *deafen their ears*

        C. *and blind their <u>eyes</u>;*

        C. *otherwise, they might see with their <u>eyes</u>*

    B. *and hear with their ears,*

A. *understand with their **minds**, turn back, and be healed*

(Isa 6:10-30, CSB).

In some chiasms, there is a middle element that sits alone between the inverted parallels. In the example above there would be only one "C." This middle element may be the climax of the chiasm, or it may serve some other purpose.

Like other forms of parallelism, the chiasm found its way into prose literature. In antiquity it was used to help storytellers remember the elements of a story. Writers and speakers prided themselves in finely constructed chiasms with clever connections. The connections were often about similarities or contrasts.

Mark's Gospel specially makes heavy use of chiastic structure. In fact, we might say that this Gospel is written as an intricate pattern of larger and smaller chiasms. Mark loved to wrap one narrative around another narrative. In using this structural pattern, he would contrast characters and events. These structures are sometimes referred to as "Markan Sandwiches." Consider the following Markan chiastic sandwich of Jairus and the Woman with the Hemorrhage (Mark 5: 20-43).

A. Prelude: Jesus instructs the demoniac to go and tell others what he had done for him (5:19-20).

    B. The story of the synagogue leader named Jarius begins in a crowd. (5:21-23).

        C. Jairus begs Jesus to come to his home and heal his daughter. Jesus goes with him toward his home with a large crowd following (5:21-24).

            D. An inner story about a woman with a hemorrhage is inserted; she touched the garment of Jesus and was healed (5:25-34).

        C. Messengers arrive with news of the death of Jarius' daughter. Jesus encouraged Jarius and they proceed to his house, but with only a few disciples attending: Peter, James, and John (5:35-40).

    B. The story of the synagogue leader ends in a small, secluded setting, with the girl up and walking. (5:41-42)

A. Conclusion of the story: Jesus gave strict orders no one was to know about this (5:43).

The woman with the hemorrhage is not an interruption to the narrative about Jarius but part of a larger story that compares and contrasts Jairus and his daughter with the woman. Note the following in this sandwiched story:

1. The social standing of Jarius compared with that of the woman with the hemorrhage.

2. The movement: Jarius moves from public space to the private room where his daughter is healed. The woman moves from the hidden space required of unclean persons to the center of a crowd.

3. In the inner story, the woman breaks a social taboo by touching Jesus. In the outer story (Jarius' daughter) Jesus breaks social taboo by touching a dead young woman.

4. Jairus fell at Jesus's feet before his daughter was healed; the woman also fell at his feet only it was after she was healed.

5. Jairus begs Jesus to act; the woman acts in faith.

6. The woman had endured her malady for twelve years. The girl was twelve years old when Christ raised her up.

There may be more similarities and contrasts revealed in this chiastic structure if you look for them.

Inclusio

When an author repeats words, phrases, or concepts from the beginning of a unit of literature at the end of that unit, he or she is using an *inclusio*. An *inclusio* provides a bracket effect, drawing a nice boundary around a thought or narrative. This tool also had its origins in Hebrew poetry as a form of parallelism. Just like in a chiasm, a line, word, phrase, or concept that appears at the beginning of the poem is repeated in parallel at the end. The Psalms are replete with *inclusios*. For instance, Psalm 73 begins with…

> God is indeed good to Israel,
> to the pure in heart.
> But as for me, my feet almost slipped;
> my steps nearly went astray (Ps 73:1-2, CSB).

And ends with

> But as for me, God's presence is my good.
> I have made the Lord God my refuge,
> so I can tell about all you do (Ps 73:28, CSB).

The initial use of the phrase, "But as for me" introduces the writer's testimony of wavering faith (Ps 73:2-16), and the ending bracket uses the same phrase to introduce the conclusion to a testimony of how his or her faith was renewed in the presence of God (vv. 17-28). Also, both elements of the *inclusio* contain a reference to God being good. Note that by their very nature, chiasms have *inclusios,* but not all *inclusios* belong to a chiasm.

Relational Connections

The most prominent type of literary devise is that of relational connections. For most books of the Bible, these constitute a major portion of inductive observations. Remember, an observation is essentially connecting the dots, seeing what the author wanted you to see. How do the various elements of a book or segment of a book relate to each other?

As you study the Bible, you will see many ways in which events, people, places, and things are placed in relationship. Structural patterns are but one means of accomplishing this. There are also relational connections that lack prescribed structure. Because of the lack of defined structure, they may be more difficult to identify, but observing these relationships provides powerful clues to the author's deeper meaning.

As you read through the items below,[4] you should notice that there can be overlap in relationships. Items observed in a book may exist in more than one type of relationship or one of their relationships may exist as a sub-type of another. Focus on the type that most precisely describes the relationship.

Quantitative Relationships

Quantitative relationships express relationships in size, number and/or amount. Whenever we indicate that something is equal to, greater than, or less than something else, we are indicating a

---

[4] This list is greatly modified from Leigh, *Direct Bible Study*, 178-179.

quantitative relationship. Any time an author provides a quantity, it is wise to ask *why* the quantity was given and then to look for other quantities that might be related to it. It may also prove helpful to consider the precision given to the quantities mentioned: "twelve baskets full" is different from "several" or "many baskets of."

The Book of Mark contains many quantitative relationships. As mentioned above, the age of Jairus's daughter (twelve years) is obviously connected to the length of time the woman with the issue of blood had been afflicted (twelve years). Unlike other Gospels, Mark records two accounts of Jesus feeding the multitudes. Here, he seems almost obsessed with quantities: five loaves and two fish vs. seven loaves and a few small fish, twelve baskets of leftovers vs. seven baskets, "five thousand men" vs. "four thousand" (without gender reference), and sitting down in groups of hundreds and fifties vs. the crowd sat down. Why did Mark give so much quantitative data? What does this reveal about Mark?

In Mark, you may also pay attention to the numbers of persons following Jesus at any given time, the presence and absence of the crowds, the occasions where the Twelve are included compared with those occasions with just the Inner Three, etc.

Quantitative relationships are easy to spot when clustered together but take care not to miss those widely distributed in the book. Once identified, you should consider whether these quantities are part of another type of relationship—one of the ones discussed below. Quantitative statements are seldom given without a connection to other quantitative statements; look for them and ask what they signify.

Spatial Relationships

Take note of how things are located in relation to other things spatially. Are some things close together? Are they far apart? In the Gospel of Mark, there are occasions when some people "press in" on Jesus and other occasions where others stand at a distance. There are references to people touching Jesus and of Jesus touching persons. Peter's spatial relationships with Jesus in the Gospel are especially telling.

Sequential Relationships

A set of events or concepts that have an intentional, specific order is said to exist in a sequence. Obviously, all the events of a narrative are sequential; the author placed them in a specific order. Within the narrative, however, there are sequential relationships that take on special meaning. The ordering of those events may or may not be tied to fixed times. In sequential relationships, the calendar date of an event is irrelevant compared to the order in which the events took place.

Sequential relationships sometimes appear in lists. Note the sequence in Mark 9:31 where Jesus states, "The Son of Man is going to be betrayed into the hands of men. They will kill him, and after he is killed, he will rise three days later" (CSB). It was important for the disciples to take note of this sequence of the events that awaited them in Jerusalem. Unfortunately, they did not recognize the sequence of events as the events unfolded. Only in hindsight did they remember what Jesus had told them.

Sequential relationships are not limited to narratives. The Apostle Paul frequently used sequential relationships to describe aspects of the Christian life: "And not only that, but we also boast in our afflictions, because we know that affliction produces endurance, endurance produces proven character, and proven character produces hope (Rom 5:3-4, CSB).

On occasion, Paul emphasized a point by reversing the order of a sequence:

> For everyone who calls on the name of the Lord will be saved. How, then, can they call on him they have not believed in? And how can they believe without hearing

about him? And how can they hear without a preacher? And how can they preach unless they are sent (Rom 10:13-15, CSB)?

Keep in mind that when observing sequential relationships, other types of relationships may also be present. What comes first may be more important than what comes last. On the other hand, what comes last may be more important than what came first! When compared, the quantitative nature or spatial aspects of the events in sequence may be significant. There are several sub-categories of sequential relationships.

Cause-Effect Relationships

One special type of sequential relationship is cause and effect. One event may follow another because the first brings about the second event. One person's actions may cause one or more other events. Pay attention to any action clearly linked to an effect.

In cause-and-effect relationships, the effect is determined by the cause. We may observe this in the first chapter of Mark's Gospel where it reports on the actions of a man healed of leprosy: "he went out and began to proclaim it widely and to spread the news, with the result that Jesus could no longer enter a town openly" (Mark 1:45, CSB). The man's actions were the direct cause of Jesus retreating to the desert.

Agency or Means-End Relationships

Agency or means-end relationships are also sequential in nature and similar to cause-and-effect relationships, only they focus on agency rather than cause. Sometimes a person or an event can serve as the tool (agent) that facilitates an event. Agents do not cause a response; they are merely a link in the process. For instance, Judas, the disciple of Jesus, was the agent for the arrest of Jesus. It was the chief priests, scribes, and elders who authorized the arrest.

Another example in Mark's Gospel is in the story of Peter's denial of Christ. Upon hearing the rooster crow for the second time, Peter remembered what Jesus had said, and as a consequence he wept bitterly. The crowing rooster was only an agent. Peter's memory of the words of Jesus was the cause of his sorrow.

Be careful in Bible study not to confuse a cause with an agent or vice versa. Also, take care not to read cause and effect into events that are merely sequential or chronological in relationship. In cause and effect, there will be observable indicators that sequential events are in fact cause and effect in relationship.

Chronological Relationships

Chronological relationships are yet another type of sequential relationship, only they are connected as events in time. Chronology keeps record and marks the time in which an event occurred. For our purposes, "time" refers to a year, a season, a day, an hour, or any other means of marking time. No one wore a wristwatch or carried a smart phone in biblical times. Time was marked by months and days on the Jewish calendar, but things like the period in which a ruler reigned, or natural events such as earthquakes and seasonal rains, also marked time. Jesus's comment about a rooster crowing was a reference to time, that is, the early dawn of the day.

Chronological time is sequential regardless of the way it is measured. It is used to identify how one event relates to another event or set of events in terms of the order and/or duration of the events. When making observations about time and timing, ask yourself why the author set this event in a fixed timeframe. Is there something significant about an identified time? Does it carry special meaning? Is the reference to time significant just for the one event, or does it connect this event to others?

Chronology is a multi-dimensional literary tool; in ancient times, it was common for authors to alter the actual chronology of events to better serve his or her literary purposes. References to time markers are more complex than simply marking when a series of events took place; they may speak primarily to how and why the events took place.

Cyclical Relationships

Cyclical relationships are another type of sequential relationship. A cycle is a sequence of events that repeats itself on an ongoing basis. God has built cycles into creation: sunrises, seasons, life-stages, etc. People who lived in biblical times were more in tune with these cycles than we are. Cyclical events largely governed their lives. Everyone paid close attention to things like the phases of the moon and the seasons of planting and harvesting. The religious calendar of Israel was an established cycle of sacred events and was closely connected to the cycles of the moon.

Cyclical relationships are frequently time-bound, but that is not always the case. Human relationships may go through cycles that have no connection with specified time. In the Old Testament a major cyclical theme is how the people of God turned away from Him, worshipped idols, suffered judgment from God, repented, were forgiven, and renewed their covenant with God, over and over again. In Mark, you might observe cycles in the faith of the disciples.

Cyclical relationships may connect to other types of relationships. For instance, a quantitative relationship may be seen in changes in the intensity of cyclical events. Spatial realities may intersect with cyclical ones to shed light on the author's message.

When making observations, look closely at cyclical relationships. Do you see Jesus doing something cyclically such as going to celebrate Passover? Or do you note recurring references to the cycle of sowing and harvesting? Are there literary cycles in the plot or in the character development of the narrative?

Prerequisite Relationships

Some things must be true before another thing can be true. Prerequisite relationships are logically sequential relationships. In Mark 8:34, Jesus, speaking to His disciples and to the multitude, gave a prerequisite for being His disciple: "If anyone wishes to come after Me, let him deny himself, and take up his cross, and follow Me."

Principle-Application Relationships

Another type of logically sequential relationship is that of principle-application. Often a writer or a speaker will give a principle followed by an application. These are like cause-and-effect relationships, except that in the principle-application relationship, the application is reasonable but voluntary. Be careful to distinguish cause and effect relationships from principle-application relationships.

Note Paul's use of "therefore" in his epistles. He often develops a doctrinal theme followed by how his readers are to apply the doctrines he taught. Jesus also used this communication structure. Consider the conclusion to the story of the withered fig tree.

> The principle: Jesus replied to them, "Have faith in God. Truly I tell you, if anyone says to this mountain, 'Be lifted up and thrown into the sea, and does not doubt in his heart, but believes that what he says will happen, it will be done for him (Mark 11:22-23, CSB).

> The application: Therefore, I tell you, everything you pray and ask for—believe that you have received it and it will be yours. And whenever you stand praying, if you have anything against anyone, forgive him, so that your Father in heaven will also forgive you your wrongdoing (Mark 11:24-25, CSB).

Comparative or Contrastive Relationships

One of the best ways of making observations on the text is to do a comparative or contrastive study. This study looks for things, events, people, or ideas that may be identical, similar, overlapping, different, mutually exclusive, opposite, etc. As you read and study, identify elements to compare and contrast, asking yourself, "How does this element compare with other elements that are the same or similar? How is this event different from similar events in the book? How is this character like or different from other characters? How is this idea comparable to other ideas?"

Returning to the two accounts of the feeding of the multitudes recorded in Mark's Gospel, we have already noted the multiple quantitative connections that may be compared and contrasted. Other elements of the two stories beg for comparison. One might compare the role of the disciples in the two events, or their faith/lack of faith. Compare the interaction between Jesus and the disciples. Compare the expressed attitude of Jesus toward the crowds, and more.

Supportive Relationships

In some relationships, one character serves as support for another character, one event supports another event, or one concept undergirds another. Often a clue to recognizing supportive relationships is as simple as noting whose name comes first. In the book of Acts, Aquila's name appears before his wife's name initially, but the team quickly shifts from "Aquila and Priscilla" to incidents of "Priscilla and Aquila." (Note: the translators of the King James Version of the Bible erroneously and with intent reversed the names of the couple, giving preference to "Aquila and Priscilla.")

This pattern is made explicit in the evolving relationship of Barnabas and Paul. Their relationship began with Barnabas defending Paul before the leaders at Jerusalem. It picks up with Barnabas recruiting Saul (Paul) to assist him with his teaching ministry at Antioch. Paul's supportive role continues into their first missionary journey. However, a shift in their relationship takes place as they travel through Asia. "Barnabas and Saul" becomes "Paul and Barnabas." From that point forward, Barnabas supports Paul, at least until their great disagreement over Mark.

Inclusive/Exclusive Relationships

In some relationships, one element is included within the whole. In other relationships, one part excludes the other. Noting inclusion and exclusion is an excellent means of observing relational structure. For instance, note Jesus's conversation with the Syrophoenician woman (Mark 7:24-30). She asked Jesus to heal her daughter, but He responds, "Let the children be satisfied first, for it is not good to take the children's bread and throw it to the dogs." She is excluded from the people and blessings of God. Yet, as the story unfolds, her response, "Yes, Lord, but even the dogs under the table feed on the children's crumbs," places her in an inferior but inclusive relationship. Jesus, noting the faith expressed in her answer, acknowledges her place and heals her daughter, making her to be more fully included.

Implied/Inferred Relationships

At times, relationships can be implicit rather than explicit. We can only infer that if one thing is true, then another must be true also. The author has chosen to draw us into the text by not stating explicitly that a relationship exists but rather inviting us to infer the existence of the relationship. For instance, as demonstrated in the account of the Syrophoenician woman, faith is often a stated prerequisite for miracles. But in some instances, miracles take place without any reference to faith; faith is implied by the act of coming to Jesus. For example, in the account of the healing of a deaf mute that immediately follows the story of the woman (7:31-37), faith is clearly implied but not mentioned.

Inferences not built on solid observations
are just assertions of an unfounded
opinions.

We must take care when noting inferential relationships. Identifying inferential relationships is always the product of interpretation with varying levels of certainty. Whenever we infer, we are interpreting the author's meaning. Look for implied truths but resist the temptation to move quickly into unfounded interpretations. Inferred relationships should be stated only after one has made careful observations. Inferences not built on solid observations are just assertions of an unfounded opinions.

Evaluative Relationships

In an evaluative relationship a character, event, idea, or concept of known value points to the worth or value of something else. In Mark 9:36-37, Jesus embraces a child and tells the disciples that whoever welcomes a child welcomes him and whoever welcomes him welcomes the one who sent him.

In this event Jesus uses the disciple's value of him, their devotion to him, to establish the great value of a child. Evaluative relationships may, or may not, indicate the two things are equivalent in value. In his words and actions, Jesus established the great value of the child by associating the child with himself. He is saying children should be valued in the same manner he is valued.

Contrasting-Value Relationships

Similar to evaluative relationships are contrasting-value relationships. The difference lies in the purpose of the relationship. As seen above, evaluative relationships use one thing of known value to establish the value of another. Contrasting-value relationships establish the relative value of two things. The author is saying "Don't be like this. Be like this."

Sometimes an evaluative relationship is placed inside a contrasting-value relationship. For example, the evaluative relationship of Jesus and the child found in Mark 9:36-37 is part of a larger story (Mark 9:33-37). In the larger story, Jesus overhears His disciples arguing among themselves regarding who was the greatest among them. Jesus tells them, "If anyone wants to be first, he must be last, and servant of all." He then contrasts their values of self with his value of a child (a contrasting-value relationship). In the process, he establishes the value of the child by linking the child with himself (an evaluative relationship).

Another example of a contrasting-value relationship is the parable of the Pearl of Great Price. In the parable, Jesus places value on the kingdom of God over and against all other human treasures (Matt 13:45-46).

Be careful to note how the Bible describes the values of the world in contrast with the values of the Kingdom God. One could argue that the entire Bible is a book about contrasting values, lessons in what to value and how to value, instructions on how to love as God loves and not as the world loves. Look for contrasting-value relationships that are stated or clearly implied in the text. Take care not to force value-based relationships where they do not exist.

Authority Relationships

It also proves helpful to note relationships based on authority. Ask yourself, "Who has authority here?" "From where their authority is derived?" "Who claims authority but does not have any?" "How is real or feigned authority either accepted or challenged?" "What is the relationship between power and authority?" For instance, in the Book of Mark, the relationship between the power and authority of Jesus is a key theme. Jesus's authority is recognized by some and challenged by others; however, as the narrative unfolds, it becomes clear that Jesus has all authority, and that this authority comes from the Father.

Attributional Relationships

At times, two things relate by the attributes or characteristics they share. Attributes can reveal commonality and/or disparity. In the Scriptures, attributional relationships serve as indicators of knowing and being known. Human attributes derive from association with others. For instance, the fruit of the Spirit in the lives of believers is a list of attributes derived from the Holy Spirit.

Illustrative Relationships

One thing may be used to illustrate another. Often in the Book of Mark, he depicts characters illustrative of faith: the Syrophoenician woman, the woman with the hemorrhage, Bartimaeus, etc. You might also note how these characters are juxtaposed with people who have little or no faith; those with faith serve both to illustrate faith and as a contrast to persons who lack faith.

Problem-Solution or Question-Answer Relationships

Often a writer or a speaker will pose a question and then answer it with an illustration. In a narrative, events may create a problem with other events providing the solution. In Mark's Gospel, the two accounts of Jesus feeding the multitudes begin with comparable descriptions of how the crowds were closely following Jesus to hear Him teach. In both, a logistical problem arose concerning how the people could get food. In both cases, Jesus provided a solution that also served as a lesson on faith; He miraculously multiplied a miniscule amount of food to feed thousands.

Conclusion

When studying the Bible, pay attention to literary devices. They provide more than variety and creativity in style. Each devise is a tool for connecting the author and the reader on a level that transcends grammar and vocabulary. They humanize the book by tapping into common human experiences and draw the reader closer to the author's meaning. In essence, they paint a three-dimensional picture.

Chapter 7

Observation—The Key to Discovery

"We need the same Spirit to understand the Scripture which enabled the holy men of old to write it."

—John Wesley

Making good observations on a Biblical text is the heart of inductive Bible study. To observe is simply to see, but to see in the sense of watching. It is to see what you are seeing. An observation then is a statement about what you have seen. The key to making good observations is to write them down and check them for accuracy. This is the most critical step in inductive Bible study.

From the perspective of RIBS, making observations is both the strength and the weakness of the inductive approach. Its strength is that it trains us to pay close attention to what the Bible says and helps us to not add to or take away from what is written. Its weakness is that it can incline us toward treating the Bible like a lifeless object, an artifact of a time when God spoke. Indeed, the classic metaphor for making observations is that of a science student carefully dissecting a fish on a laboratory table.

In relational inductive Bible study, we must ever be mindful that the Bible is a living book inhabited by God. It is the eternal Word of God wed to human literature, a limitless fountain of truth and beauty. Yes, it is an object to have and to hold, to analyze and to interpret, but it is also a subject that lays claim on us. Through it, the Spirit of God is interpreting us more than we are interpreting it.

Relational observations are like an apprentice being guided by a master gardener through her flower garden. The master is not interested in telling the apprentice what he should see. She wants to see the joy on his face and in his voice as he discovers the intricacies of her beautiful creation. The apprentice will no doubt first see the design of the garden as a whole and then be led through the interweaving pathways to take note of the great varieties of flowering plants and how they are positioned. In time the apprentice will focus on each of the varieties one at a time and observe how the master cares for each.

RIBS should be more like thoughtfully strolling with God through his vibrant garden than dawning a lab coat, sitting at a cold table under florescent lights, and slicing and dicing a lifeless fish. If we are sensitive, the Holy Spirit will nudge us into seeing the intricacies of the written Word of God.

Developing this skill requires harnessing our abilities to focus on what a text says and how it says it. Careful observation keeps us on track with the author's message and helps us control our tendencies to jump too quickly into interpreting the text, making it say what we think it should say.

But skill alone is not enough. Skill must be guided by love. If we love the Word of God, we will revere it, hold it with integrity, and study it responsively. We will be careful to not add to or take away from what has been written.

Inductive Observations

Good observations are the product of carefully observing the details of what is written in a book and how those details work together to convey the author's message. Making observations of literature requires paying close attention to the subjects who act, the objects acted upon, the actions that take place, the descriptive features of that which is being observed, the location of events, and the relationships of the things observed. This is a time-consuming process that requires us to slow down and concentrate on what is written.

Observations are about how the text is written, and not about restating what is written. They are about literary types, structures and devices and how they are used to establish textual relationships. For example, in Ephesians, "The author instructs the believers to not walk as the Gentiles walk" is a true statement but not a good observation because it just restates the text. A better observation in the second division of Ephesians would be, "The image of walking recurs five times in the author's depictions of the Christian life." That observation might be followed by, "The image of the Christian life as walking reaches a contrasting climax with the image of believers standing."

Observations must be clear and accurate. Accurate observations objectively describe a truth about the text. Likewise, they are exact in how they report what has been seen. They are descriptive without being unnecessarily so. They do not add color or texture to the text. They focus on one discovery at a time. In short, they are carefully worded to precisely state a truth about how the text is constructed to help develop the author's theme(s). The most important standard for making a good observation is that any reasonable person would agree the observation is true.

Writing down observations is helpful in several ways. First, the mental processes involved in writing aid with accurately seeing what is written. Second, written observations help keep our memory honest. Quick reviews of our written observations help ensure we are building on a solid foundation of what the author said. Thirdly, the collected observations are an indispensable catalogue of facts about the book. They are a valuable resource for our ongoing efforts to see connections between different sections of a book.

The process for making observations involves three steps. The first step is to carefully look at what the Biblical text says (and doesn't say). This requires taking the time needed to see clearly what the author in fact wrote. Good Bible study cannot be rushed.

Good Bible study cannot be rushed.

During this first step ask yourself, "What does the text actually say?" Inversely, ask yourself, "As I read the text, did I unconsciously add to or take away from what the author wrote?" If you projected things into the text or overlooked things in the text, correct your preliminary observations and ask yourself why you unconsciously altered what the text said.

The second step is to ask, "How do the facts I observed in this text relate to other things I have observed within the text or within the book as a whole?" When you make an observation, you need to consider whether what you have seen is an isolated fact or a building block for a larger truth. Good observations often lead to other, far-reaching observations.

The last step is to write down an accurate description of what you observed. Use the standards for good observations given above, taking special care to limit the statement to the factual; factual observations are those that are accurately based on relationships between facts seen in the text. Again, if an observation is factual, any reasonable person would confirm the statement is true.

Observations highlight how words, events, and concepts relate to other words, events, and concepts? They help us see where the author places emphasis and how the author builds a theme. Observations expose the threads in the tapestry of the book and how those threads are connected. Observations help us see how the parts of the big picture fit together to develop the theme(s) of the book. In brief, they help us focus on the things the author wants us to focus on.

Making observations is essentially about "connecting the dots" in the manner the author intended them to be connected. The challenge is that we are all inclined to see the big picture as suddenly as possible. It may even be hardwired into our brains to quickly fill in the blanks and connect the dots in order to produce a picture that "makes sense" of what we are seeing. We must overcome this temptation. We must discipline ourselves to not subconsciously supply our own dots or borrow some from other contexts. Good Bible study requires mental discipline.

Discipline yourself to not subjectively read
into the text your own ideas or
the ideas of others.

When making observations, do not look for hidden or deeper meaning; you will do that when trying to interpret what you have observed. Look for clear connections that reveal the author's stream of thought.

Never read into the text your own ideas or the ideas of others. There always exists a subtle temptation to find evidence to support what we already believe, evidence that may not actually be there. We can too easily see what does not exist. The addition of anything to the book will distort the message of the book, even if that which is added is true. A truth that is forced into the text may distort the truth of the text every bit as much as an untruth would.

Said most simply, do not confuse an intuition or impression for a factual observation. Figure 7.1 reveals some distinctions between good observations and subjective impressions.

Figure 7.1 -- "Good Observations"

Good Observations	Subjective Impressions
Are made through careful reading	Are typically made during a. quick reading
Are based on fact(s) and the factual (how facts are connected)	Are influenced by one's preconceptions, one's set of assumed truths
Identify relationships between elements of the text	Ignore the laws of relationship
Are concrete, actual	Lack concrete backing
Can be verified by all others as being true	Cannot be verified by all others
Are clearly distinguished from interpretations	Often confused with hasty interpretations

Making good observations is a discipline anyone can develop; you can do it. It takes practice and asserted effort. Most importantly, it requires a desire to know what the Biblical text says, to know what God is saying. Our desire to hear must precede and govern our desire to understand. Bible study must be a prayer to accurately know what the Word of God is saying.

Observe the Big Picture First

When making observations, remember these important things: First, each book of the Bible is a piece of literature and should be studied as literature. Good literature always has a main message grounded in the author's purpose for writing, and everything in the book contributes to that message.

Second, good literature also has structural design, and everything within the work of literature is connected through that structure. Through the structural design, the elements within the book contribute to the main message of the book. In other words, you cannot fully understand a verse in the Bible without understanding how it contributes to the message of the book in which it is found.

Third, inductive reasoning always moves from the specifics to the general. In part, this means that observing what a text actually says (and does not say) must be done before one attempts to interpret what it means; interpretation always follows careful observation.

However, moving from the specifics to the general is not the same as moving from the small to the large. While it is possible to apply inductive methods to any portion of Scripture, inductive Bible study is best done when applied to a book-as-a-whole. Keep in mind that nothing in the Bible is written in isolation. Everything written is in relationship with everything else. This is especially true when doing a book study.

The inductive approach, therefore, begins with looking for those things that paint the big picture. Think about a picture puzzle; the first thing you do when working on a puzzle is to look at the picture on the front of the box. You look for shapes, colors, and hues. Then you keep that picture before you until the puzzle is finished. The first movement in making observations is to observe the big picture.

The big picture of a book is recognized by asking questions such as who wrote to whom, when was it written, why was it written, and what is the primary message (theme) of the book? Then ask, what is the structural design (the outline) of the book? Answers to these big picture questions provide the context for understanding the shorter portions of the book.

We will learn more about seeing the big picture when we come to Chapters 11 & 12.

Types of Observations

There are three main types of observations that should be applied at every stage of an inductive Bible study beginning with looking for the big picture.

1. Answer the six standard questions: Who? What? When? Where? Why? How?

2. Identify the structural design of the portion of the book under review.

3. Recognize literary devices: figures of speech, illustrative stories, literary techniques, structural patterns, and relational connections.

Often, there is overlap between these categories; an observation in one category may also fit in another category. Also, remain open to observations that do not easily fit into any of these categories.

Answering The Six Questions

The six standard questions constitute the first phase of "big picture" observations, but they should also be asked in some form at each of the other phases of studying a book of the Bible.

Who?

The "who" question has several dimensions. First, we ask questions of authorship: "Who wrote this book? Is the author identified, or is there other internal evidence of authorship?" While you are learning inductive study, it is important to resist looking at outside sources to identify the author until you have thoroughly looked for clues from within the book itself. Looking for yourself will help you gain a better sense of the author's character and purpose in writing, even if you cannot decide who the author was.

The second dimension of the "who" question is audience: for whom was the book originally written? At times the audience is clearly stated, such as the case in many of Paul's epistles. In other books, the intended audience is not so clearly defined. As with authorship, it is important to resist looking at outside sources to identify the intended audience, at least until you have thoroughly looked for clues from within the book itself. Looking for yourself will serve you well later as you trace other threads through the book. As with the author, you may not be able to name the audience, but you should be able to name some facts about the audience.

The third dimension of the "who" question involves the people mentioned within the book. Ask yourself, "Who are the people mentioned in this text?" Ask this question for each of the books of the Bible, not just the narratives. As you do your study, you will want to ask yourself why the author included each person or group. Consider doing an in-depth character study after completing a study of the book as a whole.

Narratives contain main and supporting characters. Look for the protagonist(s) —the main character(s) around whom the story is woven (usually the "hero")— as well as the antagonist(s) —the opposing character or characters in the story. For instance, in the Gospels, Jesus is the protagonist. Several characters and character groups fill the antagonist role.

In narratives, especially look for character development, that is, changes within a character and the reasons for those changes. Do not overlook the character development of groups. For instance, in the Gospel of Mark, major character groups include the disciples, the scribes, the sick, the demoniacs, and others. Be careful to note characters who transition from a protagonist role to an antagonist role or vice versa.

What?

The "what" question focuses on the main theme of a text as well as any supporting theme(s). Ask yourself, "What actually is written, and what is the author trying to say by what is written?" In other words,

"What is the author's main point, and how is that point developed and supported?" Here, you must be very careful to limit your response to factual statements and avoid interpretations of what the theme might be. That will come later.

When?

The "when" question is twofold. First, look for the date the book was written. Sometimes you can readily see internal evidence for dating. For instance, the Book of Amos begins with, "The words of Amos, who was one of the sheep breeders from Tekoa—what he saw regarding Israel in the days of King Uzziah of Judah and Jeroboam son of Jehoash, king of Israel, two years before the earthquake" (Amos 1:1, CSB).

Notice that the author is precise regarding dating. He notes both a specific king of Judah and a specific king of Israel, and he places his oracle two years before a major earthquake. In cases like this, look through the book for other internal evidence for dates. Then turn to outside sources that can help you quickly pinpoint the dates and the circumstances of the internal clues.

Several books in the Bible, however, have little to no internal evidence as to dating. In these cases, it will be necessary to consult outside resources to gain the historical context in which the book was written. But don't be surprised if there is no consensus among the scholars. Again, always look internally before you turn to external resources.

The "when" question is also needed for noting the chronology of events within a book. For instance, it is helpful to note the chronology of Jesus's life and ministry as presented in each of the Gospels. However, be careful not to make chronology more important than it is. For instance, the writer of Mark's Gospel does not seem to emphasize the chronology of the events in the ministry of Jesus (at least until the Passion Week). Furthermore, chronology within a book sometimes serves literary purposes beyond the straightforward recording of historical data.

Where?

The "where" question looks at issues of location. First, note the location of the writing of the book. Sometimes the location is mentioned, but in most books, this is not the case. If it is mentioned, it is probably important. Also, ask the question, "Where is this book being sent?" This question relates to audience. This is especially helpful when considering the location of the recipients of books like the epistles. Geography can help resolve important issues related to context. It points toward social, religious, cultural, and theological matters that may help clarify the message of the book. Next, ask, "Where do the events occur in this book?"

Why?

The "why" question looks at the rationale behind the writing of a book. This question relates to the main theme identified in the "what" question. Sometimes the "why" is explicitly given. For instance, the writer of the Gospel of John clearly states why he wrote:

> Now Jesus did many other signs in the presence of his disciples, which are not written in this book. But these are written so that you may come to believe that Jesus is the Messiah, the Son of God, and that through believing you may have life in his name (John 20:30-31, NRSV).

At other times, you may deduce the intentions of the writer by taking note of what he or she is stressing as important.

How?

The "how" question deals with the literary type and style of the book. Is the book poetry? Is it narrative? Or is it one of the other types discussed in Chapters 4 and 5? Is it oriented toward remembering the past or toward preparing for the future? Sometimes one book may include a variety of literary types and styles. For example, the Gospel of Luke is primarily written in narrative form. However, in the first part of the book, Luke records the beautiful poetic songs of Mary (1:46-56) and Zechariah (vv. 67-79). Several brief poems are included elsewhere. While the dominant form is narrative, the story is largely told as a series of dialogues, but the narration does include parables and discourses.

Identifying the Structural Design

A second set of observations are those made about the structural design of the book. As we saw in chapter 5, the structural design reveals how authors organized their thoughts. In that chapter, we noted that the way modern translations of the Bible divide the books is somewhat artificial and represents interpretations by the translators. The original documents of the books of the Bible did not mark where divisions were to be placed. We should decide for ourselves where they should be.

The design of the structure of a book is found in the author's carefully planted clues as to where it is to be divided. One of your primary tasks in inductive Bible study is to find those clues (through observation) and then interpret what they mean; how did the author intend for his flow of thought to be understood?

Thus, identifying the structural design of a book or of a section of a book is often a mixture of observation and interpretation. The question of "Where do I think the author makes transitions in the development of his or her message?" may sometimes be made with the certainty that any reasonable person would agree with me. But sometimes it is a matter of opinion, an interpretation. Just always remember, interpretations about the structure of a book must be based on observations about the structure.

We provide more assistance in the process of identifying the structural design of a book in Chapters 11 through 13.

Observing Literary Devices

A third set of observations includes those made about literary devices. We identified these devices in Chapter 6. We will look much more closely at making observations on the devices in Chapter 16. For now, think of the devices as attempts to connect with the reader by providing more clarity to the main concepts being presented. They are a primary medium authors use to make clear the meaning behind the words. They provide the tone, texture, and color for the literary edifice being built. They are "dots" that beg for connections.

Miscellaneous Observations

Most of the observations that can be made fit into the three categories discussed above, but do not limit yourself to those categories. There is a very real danger of forcing the categories onto the text.

Conclusions

We have all said something like "I have never noticed that before." We tend to see what we expect to see, or what we want to see and to overlook other objects placed in plain view. We also tend to plan our response before we have heard the other person's complete statement or question.

Honest Bible study requires desire and discipline. We must have a deep desire to see what the text says and to hear what God is saying to us. But desire is often not enough. We must also discipline ourselves to become keen observers, to see the big picture, the details, and how the details fit together to form the picture.

There is a danger in making careful observations about what is written in the Bible. In making observations we are the subject handling the Bible like an object. There is a temptation to treat the Bible like a dead text. We must constantly remind ourselves it is the living Word of God given to us to hold and study.

Making observations must be done as a form of reverent prayer. We are asking God to help us know him better by knowing his Word better. We hunger to find his meaning that lies behind his words. But we know that his words are the sure path to his meaning.

We must discipline ourselves to listen for the voice of God as we make observations. Careful listening requires that we not put words and ideas into the mouth of God. It requires a humble spirit, one that knows it has much to learn and accepts that the Word of God comes both to affirm and to correct.

Observe! Observe! Observe!

Chapter 8

Interpretation Follows Observation

"Is there a doubt concerning the meaning of what I read?
Does anything appear dark or intricate? I lift up my heart
to the Father of Lights: Lord, is it not thy word,
'If any man lack wisdom, let him ask of God?'"

—John Wesley

RIBS is a spiritual exercise that follows a normal pattern of observation followed by interpretation followed by response followed by more observation, interpretation, and response. This pattern is applied to every phase of Bible study. It should guide how we study without inhibiting our openness to the Holy Spirit. Instruction by the Spirit-Word must not be constrained to this or other logical patterns of study.

In the RIBS pattern, we move from insight, to understanding, to life. This process is not time governed; it can take place instantly or it may require lengthy mulling over each component. Sometimes the Holy Spirit even changes us and the way we exist in the world before we understand the why and the how. It should not surprise us for this to happen during Bible study. However the Spirit chooses to teach us, Bible study should always culminate in our living in the light of what we are discovering as we journey with Christ.

In this chapter, we turn our attention to the second element in the RIBS pattern: interpretation.

We should constantly move in and out
between understanding and meaning
and living in the light of what
we are discovering.

As Spirit-Word, the biblical text is living and multi-dimensional. Interpretation attempts to answer the question, "What do the observable truths I have seen in the Bible mean?" Good interpretation requires that we be open to all the living dimensions of the text and to the entire audience of the text. We must always be aware that God is speaking to us personally through the Bible, and that He is simultaneously speaking to the whole of humanity. Bible study should always be personal which is not the same as being private.

These realities demand reasoned interpretation combined with spiritual discernment. Good interpretation takes place when the head and the heart work together. It requires that we integrate reason and discernment into one process in which the freedom of imagination is anchored to the confines of logic. This is one of the leading ways the Spirit leads us into truth.

Interpretation naturally follows observation, but that does not mean there will always be an interpretation immediately following an observation. In the early phase of study, there may be many things you observe for which you have no idea how to interpret. In fact, you may never interpret some observations. That is okay. The more you progress in an inductive study, the more interpretations you will make, and those interpretations will become more and more certain. For this to happen, you need to make some less certain interpretations from the very beginning of a book study and continue refining them throughout the process.

Always remember, interpretation is never an end-in-itself. Interpretation should always be moving toward a response to what

God is saying. The goal is to achieve truth-filled interpretations and for them to nurture our being and guide our doing as followers of Christ. Good Bible study must never be a one-step process that begins and ends with interpretation.

The RIBS approach requires faithfulness to the inductive cycle but that does not mean it must be a dense and difficult task. If you have read a book of the Bible and observed its literary patterns and its structural relations, you will usually find that interpretation of the meaning behind those patterns and relationships flows naturally out of your observations. It is human nature to interpret what we see. It is not human nature to always be careful in how we interpret what we read.

As we have seen, an observation is merely an objective statement about the construction of a biblical text. Observations are concerned with the factual. They approach the text as a work of literature asking, "What does it actually say, and how does it say it?" An interpretation, on the other hand, has to do with the meaning of the text, the truth that lies within and behind the words. Structural and relational patterns can be observed, but the significance of those patterns must be interpreted with discernment.

It is all too easy to read our own beliefs and understandings into a text, thinking that we are making an observation or a reasoned interpretation, when in fact we are adding to the text something we already assume to be true. Instead of hearing what God is saying, we fill in the blanks with what we assume God *would* say on the topic and/or *how* He would say it. Remember, it is human nature to interpret what we see, but all too often we interpret too quickly.

We are prone to misread the text and jump to the question, "What does this text mean?" before we have adequately addressed the question, "What does this text say?" Premature interpretation is like interrupting someone who is talking by finishing their statements for them. We often interrupt the Word in mid-sentence and interject our own thoughts. Don't do this! Be very careful to separate interpretation from observation. Good interpretation is almost always preceded by a pause to reflect on that which has been observed.

Premature interpretation is like interrupting someone who is talking and finishing their statements for them.

Good interpretation is both a science and an art. As a science, interpretation is a process of sound reasoning. I have these facts before me, i.e., specific observations, and I must ask myself, "What do these facts mean?" In other words, "What general conclusion can I draw from my observations?" The conclusion we draw forms a hypothesis. This is the heart of the scientific method. The next step would involve testing the hypothesis to see whether the conclusions are true. In inductive Bible study, the application step serves the role of a test for the hypothesis. In RIBS, we have replaced "application" with "response" to promote a more holistic response to the Word of God and to resist treating the living Word like a dead object. (You may wish to review the strengths and flaws of deductive reasoning, which we addressed in Chapter 2.)

This scientific aspect of interpretation sounds very objective. The conclusions drawn are obvious deductions from the discovered facts. It is all just a matter of following the method, or is it? In reality, everyone brings to each step in the inductive process their own biases shaped by their life experiences. We all have our own abilities to see and our own blinders that hinder our ability to see. Our "objective" conclusions are always influenced by the subjective limitations of our perceptions of truth.

Art is the creative expression of an interpretation of some aspect of life. When interpretation remains solely in the domain of logic and reason, it can never capture the richness of life. The Bible is literary art. By the Word, God created all things, and by the Word, God is now in Christ Jesus recreating all things. The Bible is creational in nature and affect. The Word of God is life-giving and not just intellect-building, truth nurturing and not just truth revealing.

To truly know (*yada*) the Word is to become one with the Word, which calls forth participation in the creative power of the Word. We were created to function as creators with God, to create ways to care for creation, tend the garden, and replenish and nurture the earth. Relational Inductive Bible Study should fan into flame that aspect of our created nature.

When we teach seminary classes on inductive Bible study, the term project is for the students to express an interpretation of the Gospel of Mark through an art form: drawing, painting, sculpture, music, etc. The purpose of this assignment is to challenge students to interpret the book on a different plane than they normally think and in a different "language" than they normally speak. For most students, this is the hardest part of the class. They struggle to get started and must overcome fears of public embarrassment. By the end of the semester, though, they are so in love with Mark's Gospel their creative juices are flowing. Over the years many of these pieces of art have been near museum quality portraits of the Gospel of Mark.

Imagination is the wellspring of creativity. Both flow from the same region of the human brain that allows us to hold together things that seem disconnected—the region that allows us to see how the dots in our lives can and should connect. It takes imagination to make good observations, to see connections that others may have missed. They will see what you see if you point out for them what you are seeing. It takes even more imagination to draw true and wise interpretations out of our factual observations, to help ourselves and others see the meaning and beauty that lies behind our observations. Reasoned deductions are dependent on imagined possibilities with reason serving as the bumper guards for imagined truth.

Observations vs. Interpretations

The fundamental difference between an observation and an interpretation is verifiability. Observations can be verified and affirmed by everyone. Interpretations are opinions about purpose and meaning. Not every reasonable person will agree. But every reasonable person should be able to understand our thought processes even if they disagree with our conclusions.

Consider the following differences between an observation and an interpretation.[1] An observation is a factual comment about the contents of the text. An observation may be …

- an isolated fact

- a relationship between facts

- a pattern of relationships between facts and other factual observations.

Observations begin with taking note of the facts and then connecting the facts in accurate ways. Observations on relationships between facts must be factual and true. There should be no need to defend them as true. The author has laid them out for all to see.

An interpretation is a personal opinion about the author's intent for writing what you have observed—a statement about the author's purpose for the things in the text. It states:

- an explanation of the of the author's purpose.

- a generalized conclusion about meaning. (Note: a summary statement is an observation, which is not the same as a generalized conclusion.)

- a principle derived from a set of observations.

---

[1] Adapted from Leigh's *Direct Bible Study*, 60.

- a statement about the significance of things observed.

- an implication or an inference drawn from things observed.

- a judgment about things observed.

Thus, a primary distinction between observations and interpretations is the certainty of the statements. An observation must be absolutely certain. Any reasoned person who reads the observation and examines the textual evidence for the observation would agree that the observation is true. On the other hand, interpretations have an element of uncertainty; interpretations are human opinions about meaning. Reasonable people may disagree with your interpretations.

In the inductive process, it is normal for one's interpretations to progressively increase in confidence. Early interpretations should be less certain than final interpretations. However, it is important to start making interpretations at the very beginning of an inductive study. Early interpretations, while having less certainty, serve as markers for finding more observations that will lead to more certain interpretations. Early interpretations often are theories to be proven or disproven by deeper study of the book.

Think of your interpretations as existing on a sliding scale of confidence. On one end of the scale are opinions that are little more than hunches. These interpretations might appear in the form of questions such as, "Could it be that the author wants the reader to think or conclude ...?" Informed questions become the impetus for deeper study. Early interpretations serve to provoke you to ask yourself, "Am I seeing what I think I'm seeing?" and "Is what I am seeing significant?"

In the middle of the scale of certainty are interpretations that make a qualified statement, including phrases like, "It appears to me ...," or "It seems reasonable to conclude ..." These statements are opinions the student should stay open to reconsider. Like earlier interpretations, their primary purpose is to point the student toward more certainty as to what the author intends the reader to know.

Hearing God's voice demands a response.

On the other end of the scale are personal interpretations made with a strong sense of certainty and confidence that the student has rightly "connected the dots" of a text and found the author's message. In effect, these interpretations say, "Recognizing my own human limitations, for me it is beyond any doubt that the author intends for the reader to think or to conclude ..." or "It seems abundantly clear that ..."

Interpretations made with a high level of confidence require a response. If God is indeed speaking these things, He expects us to conform to them. Hearing His voice demands some type of action. We will return to this thought later.

RIBS Principles of Biblical Interpretation

Below we have listed some principles for good biblical interpretation drawn from what we have written so far. We offer them here as a summation of what we have written in the preceding chapters and a foundation for making good interpretations drawn from good observations. These concepts should constantly be in the background of your mind as principles for Relational Inductive Bible Study.

In the Scriptures We Come to Know and Love God Better. We often read the Bible to know things about God. It is good to know about God, but *knowledge about God* is not the same as *knowing God*. As was noted in an earlier chapter, the Hebrew word for "to know" is *yada*, a word conveying knowledge that comes through experience. This type of knowing is more by the heart than the mind and comes from active, intentional engagement in lived experience. In the Old Testament, *yada* is the word used for lovemaking.

This type of knowing is in stark contrast with the basic Greek approach to knowledge, which involved a standing back from something to know it objectively. Biblical writers make clear that if a person knew God, he or she was encountered by a living God who required a response from the total person. In other words, one could not truthfully say they knew God unless they were living as if they knew Him.

In this biblical concept of knowing, our knowledge of God is not derived primarily from the information we possess but from how we respond to God's loving and holy presence. Our knowledge of God is grounded in loving relationship. We read and study the Bible to go more deeply into this relationship. In the Scriptures we encounter a living God who desires to be known, not just known about.

In the Scriptures, We Are Known. Knowledge in the biblical paradigm of *yada* not only means that we come to know and love God, but it also conveys that in this process of knowing, we the readers are transformed. As we come into the presence of God through His Word, there is a wonderful, frightening, and amazing "figure-ground reversal" that takes place. Through the text, God reads us. We come to know ourselves as the object of God's divine love as He exposes to us the mysteries of our inner self.

This reversal means that as we come to know and love God more fully, we discover more fully how we are known and loved by God. Thus, reading the Bible should be a two-way relationship, one of intimate encounter. It is wonderful to know that God's Word reveals to us our true selves. Sometimes we hide, not only from others, but also from ourselves. The Word of God opens us up, cutting away our self-deception and exposing what is hidden. Herein lies the possibility of true transformation. As we yield to the Spirit of God speaking through the Word, we are transformed more and more into the image of Christ.

Biblical Interpretation Must be Trans-rational. Bible study must not be irrational, bypassing human understanding and reason. However, through and with the Holy Spirit, it should transcend human reason. We are gifted to know, but we know in part. We understand in part. But the Holy Spirit, the *Paraclete*, transcends our reason, granting us discernment, knowledge, wisdom and understanding beyond our abilities. The Spirit flows in ways we cannot dictate or program. By the Spirit, we can know more than we can understand.

Bible study empowered by the Holy Spirit takes reason and sharpens it with a keen awareness that is beyond our natural abilities. We come to know the Word of God with knowledge that is of the Holy Spirit. We study hard. We apply ourselves, and God takes our efforts with our limited abilities as an offering. The Spirit adds to this offering rich gifts of grace, and we see the truth, embrace the truth, know the truth, and are enabled to live the truth.

There is No Private Interpretation of Scripture. Bible study is deeply personal, and God's Word addresses us as individuals. Whatever we come to know about the Bible, it is distinctly our knowledge. However, the Bible is not given to us to be a private possession. Rather, the Bible was given to the church, preserved by the church, and speaks to the church. It is the church's book as well as every believer's book.

The relatively few followers of Christ who were gathered on the Day of Pentecost has expanded to become a worldwide communion of saints. The Holy Spirit resides in this holy communion of saints and remains equally present wherever "two or three [are] gathered together" in the name of Christ (Matt 18:20). In this we rejoice: Jesus is always present when we gather around the Word.

The Scriptures are to be read, studied, taught, and preached within this community of saints. In this context, the Word is especially encountered as living and powerful. It is nourishment for the body

144

of Christ always working to make the church a healthier expression of God's presence in the world.

Interpretation of Scripture Must Not be Separated from its Nature as Literature. The Bible came to us in the form of great literature. It contains wonderful narratives, beautiful poetry, and vivid apocalyptic images. To know the Word of God means that we

- learn the form and structure of narratives and how meaning is conveyed through story.

- appreciate the depth of poetry as it unveils the human heart and our longing for God.

- understand how truth is embedded in visions and dreams and symbols.

God's Word came to us in history through people who used their skills in writing so we could better know the mysteries of God. The Spirit of God worked with human writers, and they produced for us the most eloquent forms of story, rhetoric, and poetry that convey deep and eternal truths.

As you study the Bible inductively, you will increase your skills in recognizing literary forms and observing how these forms convey meaning. You will learn how to see patterns in the books, and in doing so, learn to love and appreciate the wonderful treasure that is the Bible.

Interpretation of Scripture Must Not be Separated from the Historical/Cultural Context out of Which It Arose. God's revelation did not come down to humanity as a pristine, ahistorical artifact. Rather, it came to us in the messiness of history. Jesus Christ, the Living Word, became flesh and lived among us (John 1:14). So too, the written Word, as a sanctified vessel of the eternal Word, came to us through vessels of flesh.

Thus, we need to say that just as Jesus is both fully divine and fully human, the Bible is both fully God's divine Word and fully human words. As God's divine Word, it is Spirit-given and Spirit-anointed. As human word, imperfect people were the instruments of this divine Word coming and living among us.

As a human document, the Bible reveals much about humankind. It shows the messiness of history. It shows how we are finite in our understanding. It even shows the depths of human depravity. Read the Old Testament and you will see how people repeatedly ignored the Laws of God and "did what was right in their own eyes" (Judges 21:25). The books of *First and Second Kings* expose the good, bad, and ugly of the rulers of Israel and Judah. A quick reading of 1 Timothy gives a glimpse into the passion of Paul as he attempted to guide a young minister in shepherding the people of God. A look into the books of *First and Second Corinthians* reveals the difficulty Paul faced with the greatly divided and immature church at Corinth.

Yet, despite human limitations, or possibly because of them, God's Word speaks to humans. God's Word transcends human frailty, sinfulness, and prejudices to speak to us. There is great peace in knowing that as a sanctified vessel set apart as God's divine revelation, the Scriptures remain trustworthy—because God is trustworthy. People do not have to "get it right" all the time for God to speak to them and through them.

Also, it is helpful to learn about the cultures represented in the Bible and about the lifestyles, governments, and people of biblical times. The Word of God directly addresses these rulers, governments, and people where they were living. We do not live there, but we can see how God spoke directly to their specific issues.

We can further know that the Word of God is not limited to a particular context. Just as the Bible is a divine-human book, it is a time bound and timeless book. Hold these things in tension. God is a God of history, but God is not limited to history. We can read the

Bible as history, but we should also read the Bible as the eternal Word of God. What a wonder!

Knowledge of Scripture Cannot be Separated from Our Own Historical/Cultural Realities. It would be nice to say that we read the Bible objectively. However, there is no totally objective person. We are born into specific families, cultures, and geographical locations. These givens and our life experiences within them color our reading of the world and our reading of the Bible. They influence what we see and what we don't see.

> Bible study as an act of worship demands that we let go of our own attempts to manage, control, or manipulate the truth of God's Word.

While the inductive approach to Bible study will help us "let go" of many of our faulty preconceptions, it does not free us from ourselves. We live in our own skin, and we read with our own eyes. We can take comfort in knowing that with the inductive approach, we can come to the text with open hands, open minds, and open hearts. We can in faith prepare ourselves for the Holy Spirit to remove our personal blinders.

The posture of worship is one of surrender. As an act of worship, Bible study demands that we let go of our conscious and subconscious attempts to manage, control, or manipulate the truth of God's Word. We must surrender ourselves to the Holy Spirit who will take us into truth, including the truth about the things we cherish.

With these things said, we must never forget that the Word of God is speaking within and to our historical/cultural realities. We can only truly know the Word of God by allowing the Word to know us. We can only know to the extent we are willing to be known. When we bring ourselves to Bible study, we are bringing everything that has helped to make us who we are. This includes everything we cherish about our heritage and those things we wish we could escape.

Just keep in mind that there is a difference between surrendering one's contextual identity so that it can be judged in the light of God's Word and attempting to suppress our identity in order to better interpret the Bible. We cannot truthfully understand the Word of God without openness to hear what God is saying about us and our world. Proper interpretation of the Bible requires open and honest interpretation of ourselves and our contextual realities.

Some Guidelines for Interpretation

Having already considered some differences between an observation and an interpretation and having considered some principles for interpreting the Scriptures, here are some guidelines for making good interpretations:

Be Prayerful. As we discussed in Chapter 3, we should view Bible study as worship and especially as prayer. Good Bible study is a process of listening for the voice of God. This is most critical at the point we are attempting to interpret the meaning of Scripture. Interpretation should be an effort to speak God's words after Him. The process centers on our attempt to understand the meaning of the Bible, but it results in our expression of meaning; it is our attempt to name the truth of God's Word. With varying levels of certainty, we are announcing, "Thus says the Lord."

Therefore, we must approach interpretation as something we do before God and with God. Jesus promised that the Holy Spirit would teach us. We must believe Him and have faith that the Spirit is with us to do just that. We should approach biblical interpretation as interaction with the Holy Spirit, who is present to guide us. In this, the Spirit binds our heart with the heart of God, and the light of God's Word shines more brightly on our path.

Be Humble. It is repeatedly stated in the Bible that the Lord resists the proud but gives grace to the humble. It is also repeatedly stated that all knowledge and wisdom come from God. We cannot rightly interpret the Scriptures on our own. We need help. We need God's help. Humility strips us of any sense that we are mastering God's Word. It removes from us the pride that so often accompanies knowledge, and it leaves us with a sense of awe that the God of all creation is speaking to us.

Interpret Observations. The central premise of the inductive approach is that our interpretations of the Bible should be based exclusively on what is written. We make observations as a means of disciplining ourselves to carefully see everything that is written without adding to it or otherwise distorting it.

Interpreting a text begins with interpreting what we have seen in the text. Interpreting what we have seen is not precisely the same as interpreting what is written. Because of our limitations, we never fully see everything that is in the text.

We might think of it this way. Interpreting our observations is part of the study process. The process climaxes in clear statements of what we understand the text to mean. Interpretations of observations do not have to be statements about the meaning of the text. They may be statements about how the author structured the text so that the meaning might be discovered.

Recognizing this procedural difference between interpreting our observations and interpreting the text helps us appreciate the sliding scale of certainty in our interpretations. Making good observations followed by good interpretations of our observations are the primary building blocks for making good interpretations of the meaning of the text.

In other words, it is helpful to distinguish those interpretations of observations about how the author built his argument from those interpretations about the meaning of the text. Interpretations of meaning are most often the product of interpretations of method.

Delay Interpreting. Too often we rush into interpretation. It is critical that you discipline yourself not to make definitive interpretations of a text until you feel certain you have made accurate observations about the text. The chapters that follow will guide you in how to do a thorough study of select passages of a text. As you study the text, noting and observing its literary structure and the relational connections within the text, restrain from jumping into interpretation until you are confident in your observations. Have patience, and your study will yield the fruit of good interpretation.

Do Not Fear Unanswered Questions. As you study the Bible, you will have many questions that linger as you move from observation to interpretation. Do not be afraid of questions; good questions are the foundation for good answers, and even bad questions can lead to good questions. Questions are not a sign of ignorance but signs of a heart searching for truth. Think of questions as open doors, inviting you into a realm of discovery. People with "all the answers" are typically more misguided than those with a lot of questions! Just remember to discipline yourself to avoid quick answers to your questions or the questions of others.

Be Imaginative. Interpretation requires an element of imagination. Interpretation is in essence a process of translation. Through it, we take factual observations from what has been written and translate those observations into statements of what they mean. That process requires choosing words and constructing phrases and sentences to create a concise statement about meaning. By its very nature, that process is one of creativity, and creativity requires imagination.

By no means do we intend that interpretation should be the product of blind intuition; rather, it must be grounded in the reality of the observations made. Interpretation must reflect the truth and truthfulness of those observations and not go beyond the reasonable limits of those observations. Interpretation must not be disjoined from good observation.

What we do intend is that when interpretation is done with the Spirit, it calls upon our imaginations to see connections between things observed and the meaning of those observations. The art of making good interpretations is a process that requires freedom of the human spirit. Good interpretation is not like a numbered painting where our job is to dab the prescribed colors in the right spaces and then to pretend to have painted a beautiful picture. Personal engagement with the Bible demands personal interpretations and responses to the Word of God.

In the end, the Holy Spirit works through our imaginations to mold our hearts and minds into the image and likeness of the only begotten Son of God. With the aid of the Holy Spirit, we can see that which God is calling us to become.

Chapter 9

Yielding and Responding

"I lift up my heart to the Father of Lights: 'Lord, is it not thy word, "If any man lack wisdom, let him ask of God?" Thou "givest liberally, and upbraidest not." Thou hast said; "If any be willing to do thy will, he shall know." I am willing to do, let me know, thy will."

—John Wesley

When we listen carefully to what the Bible is saying, with a sincere desire to hear from God, the Word of God will be written in our hearts and made evident in our lives. In the KJV there is an old English word, "hearken," that encapsulates this thought. "Hearkening" was to "hearing" what "observing" is to "seeing." It meant to listen intently with a view toward responding appropriately. It meant "to hear" in the sense a parent might mean when saying to a disobedient child "hear me when I'm speaking to you." Hearkening was more than paying close attention to the words. It included being mindful of who was speaking and being inclined to respond accordingly.

If "hearken" was still in common use, we might describe the RIBS process as "hearkening to the Word of God: hearing, interpreting, and responding." This differs significantly from the traditional inductive model of observing, interpreting and applying. The traditional model tends to reduce interpretation to studying the words, grammar, and historical context of a book in order to discover principles to live by. Principles can be very helpful tools for daily living but when interpretation of the Bible is reduced to identifying principles, the personal nature and passion of the Word are easily lost. When this happens, our opinion of what the Bible says may be given priority over the Word itself and a harmful gap emerges between God's Word and our lived response to the Word. In effect, the God who is speaking is dropped out of the conversation.

Bible study should climax in more than the reasoned application of principles. It should result in more confidence that we are walking with Jesus. This does not mean that every Bible study session will result in radical transformation or ecstatic emotional expression. It merely means that every session should be marked by our full surrender to God's Word. We should be conscious of his presence in his Word, and we should enter and exit his presence in his Word with hearts yielded to the Holy Spirit. Ultimately, Bible study should result in a deepened awareness of God's presence in our lives; our fellowship with the Holy Trinity should be renewed and strengthened.

Fellowship with God in his Word both demands and creates a wholistic response. What we think and how we behave must and will be adjusted, but so too will our affections and emotions, our attitudes and dispositions, our self-perceptions and our relationships. All that we are must be molded more and more into the "image and likeness" of Jesus Christ. The entirety of our human existence should be clay in the hands of the potter.

Responding to the Word should express our desire to live pleasingly before God. Our response must embody God's Word, making us to be the salt and light of God's Word, causing us to be living epistles of God's Word. How must I change for the Spirit and the Word to dwell in me more richly? This is a question of being more than a question of doing: being with God, being one with Christ, being in and of the Spirit. Answers to questions of being will then give rise to questions of doing.

We are not suggesting that knowing and being always come before doing. The normal pattern of human transformation is to know in the sense of understand, followed by being in the sense of conforming to what we know, followed by doing that which we know we should be doing in light of what we know and who we are: know, be, do. But this sequence is not the only way we grow as Christians. There are somethings we will only understand after we have developed the habit of doing them ("It is more blessed to give than to receive."). Likewise, there are realities in which we know ourselves as being before we even hope to understand the reality ("I know I am loved by God" precedes forever "I understand God's love for me").

Types of Responses

Responses take many forms. Perhaps the most common type of response is simply to affirm and fortify what we already know. Another type adds something new to the believer's life, a new insight, a new sense of direction and purpose, etc. Still another type requires personal transformation. We must always be open to being confronted by the Spirit-Word with errors in what we believe and how we live. Sometimes being faithful to God requires change, even radical change.

The form a response takes should be determined by how the Bible text intersects with our lives. The intersection may be related to issues in our relationships, or a recent personal crisis, or normal patterns in our lives, or even our tightly held beliefs. Our discoveries in our Bible study may touch upon seemingly minor areas of life or major aspects of our innermost being. In all cases, our responses should express our surrender to the Spirit-Word of God.

Intellectual Responses. The purpose of Bible study should not be limited to gaining knowledge. On the other hand, the results of Bible study should include increased knowledge, revision to some opinions and beliefs that we hold, and changes to our patterns of thinking. We must be willing for our Bible study to expand, improve, and correct our theology. It is a form of idolatry to manipulate the Scriptures into conforming to our preexisting, limited understanding of truth. The most fundamental response to the Word of God involves surrender of our perceived right to determine for ourselves what is true.

Heart Responses. One type of response involves change in our inner person. We might call it a change of heart. One Old Testament metaphor places our inner person in our bowels, our gut. A New Testament term for the same is "mind." We are to live as sacrifices acceptable to God through the "renewing of our minds" (Romans 12:1-2). We are to "have the mind of Christ" (Philippians 2:5).

In New Testament times, the mind was the seat out of which human thinking arose. But it was also the seat of human dispositions, attitudes, and affections. It embraced what we might call a person's mindset, and it was a near synonym for what we call the heart of a person. The mind of Christ was to pour himself out into humanity, become an obedient servant to the point of humiliation, suffering, and death on a cross. The incarnation was the result of more than a reasoned decision; it was the fruit of God's attitude about, disposition toward and affection for his creation.

Bible study should push and pull us toward the mindset of Christ. It should birth in us his attitude and disposition toward others. It should fan into flame the love of God deposited in our souls at our new birth. It is not enough to "think like Jesus thinks;" we must conform to his holy character. Having the mind of Christ will predispose our actions toward that which pleases him and give direction when we don't have time to think about how we should act.

One might think that changes to this realm of our existence can only take place through the inner working of the Holy Spirit, and one would be right. But that truth does not exempt us from initiating those changes ourselves. Take a moment to revisit some of the

156

teachings of Christ. Did he not say that we must forgive and love. Paul did not tell us to beg for the mind of Christ. He said let it be in you. We must respond in our innermost being to the instructions of God.

The transformation of our heart is the fruit of the sanctifying grace of God, and we are sanctified through the truth of God's Word (John 17:17). Thus, Bible study should convince us of God's good desires for us and simultaneously enlighten us to his expectation that we desire what he expects of us. It should also build our faith that what he requires of us he provides for us. We must believe that the grace of God works with our will to enable us to faithfully respond to his Word. Our response to God's call for changes of the heart must begin with faith that he is already at work in us both to desire and to work for his good pleasure (Philippians 2: 13).

Behavioral Responses. Behavior is what we do, the actions we take. Our actions may be subconsciously guided by our attitudes or consciously determined by our will. Behavioral responses to the Word should be based on certainty that we have rightly interpreted the Bible. But we do not have to understand everything the Bible demands of us before we act accordingly. Sometimes the formation of a habit comes before understanding the purpose behind the expected behavior. In any case, Bible study should give direction to how we act. The easiest responses to make, and perhaps the hardest to keep, are commitments to change our behavior.

Principles for Responding

Out of what we have written in this and previous chapters, we can extrapolate some principles to guide our responses to our encounters with the living Word.

Responses must be personal. We think, feel, and behave as individuals. We may respond to the Word of God in a group setting, but we respond as individuals. Also, responses are made in the context of our present realities. In a different time, your response may vary significantly and still be faithful to the text. The Word does not change, but we change, our situation changes, and the Word shines light on us in the context in which we are living.

But personal does not mean private or segregated. How you respond should be in harmony with the responses of others. Just like your interpretations, your responses must be consistent with Christian tradition. The light that shines on us is the same light that has lighted the Way of the Cross for two millennium. Furthermore, because responses are personal, we must never impose our responses on others.

Responses should be reasonable. We have suggested that some responses may occur as we study and may seem spontaneous. But most responses will be based on reasoned reflection and meditation. All responses should be reasonable. There should be a logical connection between what we believe the Bible is saying and how we respond to what it is saying. If shared, others should be able to appreciate the connections we have made between the Word and our life.

Responses should be wholistic. Our response to God's Word should not be limited to our reasoning. They should be transrational. Every aspect of our lives must be responsive to the Word of God. We must reason to the best of our abilities, but we must not allow reason to shackle other aspects of our humanity. We respond as human beings, not as thinking machines.

Responses require introspection. You cannot properly respond to the Word of God without examining yourself. The Bible is a mirror for looking into our innermost being, helping us see ourselves more clearly. In it, God is speaking to us about us and about our place in the world. At the heart of Bible study must be the question, "how must I change in order to conform to Christ and fulfill God's purposes in my life?"

Responses are always confessional. Whatever form they take, responses are confessions of what we have come to believe and what we think. Responses to the Word of God are thus expressions of our faith. They are testimonies of our current spiritual realities; they express what we consider important in our Christian journey, what we are willing to commit ourselves to.

Responses may be conditional. Not every interpretation will result in radical change. Just as interpretations are made on a sliding scale of certainty, responses should exist on a sliding scale. On one end of the scale are responses to interpretations that lacked certainty. It is only reasonable that our responses would also lack certainty. Typically, responses to uncertain interpretations express our resolve to do further study. On that end of the continuum, we are saying (1) I see something that seems important, (2) I am not certain of the meaning of what I am seeing, and (3) I will do further study to better understand what I am seeing.

On the other end of the sliding scale are interpretations that seem absolute, those things for which we are fully persuaded we understand what God is saying. On that end of the continuum, we are saying (1) I have observed something in the text that no reasonable person could deny is true, (2) It is clear to me what the author intended by what I observed, and (3) God is saying to me that I must act or change in a specific way. These responses may include specific plans for action but more importantly they should be expressions of who we are committed to become.

Responses may grow out of a time of prayerful meditation, or they may seemingly be instant. Because our responses may be deeply personal, we may at times have to wrestle with God and/or wrestle with ourselves before we know how we should respond. On the other hand, encounters with the Word of God may result in instant insight to the text and to ourselves. Without hesitation, we know what we must do. Therefore, a response may happen at any time within a study session, but most responses will be based on critical reflection on what we have discovered.

Some Guidelines for Responding

There are no hard and fast rules for how to respond to Bible study discoveries. Every response must be your personal response. Your responses should flow out of what you believe God is saying to you personally. Here are some guidelines to help.

Always keep in mind that your responses are to and before God. We are not responding merely to ideas and concepts. We are responding to a person, God. Be constantly aware of God's presence when you study his Word. If you do this, your responses to his Word will be responses to him. Do not allow the medium of literature to become a barrier when God intends it to be a bridge. Hold tightly to your belief that God is speaking as you read and study. Form your response with his presence in mind.

Respond during every RIBS study session. In general, you should respond immediately after you have interpreted a set of observations. Every study session should include one or more pauses to prayerfully formulate responses to the things you have discovered.

Always write your responses down. You should do this alongside your other notes on the book you are studying, i.e., next to your observations and interpretations. Composing a written response helps ensure your responses flow out of your observations and interpretations of the text. Also, written responses can be revisited and are more likely to be remembered and adhered to.

Make your pauses to respond times of worship. As is appropriate to your discoveries, offer up prayers of thanksgiving, praise, and adoration. Petitions for assistance in knowing how to respond and for faithfulness to your responses are appropriate. Don't hesitate to worship in song even if it is with inaudible melodies in your heart. Obedient response to the Word of God is the essence of worship.

Summation

If we truly believe the Bible is the Word of God and God is speaking to us personally through it, we must respond to what we hear God saying. Our response must be true to the Scriptures and to the realities in which we live. We must respond with integrity and be able to say with confidence how God's Word is speaking into our lives.

Yet, some of our responses will reflect our limitations. Sometimes, our truthful response is to admit we do not understand the meaning behind the words of Scripture; we do not grasp the connection between the Word and our lives. The best we can do in those times is to pray for wisdom and formulate questions that will lead us toward further discoveries. Honest questions are valid responses.

As we journey with God through the garden of his Word, insight may leap out at us and call forth an instant response. Most often, however, our response to God's Word will be the product of reasoned application of our careful interpretations of the text. Likewise, our response may be spontaneous expressions of worshipful communion with God. In any case, we must continually be working toward thoughtful conformity to God's Word.

Always be sensitive to the Holy Spirit, letting the Spirit through the Word help you interpret yourself. The Spirit knows the deep things of our hearts and the Spirit knows how to best connect the Word to our lives. The Spirit-Word will help us bring our full humanity into conformity with God's desires for us. A proper response to the Word of God is surrender of all that we are to the will of God.

Chapter 10

Preparing to Study

"Serious and earnest prayer should be constantly used,
before we consult the oracles of God, seeing scripture
can only be understood thro' the same Spirit
whereby 'it was given.'"

—John Wesley

Many metaphors offer wisdom on how to approach the Bible. We have already identified a couple. The Bible is a field of unearthed treasures, each waiting to be discovered. The Bible is a love letter from God to us. Another helpful metaphor is that of an art exhibit. The Bible is literary art on display for all to see. It is like the collected works of a great artist who has mastered many differing styles and mediums.

Most of us have low opinions of ourselves as art critics, but all of us know the art we like when we see it. What we lack is the discipline to study the art we like until we can tell others why we like it. Let it become your goal to study the Bible until you can confidently tell others what it is saying to you.

Become a Lover of Art

A lover of art does not walk through an exhibit quickly and leave. No, that person wants to linger, often surveying the whole exhibit before returning to gaze at individual pieces. Art lovers know that the longer they look at a single painting, the more they can see; colors and shapes give way to styles and techniques until a single brush stroke is seen in light of the whole. For these students of beauty, the art speaks to them and stirs thoughts and feelings from deep within.

Bible study can be that kind of exploration—a life-long adventure of gazing at the Word of God, finding wonder, beauty, meaning and purpose in each of the sixty-six books. Unlike ordinary art exhibits, this treasured collection of literature is living. It is not a repository of past genius being put on display. The artist is present with and in that which is admired and studied. The exhibit itself is God personally reaching out to humanity, offering to be known as our Father in heaven. Through the Scriptures, God invites us to journey with Him into the joy, wonder, and beauty of His presence on earth.

If we can stretch this metaphor a little further, at least for believers, we can think of this art exhibit as an interactive museum of art where the faithful get to enter into the art, touch it, and be touched by it. Without altering a single syllable, we can add our voices to the lament, joy, and praise of the Psalmists. We can enter the lion's den with Daniel as we welcome God into our own tribulations. We can experience Paul's radical transformation on the road to Damascus as we ourselves are transformed. We can travel through the wilderness with Israel and know that a great heavenly host is journeying with us in our wilderness. We can become artists with God, living epistles creatively adding our story to the story of God's love for His creation.

Studying art is in many ways different from studying history, science, or other academic subjects. Yes, there is much to be learned about art. There are scholars of art who write textbooks on art history and art appreciation. Their books can help us gain knowledge about styles and techniques of art and how they have evolved over the centuries—knowledge needed to become a serious student of art as a discipline. But there is a difference between studying about art and studying works of art. That difference is much like the difference that exists between studying about the Bible and studying the Bible.

Bible scholars are a great gift to the Church. Their work should be honored, and the fruit of their labors should help guide the Church in what to believe and how to act. But no one must become a great scholar in biblical studies before becoming an excellent scholar of the Bible. Good Bible study requires that we approach the Bible both as a written text to be studied and as a work of art to be gazed upon with curiosity and wonder.

RIBS is more closely aligned with those who are lovers of sacred art than with those who desire to be scholars of sacred writings. For this reason, inductive Bible study has often found a home with Christian groups that deeply love the Bible. Those who deeply love the Bible are never fully satisfied to "live by the Word;" they hunger to "live in the Word." They are the ones who keep gazing at the Scriptures with a sense of awe at what they see. Those who equip themselves with the methods of inductive study are prepared to move out of the classroom and into the art itself. You can become that kind of scholar of the Bible.

Those who deeply love the Bible are never fully satisfied to "live by the Word;" they hunger to "live in the Word."

Throughout the centuries, the church told the stories of the Bible through music, paintings, sculptures, and statues. Through this art, the church did more than tell stories; it interpreted the theological meaning of the stories. We seriously encourage you to set aside some time to visit an art museum or google "classic Christian art." Select one piece that draws your attention and look intently at it. Gaze at it over and over again. Set it aside and return to it later, each time looking for something new. It will help you become a better student of the Bible.

One of the most famous examples of using art to teach is the Christian icon named *The Trinity* (also called *The Hospitality of Abraham*) by the Russian monk, Andrei Rublev, in the fifteenth century. A copy of the original appears here, printed in grayscale. Please take the time to Google the icon and view it on your computer screen. You may also wish to locate a good replica of the piece on the internet for more visual clarity. (The original has been exposed to the elements and is quite faded.) But keep a copy of the original handy to verify what you see in the replica.

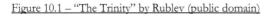
Figure 10.1 – "The Trinity" by Rublev (public domain)

Now, let's look at the icon as if we were doing an inductive study. First, imagine yourself in a church where the painting is on display. Look at it from a distance. What do you see? At first glance you probably notice that it is a picture of three angels sitting around a table. You believe they are angels because they have haloes and wings. Step closer and look again. You might notice the colors: each is dressed differently, but each one's clothing includes royal blue with the central figure's being more prominent and brighter.

Without moving closer, look again. Now you may notice more elements in the picture such as the chalice or bowl that is front and center on the table. You might also begin to notice the structure of the painting: the three figures are centered in the painting; the figure in the middle is higher, more focused, and brighter. The three are seated so as to approximate a circle on the canvas (it was actually painted on wood). There are images above the heads of the figures appearing as if one for each figure: a building above the head of the being on the left, a tree above the central being, and a shape that looks something like a mountain above the one on the right.

Focusing on the three figures, you might observe further that they are at a table but not eating or drinking. Neither do they appear to be talking. Their mouths are closed. Each has the appearance of contemplation. The faded outer garment of the one on the left appears to originally have been gold in color, and the outer garment of the one on the right is green. The inner garment of the central figure is brown but was possibly originally crimson.

You might begin to ask yourself, who are these figures? What is the setting? What, if anything, do the building, the tree, and the mountain represent? Does this painting depict an event in the Bible? If so, what event? You might remember the story of the three angels who visited Abraham, sat down under a tree, and ate a meal prepared for them.

Now step closer and look more deeply. You will see that the faces of the three figures are the same. Each holds an identical rod. The way the figures are seated around the table creates the image of a chalice when seen as a "figure-ground reversal." The three are gazing inward with their heads tilted down. The heads of the two toward the right are tilted toward the one on the left. The two figures toward the left seem to be gazing into each other's eyes. The right hands of the three figures have two fingers that are extended as is often done in ecclesiastical blessings. The feet of the two seated forward are on pedestals and do not touch the ground. In the bowl is the head of a calf.

More questions arise, and theories might emerge. The painting very much seems to depict the story of the three angels visiting Abraham and Sarah and eating a meal under an oak tree. The tree centered at the top strengthens this thesis, as does the calf's head in the bowl. The building then might represent the human couple's dwelling place, except that the biblical text refers to it as a tent. Also, why are Abraham and Sarah not represented in the painting? The biblical text makes a point that when he brought the food, Abraham "stood nearby" while they ate. It is also interesting that in the biblical text, Abraham engaged the three both in the plural and the singular as "my Lord."

With our observations in mind, we might do some more interpretation. In addition to representing the three angels of the Old Testament story, the figures in this picture can easily be construed as representing the Trinity. Their faces are the same. Their rods seem symbolic of equal authority. The levels of brightness for their clothing might indicate their visibility on earth. The figure on the left is most faded in appearance and might represent the Father, who is largely unseen on earth. The central figure would represent Christ, who has been seen and touched. The Holy Spirit, who is active in the church, would then be on the right and appears to be somewhere between the other two in brightness.

Look again and again, and you will no doubt see more and more details that beg to be interpreted. Now think of any book of the Bible. That book is like the icon; it is a portrait of divine revelation—waiting for you to gaze until you see what the artist wanted you to see. Then, as you begin to see how the details come together to convey meaning, you might just hear the artist beckoning you to tarry until you more and more understand the meaning of the portrait.

Develop Faith in Yourself

If you have a poor opinion of yourself as a Bible scholar, join the crowd. Many people from all walks of life feel the same way. Why? From where does this attitude come? Well, in some respects it has come from those of us who are ministers. At times we feel as though we have a monopoly on the deeper things of God's Word. We may stand in the pulpit Sunday after Sunday and utter sayings such as, "I have labored long over this passage, and I have come to understand it to mean…" or, "In the original language, the true meaning of this word is…" Unwittingly, we have intimidated the average person away from serious study of the Bible for himself or herself. We have blocked the doorway of the greatest of all art exhibits.

For centuries, the clergy opposed the translation of God's Word into the common language. People who dared translate the Bible into the vernacular were sometimes tortured and killed. Clergy would seize copies of translations and burn them. This attitude came from a fear that if the Bible was placed into the hands of ordinary people in their own language, the true meaning of God's Word would be perverted. False doctrines would abound, and the church would fall into apostasy. While there are few ministers today with this extreme attitude, the idea still exists in many minds that the Bible needs to be filtered through the eyes of a special group of people before it can be understood by the rest of the world.

We are not saying that we have no need of teachers or church doctrine. God's Word is clear that He has given us apostles, prophets, evangelists, pastors and teachers to equip us to do works of ministry (Eph 4:11). We need teachers and preachers to nurture us, but no one can learn for us. Learning is an active state of being, one in which we must participate with the teacher in discovering truth. It is not a passive condition in which someone studies for us, digests the material and then pours it into our heads.

We need teachers and preachers to nurture us, but no one can learn for us. Learning is an active state of being.

Learning is a quest, an adventure, and no one can make the journey for others. Therefore, the teaching-learning situation should be a dialogue between the learner and the teacher, both of whom should be in dialogue with God's Word. Both are to be changed in the process. Each is to learn from the other.

Even preaching should not totally be a one-way situation. In many cultures and especially in the traditions of the Black church, Pentecostalism, and others, the congregation 'helps' the preacher preach by interjecting blessings and affirmations ("amen") that affirm that the minister is indeed speaking the Word of God. In this wonderful tradition, the minister and congregation together fulfill the role of preaching the Word. Other traditions may frown on such overt expressions, but there is always a discernable response to the preached Word.

Clergy are not totally to blame for indifference to God's Word. Many people just prefer to have someone else study for them and then tell them what God expects. They distance themselves from God's voice, making it easier for them to accept or reject what they hear. They do not want to be directly responsible to God's Word. This approach creates a secondhand faith. It is an attitude that causes people to shift in opinion from preacher to preacher and teacher to teacher.

We should desire godly teachers but also remain aware that the words of teachers are subject to confirmation by the body of Christ. No Scripture is of private interpretation (2 Pet 1:20). It is God's plan for the Church to be a community of Bible scholars, growing and learning together.

As Christians, we have the opportunity and responsibility of going privately and corporately to God's Word for direction in life. When studying with others in an atmosphere of love and respect, we can allow the Holy Spirit to make God's Word alive for the community. We share this wonderful privilege as members of the body of Christ; we are priests together in the household of faith. In Chapter 19 we present a model for group Bible study designed to help in this process.

Preparation for Bible study should include remaining intentional about having faith in God's Word and consequently having faith in oneself as a student of God's Word. Have faith in yourself because God has faith in you. Each of us has a God-given right and responsibility to discern what He is saying through His Word. Think of it this way—you have been appointed by God to study His Word for the good of yourself and others, and whatever He has called you to do, He is equipping you to do. It is impossible to believe that you will hear God speak without also believing that you can hear God speak.

Spiritual Preparation

The most important thing to do before Bible study begins is to spiritually prepare for communion with God. Spiritual preparation is always personal. Each of us has our own set of challenges to prepare our spirits for study, and we have our own patterns for conquering those challenges. The critical issue is that we learn to discipline ourselves to listen for the voice of God. This proves essential for good Bible study. Thanks be to God; He has sent the Holy Spirit to help us prepare to study.

Spiritual discipline for Bible study must include nurturing a right attitude about the Bible. We need to cultivate a mindset that the Bible is not just words on a page but sacred space where God dwells.

When we do Bible study, we enter the realm of the reign of God where His plans for creation are already being fulfilled. To read and study the Bible as Spirit-Word of God is to be in the very presence of God!

A right attitude about the Bible will lead us to quiet our spirits and open our hearts to hear God speak. God is always at work in the Scriptures speaking to us personally. Furthermore, the Holy Spirit is with us and in us to help us know what God is saying through the Bible. Spiritual preparation requires faith that God rewards those who seek him (Heb 11:6). Preparation for Bible study should include sincere prayer that God will help us have ears to hear and eyes to see what He is revealing. We should then enter Bible study as an event of worship, especially worship through prayerful listening.

The love of Christ is the preeminent sign that one is prepared to hear what God is saying. Paul's prayer for the Ephesian Church should be adopted as our prayer for ourselves: I pray that through the reading of God's Word I may be able to more fully comprehend with all the saints what is the length and width, height and depth of God's love (See Eph 3:17-18). May our Bible study always lead us along with all the saints into more fully knowing the love of God. The fruit of our Bible study must always center on our relationship with Christ and with others.

Spiritual preparation for Bible study then should also include plans to reflect and meditate on what the Word of God is speaking to us about our current relationships with God and others. Bible study should never be concluded before we have examined our hearts and lives in light of what God is saying to us personally through the text. We must be intentional about letting the Word shine into the crevices of our hearts. Only then will the Spirit-Word "break up stony ground" and nurture us in the image of Christ.

We call this process "yielding to the Spirit"—an intentional movement into Christ as Lord of all. This surrender to the Spirit is letting God mold us into what we should be. It is accompanied by a desire to do what God desires us to do. In short, when we enter into Bible study, we must hunger to be formed into the likeness of Christ in our inner most being and in our behavior. Yielding must then be followed with responding to what the Spirit-Word is saying.

Some Practical Suggestions

Now that we have looked at how you can mentally and spiritually prepare for a RIBS Bible study session, we need to turn our attention to some practical suggestions on how you can best prepare to study God's Word: find the right time, find the right place, and gather the right materials.

Find the Right Time

Bible study is important business. Unfortunately, pressing and urgent things often crowd out the truly important things in life. That surely must be one of the biggest dangers in life. We allow those everyday pressing things such as grocery shopping, lawn care, housework, and so forth to crowd out some important things such as family togetherness, church attendance, prayer, and Bible study. We seem to think we always have tomorrow for important activities but tomorrow does not come because urgent things keep demanding our attention.

Yes, the pressures of modern life make it difficult for us to carve out time for Bible study—difficult, but not impossible. If you are serious about becoming an able student of God's Word, you must make Bible study a regularly scheduled part of your life. It is a matter of disciplining yourself to set priorities and then honoring those priorities. Do not give Bible study your leftover time. Fellowship with God in prayer and Bible study are the most important things you can do every day. Allow the Holy Spirit to help you discipline yourself to put the important things first. The more you intentionally schedule Bible study into life, the more natural it will become.

Take a short inventory of your weekly and daily schedules. When can you block out an hour or more of uninterrupted time for Bible study? This may sound impossible but try to find an hour that would have few interruptions and when you are at your best mentally and physically. Some people are 'morning people' and seem to function better early in the day. Others are at their peak in the evenings. You know your own schedule, life habits, and responsibilities. Perhaps there are things you can eliminate and/or things you can adjust to take less time. Whatever it takes, find a way to set aside some quality time for Bible study as a part of your regular schedule.

Find the Right Place

Do you have a special place where you can go to study and pray, a place that you can call your very own space for an hour or more every day? If you do not have an office or prayer room, this could be a corner of any room where you could have a small desk. Or it may be your kitchen table during designated times. The important thing is to have a place that can be set aside on a regular schedule as your special space for Bible study.

This place should have good ventilation and be well lit. It should be a place where you feel comfortable—but not too comfortable! Your bed or easy chair may be OK for relaxing, but for serious study, they may be a bit too relaxing! Also, your place of study should have as few distractions as possible. Try to choose a time when you are least likely to be interrupted. The TV, radio, and smart phone should all be off and out of reach. All access to the Internet and social media should be removed. Disconnect your computer router if you must!

For the best study experiences, you will need a table, a comfortable chair, and a good lamp. If possible, your study area should be a place where you can leave your materials undisturbed. This place should say, "Come here and study God's Word, I'm waiting for you!" Stop and take a few moments to think about a place that can become your special place for Bible study.

Gather the Right Study Materials

As you work through this book, you will need this text and a modern translation of the Bible. You may choose to use a computer with word processing capabilities for note taking. If so, a digital copy, along with a hardcopy, of the Bible you select will prove helpful. Or you may go old-school and use paper, a pencil, and a straight edge such as a ruler for making charts. A spiral or ring notebook would then be most helpful for taking organized notes on your discoveries. If you don't have a place, you can dedicate just for your Bible study, purchase a storage box for keeping the study materials together.

The Bible translation you choose for study is important. It should be one that you find easy to read with understanding. Each of us has our own level of reading skills and our own working vocabulary. Choose a translation that challenges you without getting you bogged down looking up words in a dictionary.

It is very important that you choose a Bible translation with clear paragraph indentions or markings. As noted in an earlier chapter, chapter and verse numberings in the Bible were added long after it was written. They do not always match the literary structure of a text. Paragraph divisions are necessary for studying the Bible as literature.

We recommend that you purchase and use either the Christian Standard Bible or the New Revised Standard Version translation. Our reasons were covered in the Introduction. You may wish to review that material at this time. There are other translations listed there that are suitable for inductive Bible study. You may already have one of those.

There are some other standard tools you may wish to collect for use in Bible study. The ones discussed below are helpful, but not necessary for learning the basics of RIBS. In this age of the Internet, each can be replaced with a Google search.

Bible Dictionary. Bible dictionaries are much like regular dictionaries with the exception that they do not define all the words in the Bible. Instead, they provide brief descriptions of selected people, places, doctrines, objects, and other things mentioned in the Bible. They are especially helpful for getting a quick description of a person, place, or concept. One of these should be near the top of your Bible study 'wish list.' You may use one when practicing the inductive methods that will be presented in the second division of this book.

Bible Encyclopedia. Bible encyclopedias are just as their name implies—encyclopedias that contain scholarship-based articles about people, places, doctrines, and things connected to the Bible. Entries vary greatly as to length. Some articles may have several pages of content. Other entries are more like a concise definition from a dictionary. It all depends on how significant the editors consider a topic to be. We suggest that you not use a Bible encyclopedia while learning RIBS, but they will prove helpful for future Bible study.

Take care in your selection of an encyclopedia and to a lesser degree, a dictionary. Most Bible encyclopedias are written by scholars who share the same theological tradition. Some theological bias will be present.

If you decide to purchase a set of Bible encyclopedias, our recommendation is that you choose one from a major Christian publisher, one that identifies with the Evangelical tradition. Do a little research to discover who the editors are and the institutions with which they are associated.

Bible Maps or Atlas. The Bible is full of references to places. The ability to visualize the location of an event can help when doing an inductive study of a book of the Bible. Geographic references are sometimes made to help reinforce one of the author's themes. Atlases can be purchased in different formats, but Bible maps may also be found on the Internet by doing a simple Google search for the place in question.

An Exhaustive Concordance. An exhaustive concordance contains an alphabetized list of all the words that appear in a given translation of the Bible, and for each word a list of all the verses where the word appears is given. To a large degree, these tools have been replaced with computer-based Bible translations that allow for word searches. For those who prefer to use books they can hold in their hands, a concordance can be helpful for quickly finding a verse that you can't quite remember its location. All you need to remember is a key word. One advantage of printed concordances is that they typically provide a concise definition of the word and an English transliteration of the word from its original language.

The most common exhaustive concordance is *Strong's Concordance of the Bible*.[1] It was originally developed for use with the King James translation but has been revised for some of the modern translations. Greek and Hebrew lexicons serve the same general purpose except they are organized around the original Hebrew or Greek words, and their emphasis is on the shades of meaning in different Biblical contexts. A basic knowledge of the Greek and/or Hebrew is needed for their use.

Computer-Based Study Resources

Not too long ago, any level of advanced Bible study required higher education and a large library of Bible reference books. With the advent of computer-based learning resources, the doorway has opened for anyone to access tools needed for a more in-depth level of study than would otherwise be possible. It still requires time and

---

[1] James Strong, *The New Strong's Concordance of the Bible: A Popular Edition of the Exhaustive Concordance* (Nashville, T. Nelson, 1985).

effort to learn how to use the various tools, but with self-discipline you can gain the basic knowledge and skills required.

There are several quality computer-based Bible study programs available for purchase. These are designed to provide ready access to broad background knowledge for Bible study. Most come packaged with varieties of commentaries, Bible dictionaries, encyclopedias, lexicons, maps, and devotional materials. They have embedded links connecting Scripture passages and resources, making it possible to access the desired information with one click of a button. Each offers additional modules for purchase containing even more expansive resources.

There are even free and trial versions of some of these programs. Some have surprisingly helpful study tools. The free programs typically also have additional modules that can be purchased. A word of warning, be careful downloading and installing free programs. It is all too easy on some of these sites to mistakenly download unwanted programs containing malware that might harm your computer or adware that is a constant nuisance. You should limit yourself to programs that can be downloaded from reputable sources.

With the better study programs, you no longer must be able to read Hebrew and Greek to benefit from a basic knowledge of the two languages. For example, when one reads in the New Testament the English word *love*, computer Bible study programs make it easy to identify which Greek word was used in the original: *agape, phileo*, or *eros*. The student can also quickly discover the distinctive meaning(s) of the particular Greek or Hebrew word used.

Most of the free programs will even provide grammatical insights to the text. Often through a simple system of abbreviations the reader can identify the precise form of the original word. Is it a verb, a noun, a pronoun, an adjective, a participle, an infinitive, or an article? Is it a masculine, feminine, or neuter word? Is it singular or plural? If it is a noun, is it in the nominative case (naming the subject of the sentence) or the accusative case (identifying a direct object or object of a preposition), or genitive, dative, or vocative? If it is a verb, is it in the past, present, or future tense? Is it an action completely in the past, the present, the future, or is it ongoing? The more one uses these tools, the more exact one can be in observations and interpretations of Bible texts.

If you decide to use computer-based programs to explore the Bible using insights from the original languages, it is important to take the time and effort to gain a basic understanding of biblical Greek and Hebrew. At the very least, learn the key differences between those languages and the English language. To begin with, unlike Greek or English, Hebrew is written from right to left.

Also, in the English language, meaning is somewhat determined by the position of the word in the sentence. The subject typically comes before the verb and the object comes after the verb. The Hebrew and Greek languages are *inflective*, that is, the form of the word determines its function in the sentence. Prefixes and suffixes are typically attached to a root word to indicate the precise meaning of the word in its context. Consequently, word order is of less importance. This trait allows the biblical languages to be more concise and more exact than English.

Be careful. Modern technology offers some very helpful tools for Bible study, but that same technology can be a stumbling block for inductive Bible study. Inductive study is based on direct encounter with the biblical text with limited use of secondary sources. Computers make it easy to 'chase rabbits' and lose sight of the big picture. It is best to limit the use of computers during an inductive study of the Scriptures to that of note taking, finding definitions of terms, doing word searches in the text, and viewing Bible maps. As we work through this book, do not use computer-based study programs. Master the skills before you play with the frills.

PART II:
Methods of Relational Inductive Bible Study

We are now ready to begin practicing some of the methods and processes of Relational Inductive Bible Study. As we go forward, please remember what we have said about the spiritual nature of the Bible and how Bible study should be an event of worship. Constantly hold to two realities: God is presently speaking through the Bible, and the Bible is an anthology of ancient literature.

It is possible to think of the inductive approach as one big method: observe, interpret, apply. It is also possible to think of it as an approach with many methods. Both are true, but we prefer to think of it as an approach with many methods. It is the approach that is most important. The methods provide structure, variety, and different lens through which to look.

However, the methods should be viewed as working together, complementing each other. There is a natural flow that calls for the basic methods to be applied in sequence, especially when doing a book study. That is, a book study should apply the basic methods in a particular order: (1) the Survey Method, (2) the Synthetic Method, (3) the Analytical Method and (4) the Charting Method. If you follow these four methods in the order given, each will build on the ones that came before.

There are other specialty methods you can apply to a book study: (1) the Character or Biographical Method, (2) the Theological Method, (3) the Topical Method, (4) the Historical Method, (5) the Rhetorical Method, and others.

The following chapters guide you through how to use the four basic methods. You will see how the four work together as if they are just one method. The five specialty methods are briefly presented in one chapter. We dedicate another chapter to how to go about doing an inductive study of a selected passage. The final chapter presents our approach for leading a group study using the inductive approach.

The guided exercises in this division of the book will be done using the Book of Ephesians. It will be best if you apply all of the methods to the entire book. If you do that you will complete a thorough RIBS study of Ephesians.

You will also discover that many of our illustrations are taken from the Mark's Gospel. Before proceeding into this second part of *Encountering*, you will find it helpful to use one of your study sessions to read through that Gospel in one sitting.

Chapter 11

The Survey Method

"The Scripture therefore … is the fountain of heavenly wisdom,
which they who are able to taste, prefer to all writings of men,
however wise, or learned, or holy."

—John Wesley

Inductive Bible study is most fruitful when applied to a study of an entire book of the Bible. This chapter is designed to help you take your first steps in an actual inductive book study which are to help you get the big picture of a book's nature, structure, and original purpose for being written. This method involves carefully surveying the book to understand its overall message and how that message is developed.

For purposes of illustration, we will use the Book of Ephesians for our study. We will direct you at certain points to set this book aside while you complete a practice exercise out of Ephesians. For your study in this chapter, you will need your Bible and your notebook. You may substitute a word processing program for the notebook. Have you set aside a time of day for study? How about your place for study? Do you remember the steps in spiritual preparation? Please be careful to follow the steps in preparation for Bible study each time you begin a new study session.

The Importance of the Survey

Relational Inductive Bible Study is like an expedition into a distant land—a journey with a beginning, stops and starts, lingering to explore, observing things you have not seen before, and connecting new discoveries with old truths. Do not approach Bible study as a task to complete or a trip to endure. The goal is not to find the quickest route to the most information. Quick trips from point A to point B require relatively little personal investment; they make the journey an obstacle to overcome. Expeditions, on the other hand, require a commitment to *live* in the journey not just *endure* it—a commitment to *engage* the world of the journey. The journey and the goal are woven together like a seamless garment.

The purpose of an expedition is not just to get somewhere. No, the purpose is to explore new territories and discover new realities. The journey and all that it contains is the destination. New and even unplanned experiences and discoveries are the curriculum. This requires general awareness of the route to follow, readiness to linger at points along the way, and even willingness to alter the route. There is a beginning point and a concluding point, places to enter and exit, but everything in between must remain flexible. You must remain open to a change of plans, to think differently about things that once seemed settled.

Expeditions have a preplanned route for the journey, it's just that the route is adjustable to the demands of the terrain and the opportunities to make new discoveries. The task of inductive Bible study is to discover the route provided by the author, the one that has been carefully marked with signposts of purpose, context, literary structure, and literary techniques. The first steps in an inductive study, then, involve surveying the book, looking for the author's intended route for studying the book: its purpose, nature, and structure. Also, why, how, when, and under what circumstances was the book written?

Each book of the Bible is a vast domain of the reign of God, just waiting for you to explore with openness and with a desire to be transformed by His presence. Each is teaming with living and life-giving truths that you can understand properly only by seeing each as a part of a whole ecosystem. All the parts are purposefully connected. To do a book justice, we must begin early to determine the main ideas and how they serve the overall intent of the author. You might think of this as doing a flyover to get the lay of the land before beginning an expedition through it.

Understanding the author's intent requires that we discover as much as we can about the author, the people to whom the author was writing, the context for writing, and the issues addressed. If we know these things, we will have a head start on knowing what to look for when we focus on the details of the book.

Surveying a book of the Bible is related to what is known as the "Critical Method" of Bible study which is a method used to study the Bible as literature. It focuses on discovering the message of a book by studying the context in which it was written and first received. This is not criticism in the sense of making value judgments about the content of the book but rather being critical in the original sense of the word—making considered and informed judgments about the origin of the book, including its purpose and nature. Who wrote it and to whom? Why was it written? How was it written and when?

The place to begin answering these questions is inside the book itself. Always begin there. After having done a thorough search inside the book for answers to those questions, you may look at some outside sources to "fill in the blanks." Remember, though, that we have designed this book, *Encountering the Living Word*, to help you develop skills in the inductive approach to Bible study. You will be best served in this endeavor by limiting your use of outside sources to Bible maps, a Bible dictionary, and a concordance. After mastering the inductive approach, you will find other resources that serve as wonderful aids in your study of the Bible. Use them without letting them become a 'prepackaged' lesson standing between you and the Bible.

How to Survey

The survey method involves reading through the book in its entirety three or four times. With each reading, you should assume a different posture as a reader—either that of a receiver, an explorer, or an investigator. Keep in mind that every component of inductive study involves the movement from careful observations to interpretations and responses. While surveying, however, you need to concentrate on making observations. After completing the survey method, you should have a good grasp on what the book is about and how the author developed the major themes of the book.

As you do the readings, keep three basic attitudes in mind: be a **receiver**, be an **explorer**, and be an **investigator**.

If possible, do each of the initial readings in one sitting. One sitting? Yes! This is not as hard as it may sound. Some books of the Bible are short enough to be read in a few minutes, many within an hour. To get a good 'bird's eye' look, you should not stop reading until you have completed the entire book. For some books, especially some of the Old Testament books, this may feel like an unrealistic goal given your personal responsibilities. For the most part, though, any of us can set aside sufficient time to read a book of the Bible in one sitting. Try not to think of how many chapters you will be reading. Rather, think of beginning and finishing the book.

As you do the readings, keep one of the three basic attitudes in mind: first be a receiver, then be an explorer, and finally be an investigator. Begin by seeing yourself as a **receiver** of a message from God. His Word is speaking directly to you. Open your heart, mind, and soul to receive what God is saying to you personally. Do not be afraid that you might mishear what God is saying. And don't feel that something is wrong if you are uncertain as to what God is saying. Uncertainty is an important step toward certainty. You are not trying to discover some new revelation; you are instead trying to let the Scriptures read you. Expect the Spirit-Word to remind you of what you already know.

For the second reading, primarily be an **explorer**. The book you will be reading was written to a certain group of people or to a certain person. The author had a specific purpose in mind when writing. You will be exploring the book in the sequence in which it was written so that you might discover the big picture of who wrote, to whom, and why the book was written. Emphasis should be placed on the "why" question. Why was this book written? Stay open to new discoveries; we cannot be confident that we understand the "why" without knowing what lies *behind* the "why."

For the third reading, keep the attitude of being an **investigator** who looks for details that might serve as clues to the main points the author was making. Look for things that affirm your previous insights and those that challenge your earlier opinions. Investigate the gift you are receiving and exploring with a desire to know more about the character, breadth, width, and depth of the gift. In the survey phase, look for the big clues as to how the author developed the theme. Look especially for clues to the structure of the book.

You need to keep the attitudes of receiver, explorer, and investigator in harmony with each other. Remember—you are always a receiver of God's Word, and God's Word is human literature to explore and investigate. Receiving God's message requires a desire to understand what He is saying. That desire requires that we give some attention to the manner in which it was first written and received.

If we only see ourselves as receivers, we may have such a magical view of the Bible that we distort it by reading into it our personal realities (and opinions) so that we ignore the realities of its historical context and meanings. If, on the other hand, we see ourselves totally as explorers and investigators, we may know all about the facts found in the book but fail to allow God to speak to us through His Word.

The First Reading

For the first reading of the book, you will want to read it straight through at a steady pace. This time, see yourself mainly as a receiver—the person to whom God and the human author have sent the book. Stay focused, and don't let your mind wander away from the unfolding message. It may help to envision the author sitting right in front of you reading the book to you. Or you may want to imagine that you have just received a signed copy of the book or personal letter from the author and are reading it for the first time. Most importantly, read as an act of worship. God is sitting with you. Our Heavenly Father is speaking to you through the words of the book. Open your ears to hear, your head to perceive, and your heart to respond.

For this reading, you are looking for the big picture. For that reason, you may opt to do this reading in one of the more "thought for thought" translations of the Bible or even one of the paraphrased translations. You might try reading aloud or listening to an audio recording of the book. If you listen to an audio recording, follow along with your open Bible and stay focused.

Read with fresh interest as if God is in the moment sending you an important personal message—because He is! Do not be concerned with remembering the details. You are just getting the lay of the land. What is the author's main message? Do not take notes as you read. Note taking will only distract you from getting an overall impression of the book. After you have finished reading, you will write down a few notes about things in the book that stuck with you.

We recommend that you write your notes in a three-column chart. Label the first column "Observations," the second column "Interpretations," and the third column "Responses" (See Appendix

C.). Keep in mind that during the survey method you will focus on making observations more than interpretations and responses.

After the first reading, ask yourself what the primary message of the book is for you personally. How does it speak to your life? What do you believe God was saying to you as you read? Continue by asking yourself what in your life may have influenced you to see that message in the text.

Typically, your notes will sequentially move from observations to interpretations to responses. But for this first reading, begin by writing these impressions of the book's personal message to you in the response column. Later, these notes will serve to help you see how and to what extent you may have been reading your life experiences into the text. This process is your first attempt at letting the text interpret you. Through it, you are beginning to intentionally discern what God is saying to you through this book of the Bible.

Next, you will want to jot down in the first column any significant memories or general observations from the first reading. These are the key points of the book's content you retained. What in the book grabbed your attention? Do certain words, phrases, events, or general characteristics of the writing style linger in your thoughts? These notes are your first set of observations. Write down only things you feel relatively certain are factual. Typically, these observations are in the category of the six questions (Who? What? When? Where? Why? How?).

Then, also in the first column, write down what you observed about the book as literature. What can you say with relative certainty about the literary characteristics and structure of the book? What literary forms and devices did you recognize? Is it prose or poetry? Does it include metaphors, allegories, narratives, parables, etc.? These general observations about the content, structure and character of the text lay the foundation for you to make your first interpretations of the book.

In the middle column, in light of your observations, what do you consider to be the primary purpose or message of the book? Remember, interpretations have levels of certainty. After just one reading, you may not feel too certain about the author's intent. It is not unusual to later refine or completely change your first interpretations of the book but write down your first interpretations anyway. "It seems to me the main message of this book is ..."

This first reading should leave you with more questions than answers. Questions about the purpose of the book are part of the interpretation process. Take careful notes on your questions and include them in the middle column. These early questions mark some areas for you to revisit as you move deeper into your study.

Some Don'ts ...

Take care not to do these things during a first reading:

- Don't run to a commentary or other study aids at this point. Trust yourself.

- Don't think that there is something wrong if the message seems unclear at this point. Later, as you study through the book, digging deeper and deeper, you will find layers of meaning waiting to be discovered. Later observations will bring the main message into clearer focus.

- Don't feel discouraged. Your wonder-filled journey has just begun.

Let's Begin

It is now time to pause from reading this book and to begin your own RIBS study of the Book of Ephesians. Take some time to prepare yourself spiritually so you stay sensitive to the Holy Spirit as you read. You have probably read Ephesians several times during your lifetime but approach it now like a "first reading" as we described above. Remember that (1) you are approaching this book with your whole being and not just your head, and (2) reading a book of the Bible is an act of worship; it should be an exercise in prayer—prayer that is more listening than speaking.

After reading, write down some notes on your first reading, the main things you remember. Follow the instructions above for taking notes in a three-column chart. First, in the third column, write down your responses to how the book spoke to you personally including your reflections on what in your life may have led to those thoughts. In the first column, add any observations you recall about the book as literature. Then in the middle column, jot down a few initial thoughts (interpretations) on the purpose of the book, that is, your preliminary opinions about the main theme of the book. After you have finished writing down your notes, take the time needed to talk with God about those things especially the items in the third column. When you have finished, return to this book, and compare your work with ours.

Don't forget, if possible, read the book in one sitting.

Welcome Back. Now that you have read Ephesians, talked with God about how it connected with your life, and made some preliminary observations and interpretations about the message of the epistle and about its literary characteristics, let's compare your notes with what we observed and concluded.

In the chart below, you will find some of our observations and interpretations. We have omitted our responsive notes (the third column) on how God spoke to us personally during this reading. You should not omit those things; these notes are just for you and whomever you wish to share them.

Don't feel concerned if your observations and interpretations differ from ours. As individuals, we should expect to see different things on a first reading. Do compare your lists with ours. What did you see that we did not make note of here? Also, pay attention to the forms of our observations and interpretations. Are we living up to our own standards for writing good observations and interpretations?

Figure 11.1 -- "First Reading"

Observations from First Reading	Interpretations from First Reading
1. Who: The author is Paul "an apostle of Christ Jesus."	1. What has been Paul's relationship with the Ephesians?
2. Who: The letter is addressed to the "saints who are at Ephesus and who are faithful in Christ Jesus."	2. Are there saints at Ephesus who are not 'faithful in Christ" or is this a parallelism?
3. Who/recurrence: The author speaks directly to Gentile believers multiple times but not directly to Jewish Christians.	3. Paul seems to be writing primarily or exclusively to Gentile Christian at Ephesus.
4. What: It is written in prose as an epistle or letter but lacks Paul's typical greetings and references to individuals.	4. A. Why are personal references absent? B. The book seems to have a tone of serious concern.
5. How: It is not a long letter, compared to some of Paul's other epistles. (We each read it in less than thirty minutes.)	5. Is there a reason for conciseness in writing style? (Based on observations 5 & 6.)
6. How: Paul writes concisely, as if he wants to make every word count.	
7. What/recurrence: The first half of the book has recurring elements of worship (praise & prayer).	7. The elements of worship seem to serve to create for the Gentile believers a sense that they belong with Paul in the presence of God; they are indeed seated in the "heavenly realms" in Christ.
8. What/themes: We noted three themes (1) worship - relationship with God, (2) unity – relationship of Gentile believers with Jewish believers, and (3) standards for Christian living.	8. The overarching theme of the book appears to be that all Christians should know their blessings of being in Christ and they should live accordingly.
9. How: The second half (last three chapters) of the book is full of 'rapid-fire' practical exhortations on how Christians should live.	9. Is Paul writing because the Ephesians do not know how to live as Christians or because they need to be reminded?
10. Structural Design: There is a major transition in style at 4:1 signaled by a "therefore."	10. The structural design appears to be based on the relationship of principle (chaps 1-3) followed by application (chaps 4-6). (Based on observations 10-12.)
11. What/Structural Design: In the first part of the epistle, Paul stresses the blessings believers have received through Christ.	
12. What/Structural Design: In the latter part of the letter, Paul writes about the Christian responsibility to live (or	

"walk") worthy of the blessings found in knowing Christ. 13. Literary Technique/Inclusio: There is an *inclusio* for the entire epistle. Paul begins his letter with the blessing of "grace … to you" (1:2) and he ends the epistle with "Grace be with all who have undying love for our Lord Jesus Christ" (6:24, CSB). [From other studies we note that it is Paul's pattern to use this *inclusio* as a standard, formulaic salutation and conclusion to his epistles. Peter does this as well but with less of a formulary style.]	13. The *inclusio* suggests that for Paul, grace is the beginning and ending of the Christian message.

The Second Reading: An Explorer

Your second reading of a book is more explorative than the first. Read as if you cannot wait to send a report back home on your first big discoveries. During this reading, you will want to (1) more carefully identify the big ideas and (2) identify how those ideas fit together. Your goal is to move closer to certainty about the main theme of the book by looking at how the author developed the theme. What is the major message the author intended to convey to the audience? How is that message developed in the major divisions of the book? Sometimes these are easy to discover. At other times, especially in historical books, the main theme and divisions are discovered only through several readings of the book.

In this reading, you are an explorer who has entered uncharted territory. In the first reading, you flew over the landscape to get a feel for the "lay of the land." Now you are back on the ground carefully trying to discover and follow the path the author laid out. You are not currently to study the plants and animals, that is, the details. You are entering the text to scout out the journey and identify the major turning points of the journey, that is, the key elements of the big picture. You will need these before you "make camp" to look more deeply into the details of the book as an investigator.

Before you read, prepare yourself spiritually for the exercise. Then, review your notes from the first reading. It is important to remind yourself of the things you thought you saw and the questions that emerged from the first reading. In the second reading, some of those things will be affirmed, and others might be challenged. Both results are good.

As you read, intentionally keep the six standard questions in mind:

- Who wrote and to whom?

- What is the major message the recipients were to receive from this book?

- From where and to where was this book written, and if it is a narrative, where did the events take place?

- When was the book written and/or did the events in the book take place?

- How is the book written (type, style, form)?

- Why was the book written?

Answering these six questions will help you further refine your initial interpretations of the book's purpose and message. You may not find answers to all of these questions during this second reading, but the prominent answers are probably significant.

Pay special attention to two of the questions: the "what," and "why" questions. The primary objective of the second reading is to answer the questions of why the book was written to the first readers and what the author's main message was for them.

The "how" question is also important. What literary types are in the book? Is it poetry, prose, or a mixture? How is the book structured? Also, look for literary devices that stand out to you. How does the author use figures of speech, illustrative stories, literary techniques (progression, climax, repetition, and so forth), structural patterns, and relational connections to develop the theme? Don't fret over trying to answer all these questions or to remember all of the details. Just keep your eyes open for any of these that catch your attention. You may wish to review the types of literary devices discussed in Chapter 6 before beginning this second reading.

Look for a key verse that potentially sums up all that the author intended to say. This kind of literary clue is not always present, but it does occur in some books. As noted earlier, John tells us in his Gospel, "These things were written that you might believe …" Thus, John developed his account of the life of Christ around the theme of belief. His Gospel contrasts belief with unbelief. He leaves the reader with the choice of becoming a believer. Does Paul do something similar in Ephesians?

Often, the main theme is discovered through the literary technique of recurrence—the repetition of key words, phrases, or event types. For example, in 1 John, the word *love* appears thirty-six times in five short chapters (just 105 verses). That is a strong indicator that a major theme, if not the major theme, is related to some aspect of Christian love.

As with the first reading, do not take notes as you read, but do read more slowly and carefully. The second reading should supplement the first and provide some facts overlooked during the first reading. For that reason, try to schedule the second reading of a book as close to the first reading as possible. The same sitting would be ideal. If that is not possible, try to schedule it the same day or the day following.

After completing a second reading, prepare another chart with three columns (see Appendix C), take a few notes in the response column on how the text spoke to you personally, and talk with God about those things. Then make notes on what you observed, focusing on answers to the six questions as discussed above.

This time, as you write down your observations, you may look back over the text to check your memory. This will make it easier to link your interpretations and responses to the specific observations from which they arose.

As you take notes on your second reading, you may find it helpful to consult a Bible map and/or Bible dictionary to clarify some of the things you observed. You may also use a concordance to find significant passages in other books of the Bible that might help provide context for things you read. This is especially helpful when studying Paul's epistles (such as Ephesians) as it can provide background information from the Book of Acts on Paul's experiences in Ephesus.

Again, you may use your computer software to take your notes, and you will find it helpful to go ahead and set up a table with three columns in which to write your observations, interpretations, and responses. Now, pause reading this book, and complete a second reading of Ephesians. Then complete your observations, interpretations and responses, especially those related to the six questions.

Welcome Back. Now compare your observations and interpretations with some we have made and given below. Your lists will probably be a little closer to ours this time compared to last time. Do not feel frustrated if they are not. The important things are that (1) you have made valid and defensible observations, and (2) your interpretations are reasonable.

We have provided more details with our observations than would be typical of a second reading. The reason for this is simply to provide more examples. Again, it is because of their personal nature (and for the sake of space) that we did not include responses.

Figure 11.2 --"Second Reading"

Observations from Second Reading	Interpretations from Second Reading
Who?	Who?
1. The letter begins with a statement that it is from "Paul, an apostle of Christ Jesus by God's will" (1:1).	1. Paul typically named individuals in the church to which he was writing. Why not this time? Does he not know persons in Ephesus? (Acts reveals that he spent considerable time there.) Is it possible "Ephesus" refers to more than one city, i.e., a region centered in Ephesus, which might explain the lack of personal references?
2. The book is addressed to "the saints at Ephesus" (1:1).	
3. None of the people at Ephesus were named.	
4. There is only one person mentioned by Paul in this book: Tychius. Paul notes that he "is a dear brother and a faithful minister in the Lord." Paul writes that he is sending Tychius to Ephesus (6:22).	2. Why is Tychius being sent to Ephesus?
	3. Why does Tychius need introduction? Do the Ephesians not know him?
To Whom?	To Whom?
1. The salutation notes that Paul is writing to "the saints who are in Ephesus." Consulting a Bible dictionary and/or concordance reveals that Ephesus was part of Paul's missionary journeys described in Acts 15-21. Acts tells us that Ephesus was the center for worship of the gods Diana (19:34) and Artemis (19:35). At Ephesus, Paul encountered some disciples of John the Baptist needing to be instructed in the fullness of the gospel of Christ. He also encountered the occult.	1. These observations lend support to the idea that the letter was intended for circulation throughout a region around Ephesus.
2. From Acts, we further learn that Paul stayed in Ephesus for more than two years (19:8, 10). Also, Paul established a strong group of believers. Further, Paul's ministry at Ephesus caused the gospel to be known throughout the region of Asia, that is, Asia Minor (19:10).	
3. The body of the text (Ephesians) makes it clear that he is (primarily/entirely?) writing to Gentile converts to Christ (see especially chapters 1 to 3).	
4. It is unclear from Ephesians whether Jewish Christians were	

at Ephesus at the time of this writing. Acts makes it clear that there were Jewish Christians present during Paul's stay there.

What?

1. Recurrence: in the first three chapters of Ephesians there are multiple references to being "in Christ," "in Christ Jesus," or "in him" (1:1, 3, 4, 7, 9, 10, 11, 12, 13, 20; 2: 6, 7, 10, 13, 21, 3:6, 11, 12, 21). There are only two such references in the last three chapters (4:21, 32).

2. Recurrence: The author makes multiple references to a mystery that has been made known (1:9, 3:3, 4, 5, 9; 5:32; 6:19). In Chapter 3 the mystery is given as "[T]he Gentiles have become fellow heirs, members of the same body, and sharers in the promise in Christ Jesus through the gospel." (3:6, NRS).

3. The body of the letter begins with a discourse on the blessings that have come from God through Christ Jesus to the Ephesian believers (chaps. 1 and 2).

4. Recurrence: These blessings are connected to the "purpose(s)" or "will" of God (1: 1, 5, 9, 11; 3:11; 5:17; 6:6).

5. One purpose of their unity is to make known "the wisdom of God … to the rulers and authorities in heavenly places" (3:10, NRSV).

6. Recurrence: There is a recurring emphasis on the union of Jews and Gentiles in Christ. Their union is described metaphorically as "a new humanity" (2:15), "one body" (2:16), "citizens with the saints" (2:19), fellow "members of the household of God" (2:19), together "a holy temple" and a "dwelling place of God" (2:21-22).

7. Recurrence: The second half of the book (chaps. 4-6) calls upon the Ephesians to "walk" in a manner worthy of their calling in Christ Jesus. (Observe the

What?

1. One theme of the book seems to be that the purposes of God in Christ Jesus are being fulfilled both in and through the believers.

2. One theme of the epistle is that Gentile Christians have an equal place with Jewish Christians in the body of Christ; they are being made one people.

3. One theme of the book is that as the people of God who are called together in Christ to be His body, believers are to live lives that conform to Christ. They are to no longer "walk" as they once walked.

4. Is it an oversimplification to encapsulate the theme of the book in the statement, "the blessings of life in Christ demand a life that conforms to Christ?" [From our first reading.]

5. It seems clear to us that the main theme of Ephesians is that God is working out His purpose/plan, which is being revealed in Christ and through the Church, for Gentile and Jewish believers to be united in Christ so as to be one and to arrive at conformity to the fullness of the stature of Christ (4:13).

6. Paul seems to be writing to the special needs of the Gentile Christians at Ephesus, instructing them in the basics of what it means to be Christian and how to live like Christians.

7. Is it possible that (a) there has been conflict between the Jewish Christians and the Gentile ones? (b) the Gentile Christians are confused about their place in God's plan and what He requires of them?

repetition of the word *walk* in the CSB translation, which culminates in the call to "stand" (4:1, 17; 5:2, 8, 15). 8. Chapters 1 to 3 are more "theological," focusing on what it means to be one in Christ while Chapters 4 to 6 are more practical, focusing on how to live in Christ.	
Why? See notes on "what?"	Why? (What is the theme?) The multiple recurrences of "in Christ" in the first half of the book combined with the multiple recurrences of "walk" or "live" suggest the purpose for writing was to emphasize what it means to be "in Christ" and what it means to live as one who is "in Christ."
Written from where? 1. We found no explicit internal evidence as to where Paul was when he wrote the epistle. 2. Paul does refer to himself as "the prisoner of Christ Jesus" (3:1), and "a prisoner for the Lord" (4:1), which, if not written metaphorically, means it was written from prison somewhere.	Written from Where? 1. If Paul's references to being a prisoner are literal, to which of his imprisonments is he referring? By consulting outside sources, we concluded that the epistle was probably written during his imprisonment at Caesarea (Acts 23:33-26:32, ca. A.D. 58-59) or his first imprisonment at Rome (Acts 28:11-31, ca. A.D. 60-62).
Where Were the Recipients? 1. Pinpointing Ephesus on a map reveals that it was located on the west coast of Asia Minor. 2. Consulting a Bible dictionary revealed that Ephesus was a major Roman seaport and served as a strategic point of evangelism. It also provided some social/cultural information that could shed light on the contents of Ephesians. (A Bible encyclopedia would provide much more helpful background information, but we will save that search until we have finished looking closely at the content of the book itself.)	Where Were the Recipients? 1. What was significant about Ephesus in the Roman world and in Paul's ministry? 2. Was this a letter to be circulated throughout the region surrounding Ephesus?
How? 1. It is a letter, but this epistle has few personal references. 2. It is written in discursive prose style and is sermonic/didactic in tone.	How? 1. Why does this epistle have fewer personal references than is typical for Paul?

3. There are two brief citations from poetic literature or songs (4:8; 5:14). [This observation is from the CSB translation; the NRSV has the citations appear as prose.]	
When?	When?
1. There is no direct internal evidence as to the date of writing.	1. If the reference to chains is taken literally, when was Paul in chains? What were the dates for his imprisonment in Caesarea and Rome?
2. Paul does allude to being a prisoner and "in chains" (3:1; 4:1; 6:20).	

The Third Reading: Investigator

For your third reading, you will approach Ephesians more as an investigator. Look more carefully for clues that point to the main theme of the book and how the structure of the book unfolds. Finding the main and supporting themes is your primary task. But the theme and the structure are often closely connected. Knowing the theme should help you more easily see the structure. On the other hand, recognizing the structure may help you discern the themes. While priority should be given to identifying the themes, make some observations about the structure.

A secondary purpose for the third reading is to find facts that affirm or challenge the results of your first and second readings. Keep your list of observations from the earlier readings before you and make notes on how they need to be improved or corrected. RIBS is a process of progressively moving closer to clarity and certainty in your interpretations and responses.

As an investigator, look for more details related to the six key questions. In addition to looking for confirmation of and challenges to your earlier observations and interpretations, fill in any major gaps about the those major events, persons, or places that you may have missed.

Give special attention to the literary technique of recurrence. Themes are typically revealed through the repetition of concepts, words, or phrases. They may be reinforced through thematic statements that serve as concise summations of a theme. Also, pay attention to the author's use of climax. Climax in action and climax in style often point to climax in theme development.

One effective tool for analyzing the author's use of recurrence is to highlight in the text those places where significant recurrence appears. In this method, the student literally uses a pencil, pen, or highlighter to mark significant uses of recurrence. This may be as simple as circling, underlining, double underlining, or highlighting key words every time they appear in the text. You might use different colors of pencils or highlighters for different items. This technique also works well if you have the text of the book copied into your word processing program in your computer.

You may develop a system of symbols and/or abbreviations to be placed in the margins of the text to mark the use of figures of speech, literary techniques, and structural patterns. For example, the abbreviation "Par" might indicate there is a parable, a stylized "X" (the Greek letter *chi*) could indicate the presence of a chiastic structure, or two vertical parallel lines could represent the use of parallelism. Be creative but consistent and create a key. Take care to translate your discoveries into observations in your notes.

A variation of the highlighting technique and of the use of symbols is to prepare a chart of significant recurrences and/or a chart of the uses of significant literary techniques. An example appears in Appendix D. Again, be careful to create a key for the meaning of symbols and types of highlighting.

This will be a much slower reading of the book. Set aside twice as much time as was needed for your second reading. As you read, write down any significant observations. Do not make interpretations and responses as you read. Save those until you have finished reading. At that point review your observations and make appropriate interpretations and responses.

Concerning structure, do not try to develop a detailed outline of the book. Look for the natural flow of the book as it presents the author's main ideas. Note the locations of obvious transitions in thought, style and content, and the presence of any literary tools used to mark them. You will look more closely at the structure of the book when we cover the synthetic method in the next two chapters.

In summation, after the third reading, you should have a firm grasp on who wrote the book, to whom it was written, the circumstances under which it was written, and why the book was written. You should also know the major theme(s) of the book and how those themes are developed. To a lesser degree, you should have an awareness of the structure of the book.

You may during this third reading make more use of a Bible atlas, a Bible dictionary, or a concordance to help you fill in any gaps. This is especially helpful concerning the background of the book and the cultural setting in which it was written. These resources may also help answer questions concerning people and places that the author assumed the first readers would have known. In a narrative, named locations often have significance.

Computer searches can be very helpful at this stage of your study. They can replace the use of printed Bible dictionaries, atlases, and concordances. But you must be very careful to not overuse them. Limit your searches to very specific quests to answer questions about the identities of people and places and to identify the recurrence of specific terms. Use your computer to look for information and not for meaning.

But above all, be careful to complete your preparations for Bible study. Do not skip your spiritual preparation. Bible study must always be approached as a spiritual task. Secondly, before moving into the text, review your observations and interpretations from the first and second readings of Ephesians.

Now open your Bible to the Book of Ephesians and complete a third reading. Don't forget to begin with a quick review of all your notes.

Welcome Back Again. Now that you have completed your third reading of Ephesians, compare your observations and interpretations with ours. For the sake of space, we have condensed our observations and interpretations and not presented them in parallel columns.

We trust you observed some of the figures of speech and connectional relationships found in the text. You may have observed the following connectional relationships:

1. Observation: Paul makes clear distinctions between the work(s) of the Father, the Son and the Holy Spirit:

    The Father:

    a. Blesses us in Christ Jesus (1:3)

    b. By His power, raised Jesus Christ from the dead (2:20)

    c. Seated Jesus at His right hand (2:20)

    d. Put all things under His (Jesus's) feet (2:22)

    e. Made Him (Jesus) head over all things (2:22)

    The Son (Christ):

    a. In Christ we are blessed with every spiritual blessing in heavenly places (1:3).

    b. In Christ we are chosen (1:4).

    c. In Him (Christ) we have redemption through His blood (1:7).

    d. In Him (Christ) we have forgiveness of our trespasses (1:7).

    e. In Christ we have obtained an inheritance (1:11).

    f. We have been brought near by the blood of Christ (2:13).

    g. He (Christ) is our peace, making Gentile and Jew one body (2:14-17).

    h. In Him we have access to God in boldness and confidence (3:12).

The Holy Spirit:

    a. We are marked with the seal of the promised Holy Spirit (1:13).

    b. We are not to grieve the Holy Spirit of God with whom we have been marked with a seal (4:30).

A. Interpretation: This is an explicitly trinitarian epistle.

2. Observation: The Book of Ephesians is developed with a principle-application structural form:

    a. Principle (Chapters 1-3): Blessings found in the calling in Jesus Christ.

    b. Application (Chapters 4-6): Leading a life worthy of the calling in Jesus Christ (Note the word "therefore" that begins Chapter 4).

3. Observation: The principle-application structural form, provides two connected themes. The first is found in Chapters 1 through 3, where Paul speaks of the benefits of being a Christian and the high calling we have to be united as the body of Christ.

4. Observation: The second theme is found in Ephesians Chapters 4 through 6, where Paul develops the theme through explicit directives as to how one is to live (walk) worthy of the blessings mentioned in the first half of the epistle.

5. Observation: We further observed that the subthemes are developed as doctrinal in nature (chaps. 1-3) and practical in nature (chaps. 3-6). Although both sections include some practical and doctrinal statements, the first section (chaps. 1-3) is theologically oriented and lays the foundation for the practical exhortations that follow in the second half of the book.

    A. Interpretation: After reading Ephesians the third time and based on these observations, it is clear that Paul's theme centers on "God's Purposes in Jesus" are being fulfilled in and through the church. God is working out His purpose/plan in Christ and through the church. God is therefore calling Gentile and Jewish believers to be united in Christ so as to be one and to arrive at conformity to the fullness of the stature of Christ (4:13) as part of God's purposes.

6. Observation: While Paul is writing to a specific set of Christians, he writes of the church in universal terms. There is one universal church, of which the Ephesian believers are members. He first describes the calling and holy purpose of the church and then proceeds to describe how the church should function as a body (1:23, 2:16, 4:4, 9-16).

    A. Interpretation: The nature of the universal church is a major sub-theme.

7. Observation: The distinctions between the works of the Father, Son and the Holy Spirit reveal all three members of the Trinity to be active in salvation (1:3-14; 2:1-10).

    A. Interpretation: In addition to the nature of the universal church, there is a theme that expresses the trinitarian nature of salvation.

If you did not see these connectional relationships at this point, don't fret. You no doubt would have seen them as you move deeper into your study. As you continue, you will note many types of structural relationships. Look for quantitative relationships, evaluative, agency or means-end. Look, and look again, and you will see how beautifully this book is written! At each stage of your study, make certain to set aside some time to review your old notes and add to them. Also, from your study thus far, you probably have come across several topics of interest to pursue. Don't do so at this point but do jot down the topics that seem important. Later, we will discuss how and when to do topical studies. Some of the topics addressed in the Book of Ephesians that might deserve a closer look at a later time include: (1) Christ (Christology), (2) the triune nature of God, (3) the Holy Spirit (pneumatology), (4) redemption (soteriology), (5) grace, (6) mystery, (7) the church (ecclesiology), and (8) Christian living.

The Fourth Reading

The fourth reading of a book is not always necessary. It may be helpful, however, to read the book for a fourth time in order to crystallize the natural divisions of the book and see other relational connections. You may also find a fourth reading helpful to better understand some difficult passages found in the text. Use a fourth reading to correct your notes from the first three readings.

Chapter 12

Sketching the Big Picture

"Do I understand the scope of each book,
and how every part of it tends thereto?"

—John Wesley

Before looking at the details of a book, it is important to look more closely at the "bone-structure" of the book, that is, the structural design of the book. (You may wish to review Chapter 5). You already have a big picture of the structure; now you are looking more deeply into the structure. How is the big picture held together? What are the major divisions, and how are they divided and further divided? What is the purpose of each of the divisions, and how do they work together? Answering these questions will make clearer the structure of the book, clarify the author's purpose for writing, and highlight how the structure supports the theme.

Without structure, a book would be nothing more than a collection of unrelated words. Each word would have its own meaning, but there would be no meaning beyond their individual definitions. Books have meaning because words are connected into structures that communicate ideas larger than the definitions of isolated words.

Sentences are combined into paragraphs to communicate a message larger than the individual sentences. Paragraphs are combined to form chapters, etc. Each part has its own purpose and is written to support the larger purpose of the book. There is meaning in how a book is structured. We must ask why the biblical authors structured books the way they did.

When trying to envision the author's structure for the book, it is possible to begin with the smaller parts and determine how they fit together to form larger parts: how words form sentences, how sentences then form paragraphs, and so forth. This may sound logical since it is, after all, the way we read a book. Repeating one of our favorite metaphors, however, it is also like trying to complete a picture puzzle without having seen the picture.

When studying a book, we should move in the opposite direction; begin with the big picture and see how it is partitioned. Determine first the major divisions and divide them into subdivisions. Then further divide the subdivisions into smaller units and so forth. Dividing a book this way is helpful for discovering how the main message is supported and developed. It provides a more detailed survey map that can guide us to treasures we might have otherwise overlooked.

Take a moment to look up and view again the icon of the Holy Trinity by Rublev. One can easily see how the artist painted the picture with five distinct sections—one each for the three figures, one for the table, and one for the space above the figures. There are a few background spaces that serve as fillers, or transitions between the major sections, but one's attention is easily drawn to the five major sections. Each section of the icon then can be studied looking for what the details say about the objects within. This also allows us to see the relationships between the various elements of the picture more readily.

Books are works of art painted with words. Those words are precisely and carefully clustered into units that express meaning. Seeing how the words are connected sentence by sentence, paragraph by paragraph, and subdivision by subdivision, etc., pieces together the author's message and reveals the depths of that author's meaning. Discovering the structure of a book is the best way to see the author's big picture, which then serves to help the student understand the significance of the details.

Identify the Major Divisions of a Book

Through the first three or four readings of the book, you should have gained a good sense of what the book is about. You should have a strong impression of the author's purpose for writing. You should have identified the literary genre chosen to fulfill that purpose. and you should have identified the people, places and significant events within the text. You should also have a grasp on the major divisions of the book, even if you cannot yet pinpoint the exact transitions between the divisions.

In this second method, we move inward to make observations and some interpretations about how the major parts of the book fit together to provide an infrastructure for the author's message. This method may be called the synthetic method of Bible study. "Synthetic" means "a putting together." Through this method, you are trying to see how the author used the structure of the book to "put together" the message.

The goal of the synthetic method is to create a model or outline of how the book is constructed, to see how the bigger pieces fit together. This process should follow the basic inductive approach of making observations that lead to interpretations. Many times, the structure is so evident that one can identify it through observations alone. In other words, no reasonable person would disagree with how you see the book divided into units of text, but some books have debatable divisions. How you see the book structured may be a matter of opinion. Make certain your opinions are reasonable interpretations drawn out of good, factual observations.

The goal of the synthetic method is to create a model or outline of how the book is constructed, to see how the bigger pieces fit together.

Dividing the text begins with looking for the natural transitions used by the author. Do not force an outline onto the text. Rather, ask yourself, "How and where does the author shift emphasis?" This may be noted through a change in literary style, type, themes, locations, characters, the use of climax, the use of transitional words and phrases, and so forth.

One challenge in recognizing the structure of a book is to distinguish between major divisions and smaller subdivisions. Not every clear transition marks a major dividing point in the book. Sometimes the transitions between subdivisions will be clearer to you than those between major divisions. Clarity that a point of division exists does not answer the question of how that transition fits in the overall structure of the book.

Most books of the Bible have no more than three or four major divisions, with each of those having three to eight subdivisions. But this is a pattern and not a rule; many exceptions exist to this general pattern.

Some Helpful Hints. When discovering divisions, whether major or minor ones, look for …

• Places where the flow of thought naturally shifts, such as transitions in topic or subject matter.

• Changes in literary style or shifts in grammar such as transitions from declarative statements to imperative ones.

- A shift in emphasis or intensity, such as added conflict, resolution of conflict, or the climax of a sub-plot.

- In narratives, a change in location or the introduction of new characters.

- Transitional phrases such as "therefore," "since," "in conclusion," "for this reason."

- Other transitional literary techniques such as generalizations, summarizations, summations, and distanced recurrence

You may find it helpful to create a chart or table of how you see the book divided. Think of this exercise as creating an early draft of your interpretations of structural transitions. On the chart, provide temporary titles for the various sections of the book. Identify the chapter and verse markings for the beginning and ending of each of those sections. If you are uncertain about how some sections fit, ask yourself whether they belong more to what went before or what comes after—or if they stand alone as a single section of the book. Seeing the structure on paper (or computer screen) will help you clarify the major divisions. As things become clearer, change the dividing points and titles as needed.

Finally, always keep in mind that when trying to discover how a book is structured, it is important to put yourself in the shoes of the author and the first readers. Set aside your preconceptions about how the book should be divided. Don't force an artificial outline onto the text. Look at it the way the author intended for it to be understood. Look for the author's big ideas and how they tie together.

Name the Divisions

Once you are relatively confident that you have identified the major divisions, give titles to each division using the guidelines below, and create a simple chart showing the major divisions of the book, marking where the dividing points are located using the chapter and verse identifiers. Chart 11.1 below provides a model for one type of chart that many find helpful for visualizing the structure of the book.

Figure 12.1 -- "Charting Major Divisions"

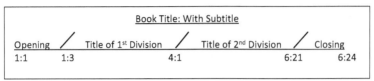

Note that the division titles are on a horizontal line with slanting vertical lines indicating where the divisions occur in the text. The vertical lines are slanted to indicate forward movement. Below the horizontal line, the chapter and verse references for the beginning of each division appear. The title of the book is placed on a separate line above the division titles.

Titles should creatively express your summative perceptions of the content of a unit in a way that also serves as a handle for remembering the content of the unit. They may convey the essence of the message of the unit, or they might capture the nature or character of the unit. They might recount a unique aspect of the unit. They should not be dry facts about the text but should be a descriptive way of remembering the contents of the unit.

One should view the naming of any unit of a book as an act of interpretation. You are attempting to capture the essence of the unit as you see it. Titles should flow out of your considered opinion as to the author's intended purpose or meaning for that section of text. For that reason, the giving of titles must always be preceded by good, even if preliminary, observations about the content of the unit and/or its relation to the rest of the book.

When possible, titles should also be creative and memorable. All interpretations involve a degree of creativity as we put into words our own thoughts about the meaning of someone else's work. This is uniquely true when assigning titles. It may be helpful to try to think of titles as words that create an image of the content of the text.

Don't worry about being "correct." Just be faithful to the text as you understand it. It is okay to let your personality or even your sense of humor shine through, as long as your title remains faithful to the content of the unit.

Titles should also be brief enough to be easily remembered—generally, three to five words in length. Typically, they will include a subject, a verb, and a descriptor. However, any of these elements may be implied instead of stated.

All titles must be unique; they should express something distinctive about the unit of Scripture under consideration. Therefore, within any book study, no title should be repeated word for word. It is okay to repeat some of the words if the unit is in fact an approximate repetition of an earlier unit. For example, Jesus fed the multitudes on two occasions in Mark's Gospel. "Jesus Feeds the Multitude" is an acceptable title for the first account. But it would not be acceptable to use the same title for the second account. It would be acceptable to title the second account, "Jesus Feeds the Multitude, Again."

All the above also applies to original titles given to entire books. Of course, every book of the Bible already has a formal title, but you might create your own title as a subtitle for the book. For example, you might give this subtitle to John's Gospel: "The Gospel of Belief." A book subtitle should distinguish the book from all the other books of the Bible and do that in a way that reflects the unique content of the book.

Your titles can be changed. As you divide the book into its smaller units and provide titles for those smaller units, you may see connections you missed before. Those new observations may lead you to alter some of your points of division and/or to change some titles. Be open to changing both the points of division and the titles. As you go deeper into your study, you may make observations that lead to other interpretations, and those newer interpretations may give rise to even better titles.

Use these guidelines for titles each time you name a unit of the text, whether large or small. In your copy of *Encountering God in the Living Word*, you may wish to mark this section on titles. You may find it helpful to return to it later when you are ready to name the smaller units of a book.

Now it's your turn. Take time to divide the Book of Ephesians into its major divisions and give each a title of your creation.

Welcome back. Now compare your work with ours.

As we saw when using the survey method, Ephesians may be divided into two major divisions, not counting the salutation and the closing. The two divisions are made clear by a change in writing style and by the content that shifts from issues of relationship with God and others in Christ to issues of Christian conduct. The division is also signaled by the transitional term, *therefore*.

The first major division, Chapters 1 through 3, consists of Paul proclaiming God's blessings upon and purposes for the Ephesians as those blessings and purposes are fulfilled in Jesus Christ. The second division, Chapters 4 through 6, describes the Christian life in terms of the responsibilities that accompany the blessings of God in Christ.

We have temporarily titled the divisions "God's Purposes in Christ" and "Living in Christ." Notice in Figure 12.2 that we have included the salutation and the closing on the same level as the major divisions, even though they are not really major divisions. These introductory and closing remarks pertain to the book as a whole and each is therefore not a sub-part of a major division or smaller unit.

Figure 12.2 -- "Ephesians: Preliminary Division Titles"

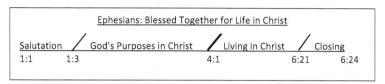

These are temporary titles. They may change as we look closer at the book. It is important that you create your own titles. Your titles are expressions of your interpretations. They belong to you. But don't be afraid to change them as you gain more insights into the book.

Studying Major Divisions

After you have divided and titled the major divisions of a book of the Bible, you are ready to make observations and interpretations on the first major division. You will complete the same study method on the second major division following the completion of your study of the first division. After you have completed studies of all major divisions of a book, you will return to the first division to study the subdivisions. After that, work your way through the book on the subdivision level. If there are sub-subdivisions, complete the same type of study on them in the sequence in which they appear. Study first the book as a whole, then the major divisions of the book, then the subdivisions of the book, etc.

In this method, you dig deeper into the book one layer at a time, finding more and more connections the author wants you to see. Seeing new connections, however, requires remembering what you have already observed. It is therefore important to review your notes each time you begin a study session. At this stage of your book study, do not linger in a division or subdivision too long. Do not think you have to see everything. Just look for things that now seem important.

Guidelines for Making Observations on Divisions

When studying the divisions and subdivisions, follow the same pattern as when looking at the book as a whole. First, make observations on major divisions by asking the six standard questions on the division: Who? What? When? Where? Why? How?

Second, look for the literary structure of the division. Then, observe the literary devices in the division. You may wish to pause here and review the list of literary devices in Chapter 6 (figures of speech, illustrative stories, literary techniques, structural patterns, connectional relationships). Pay special attention to literary techniques and connectional relationships.

You may find it helpful to divide the "how" question into basic observations and more advanced observations. Looking deeper at the "how" question may aid you in identifying the literary devices used by the author. The goal is to see the prominent connections within this division of the book. You may have observed some of these during the survey method, but taking a closer look at this point will prepare you to see them even more clearly when you look more closely in your coming study of the segments of the book. Remember, it is all about relationships! Literary devices largely serve as agents for those relationships.

Stop here and complete your own study of the first division of Ephesians, i.e., the first three chapters. Since you are still gaining skill in the inductive approach, we recommend that you continue to chart your observations, interpretations, and responses in three columns. Don't forget to complete your spiritual preparation and to review your notes before beginning.

Welcome Back. Below are some examples of observations on the first major division of Ephesians. Compare your own observations with the ones we have made. Don't fret if yours are fewer in number or differ in other ways. The ones you miss when studying the divisions will, no doubt, be seen when you look more closely at the smaller units of text. Focus on the validity of your observations and interpretations. Would any reasonable person agree that your observations are valid should you point them out?

Notice that we have not separated into columns our observations from our interpretations. We have instead sought to separate them by the level of our certainty. Our observations are stated as fact, and our interpretations are stated with less certainty, i.e., "it seems," "it may be concluded," etc. Remember, one goal is to move closer and closer to certainty with our interpretations, but we should always remember that our interpretations are limited because we are limited beings.

God's Purposes in Christ (1:1-3:21)

Six Standard Questions

Who? In this major division, the main characters are God the Father, Jesus Christ, the Holy Spirit, and the Gentile recipients. Paul references the recipients as "the saints who are in Ephesus" but with the content of the epistle being aimed primarily at Gentile converts to Christianity. The Jewish Christians are also alluded to as a group.

What? This major division describes the great blessings found in Jesus Christ. It begins with a list of trinitarian blessings (1:3-14) where the blessings are from the Father, in Christ, and sealed by the Holy Spirit. These blessings have come to both the Gentiles and the Jews, making them one body. The blessings are here and now, on earth and in heaven (2:6). The blessings will culminate when all the saints receive their inheritance with and in Christ (1:11, 14, 18; see also 5:5).

Believers have been made alive in Christ (2:1-10). They have been brought into unity with Christ and His body as full citizens (2:11-22). Paul has been God's instrument to bring the gifts to the Gentiles (3:1-13). Paul prays for them to know their great blessing, that is, that they might "be filled with all the fullness of God" (3:14-21).

When? Dating is the same as for the epistle as a whole.

Where? Location is the same as for the book as a whole.

Why? Clearly, the first major division of Ephesians is written to instruct Gentile believers in the great blessings they have in Christ and that they share these blessings equally with Jewish believers. It may be concluded that for Paul, these blessings are foundational for the life of the Church as the body of Christ. This division serves as an apologetic for the unity found in Christ, bringing Gentiles and Jews into one new community. It seems that Paul is attempting to encourage the Ephesians to live lives pleasing to God (as seen in the second division) by first instructing or reminding them of their rightful place in Christ by the will of the Father.

How? Rhetorical prose is the style of writing. It is an epistle. There is use of rich metaphorical imagery and connectional relationships. This division has the tone and language of worship: thanksgiving to God, adoration and praise, as well as prayer. Interestingly, Paul breaks the rhythm of his prose by inserting into this division of the book two prayers for the Ephesians (1:15-19; 3:14-21).

Literary Devices

What connections did you see? How are things joined together? Did you notice literary techniques such as recurrence or climax? Ask yourself:

- Did I notice any connectional relationships?

- Did I see cause and effect?

- Did I see any reciprocating relationships?

- Did I see comparative or contrastive relationships?

- Are there prerequisite relationships in the text?

You may have made some the following observations and interpretations on literary devices in the first division of Ephesians— figures of speech, literary techniques, structural patterns, and relational connections are especially present. Notice that we at times separate our observations from our interpretations, plus we have added some of our responses: observe, interpret, respond.

Figures of Speech—Metaphor

Observations: This division of Ephesians is rich with metaphors:

1. Strangers and aliens who have become citizens (2:19)

2. Household of God (2:19) built upon the foundation of the apostles and prophets (2:20)

3. Jesus himself as the cornerstone (2:20)

4. The whole structure is joined together and grows into a holy temple (2:21).

5. Body [of Christ] (1:23, 2:16, 3:6)

6. Jesus as head of the body (1:22, 2:10)

7. All things are placed under the feet of Jesus (1:22).

An Interpretation: These metaphors create a strong image of the unity of all Christians with an emphasis on that unity being grounded in Jesus Christ.

Response: I do not have a sense of Christian unity with all believers in Christ. Some individuals and some denominations are difficult for me to fully accept. Father, help me to better recognize the body of

Christ and accept those who name Christ as their lord as my brothers and sisters in Christ.

Literary Technique—Recurrence

Observation: The word *grace* occurs several times in this division. There is a multi-faceted image of grace that emerges from this recurrence:

1. "Grace and peace to you…" (1:2) (Salutation)

2. "to the praise of his glorious grace" (1:6)

3. "riches of his grace that he lavished on us" (1:7-8)

4. "by grace you have been saved" (2:5, 8)

5. "riches of his grace" (2:7) (Note that "riches of his grace" occurs twice, in 1:7 and 2:7.)

An Interpretation: It is of utmost importance that Christians know that their salvation is a gift from God (grace); clearly, this truth underlies the expectation that believers overcome their differences.

Response: Father, forgive me for sometimes acting like I am better than other Christians because of my heritage. Help me remember that we are all saved by grace.

Observation: Another term prominent in this subdivision is *faith* with its cognate, *faithful* (1:1, 15; 2:8; 3:12, 17). The first use is within Paul's formulaic salutation where he uses "faithful" as an adjective in referring to the recipients of the epistle as "faithful saints in Christ Jesus at Ephesus" (1:1). In the second use, "faith" is an object possessed by the believers, i.e., "your faith" (1:15). In the third appearance, "faith" is an agent by which the believers had received (past tense) salvation; "through faith" (2:8). Paul shifts to the first-person plural, "We have boldness and confident access through faith in him" (3:12). The final reference to faith in this division shifts back to third person plural; "your hearts through faith" (3:17). It should be observed that agency was the predominant use of "faith" in the first division; that is, there are three references to blessings that have come "through faith."

Interpretation: It seems clear that Paul is reminding the Gentile believers that it is faith in Christ alone that makes them members of the church.

Observation: Still another prominent term is *Spirit*, used in reference to the Holy Spirit. The believers have been "sealed with the promised Holy Spirit" (1:13), who is the "down payment" on their inheritance (1:14). Yet, Paul prays that God the Father would give them (future tense) the Spirit of "wisdom and revelation" in the knowledge of Him (1:17). Through Christ, believers have access "in one Spirit" to the Father (2:18). The Gentile believers are also being built together by Christ (present tense) into "God's dwelling in the Spirit" (2:22). The mystery of Christ was not made known in the past but is now being made known by the Spirit, revealing it to the apostles and prophets (present tense) (3:5). Paul prays that they may be strengthened with power in their inner being through God's Spirit (3:16).

One can further observe that (1) these references to the Spirit are dispersed throughout the first division; (2) the Spirit is described as working in the past, present, and future tenses; (3) the Spirit is portrayed as being on believers ("sealed with") and in their inner being; (4) The Spirit is the agent by which God dwells in the Church, and the Spirit is the agent whereby believers have access to the Father; (5) the Spirit is associated with wisdom and revelation (twice), power, and Christian unity; and (6) the Spirit is described as the presence of the believer's future.

Interpretation: In this recurring emphasis on the Spirit, Paul appears to be both appealing to the believer's experiences with the Spirit and instructing them about the Spirit's work.

Structural Pattern—Chiasm

Chiastic structures in prose literature are often easy to overlook. You should not think poorly of yourself if during your study at the division level you missed the following one from the second chapter of Ephesians (vv. 12-20). You may very well have seen it later when you complete your study at the subdivision level or at the segment level.

For now, notice that this chiasm includes two antithetical parallels (A/A, B/B) and one synonymous parallel (C/C).

> A. *At that time you were <u>without Christ</u>* (12)

>> B. *<u>excluded from the citizenship of Israel</u>, and foreigners to the covenants of promise, without hope and <u>without God in the world</u>* (12)

>>> C. *For he is our <u>peace</u>, who made both groups one and tore down the dividing wall of hostility ... one new man from the two, resulting in <u>peace</u>.* (14-15)

>>>> D. *<u>He did this so that he might reconcile both to God in one body through the cross by which he put the hostility to death</u>.* (16)

>>> C. *He came and proclaimed the good news of <u>peace</u> to you who were far away and <u>peace</u> to those who were near. For through him we both have access in one Spirit to the Father.* (17-18)

>> B. *So, then, you are no longer foreigners and strangers, but <u>fellow citizens with the saints</u>, and <u>members of God's household</u>,* (19)

> A. *<u>with Christ Jesus</u> himself as the cornerstone.* (20)

Observe how the pinnacle of this chiasm (line "D") places the focus of the gospel of Christ on his purpose ("so that he might") of reconciling the Gentiles and Jews to God (and to each other) as "one body" and that the cross is the means of this reconciliation. The

Cross is the agent for putting the hostility between Jews and Gentiles to death.

Relational Connection—Authority and Agency (Means-End) Relationship

Paul refers to himself as an "apostle of Christ Jesus" (authority) "by the will of God" (agency) (1:1). Paul is an agent of Christ, and the will of God is the agency of his apostleship.

Relational Connection—Sequential Relationship, Agency

Christ is the agent of our adoption by the Father (1:5) and the means to the Father (2:18). The cross is the agency for reconciliation with God and others (2:16). Grace is the means of salvation, and faith is the means of grace (2:8).

Relational Connection—Sequential Cause-Effect Relationship

Paul prays that God will give a "spirit of wisdom and revelation" so that the readers "with eyes of your heart enlightened ... may know what is the hope of which he has called you" (1:17-19). Note that it is the "spirit of wisdom and revelation" and not "wisdom and revelation" of themselves that causes persons to know the hope into which they have been called.

Relational Connection – Spatial Relationship

Paul uses spatial imagery to convey the new relationship between Gentiles and Jews: "But now in Christ Jesus you who were once far off have been brought near by the blood of Christ" (2:13). "In his flesh he has made both groups into one and has broken down the dividing wall, that is, the hostility between us." (2:14)

Relational Connection — Contrastive Relationship

From the chiasm of the second chapter as seen above, it is clear that Paul contrasts the Ephesian's life before Christ with their life in Christ.

Figure 12.3 -- "Life in Christ"

Before Life in Christ (Eph 2:12-13)	Life in Christ (Eph 2:19-22)
1. without Christ,	1. with/in Christ Jesus
2. without God	2. members of God's household,
3. excluded from the citizenship of Israel, foreigners to the covenants of promise,	3. fellow citizens with the saints,
4. divided by a wall	4. being built together on the foundation of the apostles and prophets

Interpretations and Responses

You have probably noticed that up to this point we have inserted few interpretations or responses for the first division. The primary reason for this is to save space within this book. Remember, though, that interpretations and responses should be made at each stage of an inductive study. There does not have to be an interpretation and/or response for every observation, but you should consider possible interpretations and responses for every observation.

Interpretations and responses should be made at each stage of an inductive study.

Remember that interpretations are opinions with varying degrees of certainty and responses are personal. Also, remember that every interpretation must flow out of an observation or set of observations. The deeper you go into a study, the more certain your interpretations and responses should be. Also, the deeper you go, the more specific and life-related the interpretations and responses should be. Life-related interpretations highlight our need for personal transformation, and they provide direction in how to be obedient to the Word. Life-related interpretations call for personal life changes. Don't rush; take time to reflect on your observations and interpretations. Let the Holy Spirit speak to you about you.

The next step in RIBS is to complete the same study looking at the second division of the book. Now, take time to complete a study of the second division of Ephesians, that is, Chapters 4-6. When you have completed your study, return here and compare your findings with ours.

Welcome Back. Read through our observations and responses given below. Did you see what we saw? What did we miss? What did you miss?

Living in Christ (4:1 – 6:20)

The Six Standard Questions

Who?

The only new character in this division is Tychicus. He is only referred to in the conclusion where he is described by Paul as "our dearly loved brother and faithful servant in the Lord" (6:21). Paul says he is sending Tychicus for the purpose of telling the Ephesians "all the news about me [Paul] so that you may be informed" (6:21). More specifically, he is being sent "for this very reason, to let you know how we are and to encourage your hearts" (6:22).

Interpretation: This reference to Tychicus implies that the Gentile Christians at Ephesus have become discouraged in their new-found Christian faith because of Paul's current state of "being in chains." This further implies that Paul is indeed in prison at the time of his writing to the Ephesians. It is hard not to infer that the Gentile recipients are discouraged about their place in the kingdom of God if Paul the Apostle is imprisoned. How might this be related to the question of their relationship with Jewish believers? Might it be that Paul, who was known to be a defender of Gentile Christianity, is no longer in a situation in which he can effectively defend them?

Who?

There are several groups named in this division. Apostles, prophets, evangelists, pastors and teachers (4:11) are groups of leaders given by Christ to the Church. The Gentiles are mentioned again (4:17). Also, in this section reference is made to those who are sexually immoral or impure or greedy (5:5); the disobedient (5:6), unwise people (5:15), wives, husbands, children, parents, masters, and slaves (5:22-6:9).

Who?

The word *Gentiles* takes on a double meaning for Paul in this division. In the first division, speaking directly to the Gentile Christians, Paul stresses the things they have in common with Jewish Christians, e.g., the same background as sinners and the same place in Christ. In these cases, being a Gentile is merely an identifier of heritage. In this second division, the word "Gentile" is used pejoratively as if a synonym for unrighteousness. He in essence tells the Gentile believers to not be Gentile-like in lifestyle.

> You should no longer walk as the Gentiles do, in the futility of their thoughts. They are darkened in their understanding, excluded from the life of God, because of the ignorance that is in them and because of the hardness of their hearts. They became callous and gave themselves over to promiscuity for the practice of every kind of impurity with a desire for more and more (Eph 4:17-19, CSB).

Interpretation: It appears that Paul here uses the word "Gentile" as a metaphor for all who live outside of the grace of God, that is, all who live sinful lives. Is he then implying that even Jews who live sinfully are themselves Gentiles? Is that a valid conclusion?

What?

The main theme of this section is that the blessings of God call for a new way of living. Paul contrasts life in Christ with the darkened understanding of non-believers. This division speaks to the manner of living that Paul expects of the Gentile believers at Ephesus. But first he establishes that Christ has gifted the church with ministers who are equipped to bring all believers into the ministry of Christ so that all might grow together "into maturity with a stature measured by Christ's fullness" (4:13). Each member is needed for "growth of the body for building itself up in love by the proper working of each individual part" (4:16). Paul begins this division with an emphasis on the place of all believers as ministers to the church as the body of Christ.

The blessings of God call for a new way of living.

Interpretation: It seems clear that this division is not just concerned with how Christians should live as individuals (to please Christ). It is also concerned with how Christians should live as contributing members to the body of Christ. Christians must continually grow in their relationships with one another. Ephesians is all about relationships that edify.

Response: Do I see my relationship with God as a private affair, or do I see it as being interconnected with others? Am I so focused on my personal growth that I cannot see how to serve within the body of Christ? Father, help me to better see how my growth in Christ is interconnected with the growth of the body of Christ.

When?

In terms of authorship and events, the time is the same as observed during our survey of the epistle. It seems noteworthy, though, that

Paul writes as one who expects the believers at Ephesus to live in their current time the kind of lives he describes. The growth noted above was growth in the ability to minister to the body. It was not growth into the righteous life patterns he proceeds to proscribe.

Interpretation: in Ephesians Paul does not understand sin as something out of which one grows. In the first division it was something from which one is delivered. In this second division it is behaviors to be avoided. Paul writes as if believers have within themselves (by grace) the ability to resist sin by choosing righteousness.

Where?

We gained no new insights as to from where Paul wrote.

Why?

The observations we made from our survey of the book have been reinforced. This second division was written to describe how Christians are to live in response to the grace they have received. However, building off what was noted above in the "what" question, we now observe that Paul begins this division with a challenge that the Gentile believers are being equipped to be contributing members of the body of Christ.

Interpretation: is Paul presenting a sequential priority? Should believers first concentrate on their place in the body of Christ and then on their conduct as believers? How are one's place in the body and righteous living connected?

How?

This second major division relates to the first division in the pattern of principle (first division) to application (second division). The writing style of the second division shifts from the descriptive rhetorical prose of the first division in which believers are largely seen as passive recipients of God's gifts to prescriptive rhetorical prose. This division is written with an imperative tone; believers are to act like Christians.

Interpretation: The Christian life centers on responding to the grace of God that has been received. The response must include how we relate to the body of Christ and how we choose to live as members of the body of Christ. The two are interrelated.

Literary Devices

Figures of Speech – Metaphor

This second division of Ephesians also includes rich metaphors, some are repetitions of those seen in the first division:

1. Body [of Christ] (4:4, 12, 16; 5:30) – Unlike the first major division where references to "the body" are dispersed, appearing once in each of the three subdivisions, the references here are focused in the first subdivision of the second division (except for 5:30).

2. Christ as "head" of the body (4:15; 5:23) – For the book as a whole, there are fewer references to Christ as head than there are to the church as body (four versus seven). But "Christ as head" is dispersed throughout the epistle (1:22; 2:10; 4:15; 5:23).

3. Immature believers are described as "little children," who are being tossed by the waves and blown around by every wind of teaching (4:14, CSB).

4. The Christian life is metaphorically like changing clothes; the Ephesians have been taught to "take off your former way of life" and "to put on the new self" (4:22).

5. Believers are exhorted to put on the "full armor of God" (6:11,13-17)

Figure of Speech – Simile

Amid his metaphor of armor, Paul uses a couple of similes: "truth like a belt ... righteousness like armor" (6:13-17).

Figure of Speech – Metaphor

Paul uses "light" as a metaphor for believers: "you are light in the Lord" (5:8). In the same segment he uses darkness as a metaphor for sinful living: "Don't participate in the fruitless works of darkness" (5:11).

Literary Techniques

Literary Technique – Recurrence

The word *grace* occurs twice in this division, which extends the six uses in the first division: "But to each of us was given grace" (4:7), and "Grace be with all" (6:24). It should be noted that the last reference is within the more formulaic conclusion to the epistle. That is, one would expect it to appear there reducing its significance as a repetition of the word.

Another term prominent in both divisions of the epistle is *faith* with its cognate, *faithful*. In the first division it appeared five times. In this second division it appears four more times (4:5, 13; 6:16, 21). Two of these uses refer to faith in reference to "the faith," that is, the Christian faith (4:5, 13). One use is to the object "shield of faith," an agent for believers to use to extinguish "all the flaming arrows of the evil one" (6:16). Faith is the means of spiritual protection. The final use is in the concluding comments where Paul describes Tychicus as a "faithful servant in the Lord" (6:21).

Another word that recurs in both divisions of Ephesians is *Spirit* as used in reference to the Holy Spirit. In the first division the word appeared seven times. In this second division it appears five times. Early in the second division, the author makes an appeal for "unity in the Spirit" (4:3), which is followed immediately with a reminder that there is "one body and one Spirit" (4:4). They are then exhorted to "not grieve God's Holy Spirit" by whom they are sealed "for the day of redemption" (4:30). The idea of being sealed with the Spirit is a repetition from the first division (1:13). In the final chapter there are two more, closely linked references to the Spirit. Christians are to stand against evil forces by putting on the "whole armor of God," which climaxes with taking up "the sword of the Spirit—which is the word of God" (6:17). Paul continues, "pray at all times in the Spirit with every prayer and request and stay alert with all perseverance and intercession for all the saints" (6:18).

Recurrence: "Take Off"

In his instructions to the Church on righteous living, Paul uses the concept of removing things from oneself.

- "… take off your former way of life" (4:22)

- "Therefore, putting away lying, speak the truth" (4:25)

- "Let all bitterness, anger and wrath, shouting and slander be removed from you (4:31)

Recurrence: "Put On"

In contrast to taking off some things, Paul also instructs believers to put on some things.

- "put on the new self" (4:24)

- "Put on the full armor of God" (6:11).

An Interpretation: Taken together, these observations reiterate how Paul clearly expects the Ephesian believers to accept responsibility for changing how they live; in response to God's gifts, they are to change their way of being in the world.

Flow of Intensity and Climax

This second division flows rapidly with the imagery of walking. At first, Paul is staccato in presentation, i.e., rapid-fire instruction on behaviors that all Christians must avoid and behaviors they must emulate while walking in Christ. Walking seems to build to a plateau of walking in wisdom. Here the pace slows a little, but the intensity increases as Paul becomes more direct and personal by talking about behaviors within three sets of intimate relationships—all within Christian households: husbands and wives, parents and children, masters and slaves.

After the section on households, the imagery of walking shifts to that of standing, as in taking a stand during a military battle. This brings the epistle to a climax. Life in Christ is bountiful with God's blessings but requires changes in the way we relate to those closest to us and it requires spiritual warfare.

Interpretation: The size of the "Walk as Wise" section, with its instructions to Christian households, seems to highlight Paul's theme that Christian maturity is all about relationships. The subdivision begins with the imperative that believers must submit "to one another in the fear of Christ" (5:21). Christian submission is required of all with all but must begin in one's household.

Response: Father, make me ever mindful that I must at all times be Christ-like with those closest to me, especially my wife, children, and co-workers.

Relational Connections

Contrasting Relationships

Paul uses contrast throughout the second division. Each of the subdivisions contains an element of contrast between believers and non-believers.

Contrast #1 (4:1-16) – They are to grow into the fullness of Christ and no longer be children: "we all reach unity in the faith and in the knowledge of God's Son, growing into maturity with a stature measured by Christ's fullness. Then we will no longer be little children, tossed by the waves and blown around by every wind of teaching."

Contrast #2 (4:17-5:5) – Their old life was one of the futilities of one's mind; darkened in understanding; alienated from the life of God because of ignorance and hardness of heart; loss of sensitivity; self-abandoned to licentiousness, greedy to practice very kind of impurity; stealing; evil talk. Their new life is one created according to the likeness of God in true righteousness and holiness; kindness; speaking words that give grace; tenderhearted, forgiving one another; imitators of God; living in love.

Contrast #3 (5:6-14) – Fruit of light is contrasted with fruit of darkness.

Contrast #4 (5:15) – Not as unwise, but as wise.

Contrast #5 (5:18-21) — There is a contrast between being drunk with wine and being filled with the Spirit: "Do not get drunk with wine, for that is debauchery, but be filled with the Spirit, as you sing psalms and hymns and spiritual songs among yourselves, singing and making melody to the Lord in your hearts, giving thanks to God the Father at all times and for everything in the name of our Lord Jesus Christ."

Contrast #6 (6:6) – Slaves labor as people pleasers and only when being watched. "But as slaves of Christ, do God's will from your heart."

Concluding Observation: Paul uses contrast to make clear lifestyle distinctions between the old life of the Gentile believers and their new life in Christ. While the overwhelming portion of instruction is on what life in Christ should look like, there is a consistent presence of contrastive reminders of what characterized the believers' old lives.

An Interpretation: Paul wants believers to consistently choose to behave like followers of Christ and to consistently choose to not behave like those who are outside of Christ. They must remain conscious of these things and be proactive.

A Response: At this point in our study, the Spirit may woo us into extended prayer. Allow the Spirit to be your teacher. Lord, help me to see myself and do my part in changing the way I live in Christ.

In the next chapter we go even further into Ephesians by subdividing the divisions and studying the subdivisions.

Interpretations of Division Relationships

There is a final step in studying the major divisions; how do the divisions relate? How is the main theme of the book being developed? What purpose does each division serve in relation to the others?

Our observations of the two divisions of Ephesians have led us to conclude that the primary relationship between the divisions is one of principle/application with an element of cause/effect. The first division revolves around the spiritual relationship of the believers with God and their relationships with other believers, i.e., Christ is the head of one body, which is a sure foundation.

The second division revolves around the proper application of those spiritual realities, i.e., principles. The second division is primarily a call to apply what God has done. But since it is all by grace, the second half is also a plea for believers to allow God's grace to have its full effect. The Christian life is both a gift and a responsibility.

Chapter 13

Studying Subdivisions

"Here then I am, far from the busy ways of men. I sit down alone:
Only God is here. In his presence I open, I read his book;
for this end, to find the way to heaven."

—John Wesley

Dividing the Divisions

Once you have completed a general study of the major divisions of a book, you are ready to move on to the next level by identifying, naming, and studying the subdivisions (and then sub-subdivisions if they exist). In this process you will follow the same steps you followed in making, naming, and studying the major divisions. The difference has to do with where you focus. In this step, you will look more closely at how each subdivision contributes to the book.

Small books usually have only two or three levels of divisions: major divisions, subdivisions and sub-subdivisions. Longer books may have more. Also, books are seldom uniform in the levels of divisions. One major division may have three levels of subdivisions within it, while the next major division in the same book may only have two levels within it. We will see this in Ephesians. When dividing the divisions and subdivisions, do not force uniformity. How you mark the dividing points of a book should be determined by how the author structured the book.

In the synthetic method, you should study each level of divisions sequentially. That is, complete your study of all the subdivisions before moving on to study the sub-subdivisions, etc. You might think of it as peeling back the layers of an onion, one layer at a time. Also, when you reach the level of subdividing in which the subdivision doubles as a segment of text, study it as a subdivision when you study subdivisions. This will aid in seeing the connections between the subdivisions. You will return to that particular subdivision to study it as a segment when you have reached the point of studying the segments of the book.

Generally speaking, the Pauline epistles typically have only two divisions and three to five subdivisions in each division; many of the subdivisions are small and serve as segments. A book the size of Mark typically has no more than three to five divisions with each division having three to eight subdivisions. Also, that size of book may have four or more levels of divisions: major divisions, subdivisions, sub-subdivisions, and segments. These are rules-of-thumb and not strict guidelines. The goal is to discover how the book was structured in the author's mind. Again, do not force any artificial rules on the text.

> The goal is to discover how the book was structured in the author's mind.

As noted above, subdivisions may be as short as a few paragraphs and therefore constitute a segment, or they may be much longer. When looking for subdivisions, it is important to ignore the chapter and verse designations as you seek to discover how the author structured the book. As with the major divisions, look for natural transitions in location, subject matter, emphasis, style, or tone. Look for transitional words and phrases such as "therefore," "finally" or "for this reason."

Taking note of how things cluster together provides a helpful way to identify the smaller units. For instance, look for a series of miracles, a collection of parables, or a series of imperatives. A subdivision may mark the climax of a story—an intense section that divides the narrative.

When naming subdivisions and smaller units of text, follow the same procedures as were outlined in Chapter 12 for marking and naming divisions. Remember to create titles that convey the essence of the subdivision. Short, concise titles are best. The subdivision titles should further expose the main theme of the book. In other words, show how the theme is progressing through the subdivisions of the text.

This process of studying each of the levels of the divisions one level at a time may seem redundant and tedious when you first begin using RIBS. You will be reading and making observations on the same passages over and over. This is especially true for shorter books like Ephesians. You will be tempted to skip over studying the differing levels of divisions. Resist this temptation. Keep three things in mind:

- First, repetition is an important learning tool. Each time you look at a given unit of text you should see it more clearly. Repetition helps us better retain information and it helps us better understand the knowledge we are gaining.

- Second, keep in mind that you are developing a set of skills. One of the skills is the ability to focus on different levels of the book. Think of it like focusing a pair of binoculars or using a telescopic lens on a camera. The focal point must be adjusted depending on the distance an object is from you. Focusing will also enlarge or reduce the field of vision, i.e., how big of an area can be seen. As you focus the lens, some things will move in and out of focus. They will move from being blurred to being sharp and distinguished. This process helps the viewer see more clearly what he or she wants to focus on and helps filter out unrelated items in the viewer's field of vision.

- Third, you are on a treasure hunt. Every new discovery is exciting. The excitement is enhanced each time you make a new discovery in an area you have already studied. Beautiful jewels may have been hiding there in plain sight.

Some Helpful Reminders. When discovering subdivisions, look for the following:

- Places where the text naturally divides within the division

- Clusters of types of content such as a series of similar events

- A shift in emphasis such as a change in location, the introduction of new characters, added conflict or resolution of conflict, or the climax of a sub-plot, etc.

- Transitional phrases such as "therefore," "since," "in conclusion," "for this reason"

- A unified message or component of the plot or thesis that contributes to the division

- Sub-subdivisions that work together to form a subdivision.

While the focus of your study at this time is to identify and name the subdivisions of the book, you may find it helpful at this stage of your RIBS study to do a preliminary outline of the book as a whole. Recognizing that the sub-subdivisions you will identify later can help you be more certain about where the subdivisions are divided.

It's time for you to practice further dividing and then naming the subdivisions of Ephesians. At this point, prepare yourself spiritually and review your notes on how and why you divided the book as you did. Remember, there is no absolutely correct way to divide and subdivide the book. Scholars disagree on where some of the transition points are, but most subdivisions are easily recognizable. As mentioned above, in shorter books, subdivisions may also function as segments.

Welcome Back. Once again, compare your work with ours. Also, keep your Bible open and follow our work closely. We first reviewed our notes on our study of the major divisions and noted our observations that led us to more clearly see the two main divisions for Ephesians (Chapters 1-3 and 4-6). This time, we further observed:

- After the salutation, Chapter 1 is marked by a three-fold *inclusio*. It begins and ends with God the Father as the actor. It begins and ends with references to the heavens. It begins and ends with references to being "in Christ." The entire chapter is a presentation on the believers' current blessings from God, in Christ, and in the heavens. The *inclusio* reveals Chapter 1 to be a literary unit.

- Verse 15 of Chapter 1 marks a transition with the use of the phrase "this is why."

- Contrary to the segment divisions in the CSB translation, we observed that verse 20 is linked to verse 19 by the use the word *power*. That is, the paragraph that begins in verse 20 speaks of "this power," which is a reference back to "power" in verse 19. The two paragraphs are closely linked and should not be separated as two different subdivisions.

- We further observed that the phrase "in Christ" (also "in him") used throughout Chapter 1, was replaced with the phrase "with Christ" (also "with him") in Chapter 2.

- Also, we observed that while God the Father was the primary actor in Chapter 1, Chapter 2 transitions to Christ being more the actor (see vv. 14-17).

- And in Chapter 3, Paul is the actor, with an emphasis on how the grace of salvation came to the Ephesians through his ministry.

- [For the second division we observed Paul's recurring use of the verb "walk" (concluding with "stand") to mark the subdivisions.]

Consequently, we divided and named the textual units of Ephesians as appears below in Figure 13.1. In this case, we chose to present our work as an outline. You will notice that we have divided Ephesians according to divisions, subdivisions, and sub-subdivisions. You may also notice that our study of the subdivisions has led us to change the titles for the divisions from those we gave during our survey readings. The deeper we look at a book, the clearer our interpretations become, which should lead to some revisions to our earlier work.

Keep in mind that the process of outlining a book is a process of observation and interpretation that sometimes includes an element of response. Reasonable people can disagree on how to best outline a book depending on the observations each has made. Our observations led us to divide Ephesians the way we have and suggested to us the titles we have chosen.

The Procedure for Studying Subdivisions

The procedure for studying subdivisions is essentially the same as studying major divisions. Follow the sequence of first studying each of the subdivisions, then, study the sub-subdivisions. As noted above, segments exist at the level at which subdivisions (or sub-subdivisions, etc.) are made up of a small cluster of paragraphs. The method for studying segments will be discussed in the next chapter.

Figure 13.1 -- "Outline of Ephesians"

Ephesians: Blessed Together for Life in Christ

I. Salutation (1:1-2)

II. Blessed by God (1:3-3:21)

    A. Blessed by God the Father (1:3-1:22)

      1. Every Spiritual Blessing (1:3-14)

      2. Prayer for Enlightened Knowing (1:15-23)

    B. Blessed With Christ (2:1-22)

      1. Made Alive with Christ (2:1-10)

      2. Built Together with Christ (2:11-22)

    C. Blessed Through Paul (3:1-21)

      1. Paul's Ministry of Grace (3:1-13)

      2. Paul's Prayer for the Fullness of God (3:14-21)

III. Walking (Living) in Christ (4:1-6:20)

    A. Walk Worthy (4:1-16)

    B. Walk in Love (4:17-5:6)

    C. Walk as Children of Light (5:7-14)

    D. Walk as Wise (5:15-6:9)

      1. The Will of the Lord (5:15-20)

      2. Husbands and Wives (5:21-33)

      3. Parents and Children (6:1-4)

      4. Masters and Slaves (6:5-9)

    E. Stand Against the Devil (6:10-20)

IV. Closing Remarks (6:21-24)

At this point, if a subdivision also serves as a segment, study it as a subdivision but not as a segment, that is, study it as a unit that is uniquely placed in the book but save looking deeply at the contents of the segment until you are studying the segments.

Incrementally shifting your focus to smaller units of text should help you progressively see more and more. At each level of study, make any needed revisions to your previous observations/interpretations. Then, after studying all the way through the subdivision level, turn your attention to the sub-subdivision level and repeat the process looking for additional insights. In other words, work all the way through the book at each level of dividing: work through the divisions, then work through the subdivisions, then work through the sub-subdivisions, etc.

In studying subdivisions (and sub-subdivisions, if they exist), take the following steps.

1. Review your observations and interpretations made on the division level.

2. Briefly revisit the literary structure of the division. This is essentially reminding yourself where the subdivision fits in the division (or where the sub-subdivision fits in the subdivision.

3. Ask the six standard questions for each subdivision. At this point, you should largely just be double-checking your earlier responses to the questions but ask them for each subdivision anyway—especially the "why" and "how questions.

4. Observe the inclusion of alternative literary types (e.g., poetry within a prose document).

5. Look for literary devices in the subdivision that you may have overlooked earlier. Reflect on how things are connected within the subdivision and also things that connect the subdivision to other parts of the book. Pay attention to literary techniques and connectional relationships. You may find it helpful to review the literary devices discussed in Chapter 6.

We have already seen that Ephesians has two divisions, which we titled,

"Blessed by God" (1:3-3:21) and

"Walking (Living) in Christ" (4:1-6:20).

We determined that the first division has three subdivisions:

"Blessed by God the Father" (1:3-23),

"Blessed with Christ" (2:1-22), and

"Blessed Through Paul" (3:1-21).

Each of the three subdivisions has two sub-subdivisions, and the sub-subdivisions are small enough to be considered segments. They will be studied first as sub-subdivisions and later as segments. (You may wish to review Chapter 6 for a description of divisions and segments.)

We determined that the second division of Ephesians has five subdivisions, and one of the subdivisions has sub-subdivisions. In this second division, four of the subdivisions are small and function as segments. These four should be studied as subdivisions first and later as segments. One subdivision, "Walk as Wise" (5:15-6:9), is structurally subdivided into sub-subdivisions. It should be studied as a subdivision and its sub-subdivisions should be studied both as sub-subdivisions and as segments.

Review your notes on the divisions, turn to Ephesians, and complete a study of all the subdivisions—one after the other. You should already have developed your own titles and may have divided the book differently, especially the subdivisions and sub-subdivisions. If you have divided the book differently, make your observations based upon your divisions. Then, as closely as possible, compare your work with ours.

Welcome Back. Having completed your study of the eight subdivisions of Ephesians, now compare your observations and interpretations with the observations and interpretations we have made on the first subdivision (1:3-23) of the first division. Your observations may be better than ours, and there should be more of them. To save space, we present here an abridged list of our observations and interpretations on the first subdivision.

Blessed by God the Father (1:3-23)

We focused on the six recurring questions: who, what, when, where, why, and how.

Who?

Observations: All the persons we identified when we studied the division were introduced in the first subdivision: Paul, God the Father, Jesus Christ, the Holy Spirit, and the Ephesian believers. It seems noteworthy that Paul refers to himself in the first-person singular "I" five times, all in the same paragraph and the first-person plural "we" four times, and "us" seven times. This raises a question of interpretation: who are included in the "we" and the "us?"

In addition to these eleven first person plural references, the Ephesian believers are referred to in the second person plural "you/your" nine times, all in the second half of the subdivision which we have already noted is the second sub-subdivision (1:15-23).

Interpretations: In this first subdivision, Paul establishes his two-fold relationship with the Ephesians; he is one of them (first person plural) and one who cares for them (first person singular statements). He is thankful for them and prays for them. In this, he demonstrates his commitment to the corporateness of being a Christian and his commitment to the personal dimension of being Christian.

God the Father is the preeminent person in this subdivision. He is the one who has acted to bless the believers with every spiritual blessing they have known. Jesus Christ is the second most preeminent person in the subdivision. He is the agent of the Father's blessings, that is, the blessings are "in Christ." The Holy Spirit is also portrayed as instrumental in the distribution of the Father's blessings. The believers have been sealed with the Spirit who is the "down payment" on their coming inheritance in Christ. In this opening subdivision, Paul clearly wants the Ephesians to understand that each member of the Trinity has a distinctive role in the believers' relationships with God.

What?

As noted above, this first subdivision establishes the place of believers in relationship to the Trinity. They are those who are blessed by God the Father through Jesus Christ, and they are sealed by the Holy Spirit until their ultimate blessing arrives, i.e., their inheritance in Christ (1: 10-14, 18-19a).

When?

Observations: There are no further indications as to the time of writing. It is noteworthy that the blessings named in this unit of text are distinguished as those already received (past/present tense) and those yet to be received (future tense). The blessings of the first sub-subdivision (1:3-14) have already been received. The blessings Paul prays for in the second sub-subdivision (1:15-23) are not yet received but they have already been accomplished in the resurrection and ascension of Christ (1:20).

An Interpretation: With this, Paul seems to intentionally create a tension between the "already" and the "not-yet" while at the same time offering assurance all that is promised by God has already been made secure in Christ.

Where?

There is no further information about the location from which Paul writes or about Ephesus. There is an interesting reference to the believers being "blessed us with every spiritual blessing in the heavens in Christ" (1:3). In what sense are the believers blessed "in the heavens?"

How?

Observation: Looking at this subdivision as a unit of text, one is struck with the language of worship. This first subdivision of the epistle reads like a worship liturgy:

1. There is something like a call to worship (1:3).

2. God the Father is blessed by naming the blessings He has provided.

3. Jesus is blessed by naming His role as agent of God's blessings.

4. A prayer is offered.

5. An exhortation is given.

Everything that follows in the letter is set in the context of the believers now being in heavenly places in Christ.

Interpretation: Is Paul laying the foundation for an understanding that the Christian life must be lived as an act of worship?

Observations: In our earlier study of the two divisions, we made observations and concluded that the first division should be divided into three subdivisions. As noted, the first subdivision begins with what reads like a call to worship: "Blessed is the God and Father of our Lord Jesus Christ" (1:3) and then moves immediately into a listing of blessings that come from God the Father. Also noteworthy, this subdivision includes references to each member of the Trinity as contributing to the blessings that come from God. We also observed that while the blessings in this subdivision are primarily portrayed as from God the Father, a parallel emphasis exists on the recipients of the blessings being "in Christ." The apostle then shifts his focus from what is already accomplished to a prayer for what might be accomplished in the believers.

Interpretation: This first subdivision clearly serves as a foundation for what is to unfold in the remainder of the division. There is a tone of worship and there are actions of worship: praise and prayer.

The next steps in a study of Ephesians are to study the second subdivision, followed by the third, and move through the book at the subdivision level. Due to issues of space, we have chosen to not include those studies, but we encourage you to not skip this series of studies. Make observations on the content of each of the other subdivisions.

Interpretations of Subdivision Relationships

Before leaving the study of the subdivisions, reflect on the relationships between the subdivisions. How do the subdivisions of a division connect with each other to add to the author's purpose for writing?

For example, the three subdivisions of the first division of Ephesians seem to be connected as a series of prerequisite relationships. The first subdivision (Chapter 1) establishes the "first-cause" of the Christian life; God has chosen us to be with him in Christ. We are seated in the heavenly realms. This de facto reality is the prerequisite of all that follows.

The second subdivision (Chapter 2) is in its essence the consequence of God's actions in Chapter 1. Both our salvation (vs 1-10) and our unity in Christ (vs 11-22) flow out of God's actions in Chapter 1.

God has blessed us in Christ (Chapter 1) so that we might be "fellow citizens with the saints" (2:19).

The third subdivision is dependent on the previous two. Because of what God has done from the heavens (Chapter 1) and what the Father and Jesus have done and are doing in heaven and on earth (Chapter 2), the Ephesians can be confident Christ will bring everything to fulfilment in the present and the future (Chapter 3).

The three subdivisions might also be connected sequentially as the acts of God (Chapter 1) are the foundation of the works of Christ (Chapter 2) which together authorize and empower the ministry of Paul and guarantee the coming fulness of God in believers (Chapter 3).

One might also see the relationship between the three subdivisions as one of agency. Chapter 1 is the agent for Chapter 2 which in turn is the agent for Chapter 3.

These are all interpretations and may be refined and/or replaced as we go deeper into Ephesians.

Chapter 14

The Segmented/Focused Method

"The wonderful efficacy of the Scriptures is another proof that they
are of God. When they are faithfully opened by his ministers and
powerfully applied by his Spirit they wound and heal, they kill and
make alive, they alarm the careless, turn or enrage the wicked, direct
the lost, support the tempted, strengthen the weak, comfort the
mourners, and nourish pious souls."

John William Fletcher

Once you have gotten the big picture by dividing a book into
divisions, subdivisions, sub-subdivisions, and so forth, and you have
studied them, you are ready to look more closely at the smallest
literary units of the book. Some call these "paragraph units," but that
wording can be confusing since they are most often comprised of
several paragraphs. Leigh calls these "immediate context units"
(ICU). We call them segments. Leigh's title provides a good
description of what constitutes a segment. A segment is a short
literary unit that has its own unique context. The unit may be set
apart within the book by time, place, singularity of event or content,
or literary style or purpose.

It may help to think of segments like inner rooms in a mansion. Each
room has its own function in the life of the great house, is located
according to the architect's designs and purposes, exists as a room
unto itself but in a way that helps define the rooms around it, and
each is filled with treasures just waiting for you to discover them!

A segment, then, is a series of paragraphs that cluster around a
focused topic or event. In the Gospels, most of the stories constitute

one segment. For instance, Jesus's conversation with the Samaritan woman (John 4:1-42) is a segment made up of several paragraphs that describe the one event.

A segment may be thought of as the smallest literary unit of text that is typically larger than a single paragraph. However, segments sometimes are as small as one paragraph in length.

Modern translations are divided into segments and provide titles for them, but the dividing points and titles vary from translation to translation. In light of your own discoveries, you may find it helpful to study how different translations divide Ephesians and how they name the segments within it. (For some examples, see Appendix A) However, translations seldom identify where larger units of text are to be divided. You are on your own, but you are not alone; the Holy Spirit is with you. And you have already identified the divisions of Ephesian in previous chapters.

When we reach the point of studying individual segments, we have reached the heart of an inductive book study. At this level, we are looking closely at the specifics within each segment and making observations about the connections that exist within the segment. We are also observing the connections between the segment and all that went before and, to a lesser degree, that which we already know comes after. We have moved from the big picture to focus on the colors, shapes and figures that make up the smaller sections of the picture.

The Segmented/Focused Method is not actually a different method. It is the focused application of the basic inductive approach applied to small units of text. The first thing to do in the study of a segment, then, is to review the notes you completed while doing the synthetic method of studying the book (see the previous two chapters). It is important to keep fresh in your mind where the segment that is being studied fits within the structure of the book. As with all other literary structures found in the Bible, segments do not exist in isolation. Each is a vital part of a literary matrix giving shape and meaning to the book. They connect themes and concepts, indicate progress, reveal deeper truth, and highlight characters. At this level, there may be new discoveries that arise out of the six questions: who, what, when, where, why, and how. Those questions should always be in the back of your mind, but the emphasis shifts to observations about literary devices: figures of speech, illustrative stories, literary techniques, and relational connections.

As you let go of the artificial chapter and verse distinctions, you will be more able to "rightly divide" the Word of truth.

Segments are where the rubber meets the road. As you study them, you will find outlines for preaching and teaching flowing out of the Bible itself. Preaching and/or teaching from a segment will become natural and empowering. As you let go of the artificial chapter and verse distinctions, you will be more able to "rightly divide" the Word of truth. You will find that you do not need to impose your outline onto the text, distorting it to fit your topic. Instead, you will see the outline emerging from the text itself! You will then be able to minister the Scriptures with a greater sense of authority. This process of discovery is so exciting; it gives us confidence that we are good stewards of the Word of Truth, and we are not using (abusing) the text for our own purposes.

Determining the Segment

After you have divided a book into appropriate levels of divisions with subdivisions and sub-subdivisions, etc., and given titles and studied these, you are ready to identify and study segments of the book. Keep in mind that in the dividing of a book there may be different levels of divisions. Within the same book, segments may exist at different levels of dividing. They may be positioned at the level of a subdivision, or a sub-subdivision, or a sub-sub-subdivision, etc.

It all depends on how the author structured the book. For example, in the second division of Ephesians (Chapters 4-6) the subdivisions serve as segments except for one subdivision, which needs to be divided into four sub-subdivisions. For most of that major division, the subdivisions function as segments while for the one subdivision, segments do not exist until you reach the sub-subdivision level. This will be further illustrated below.

One way of looking at segments is to think of them as the place where the downward dividing of the book meets the upward building of the book from words to sentences to paragraphs to clusters of paragraphs.

Keep in mind that segments may be as small as a single paragraph or as large as several paragraphs. For point of reference, segments are typically less than a chapter in length. However, some may be longer. Look for paragraphs that cluster around one theme, or one story or event, but stay open to finding a segment that ties two of more events together around the same theme.

As mentioned above, most modern versions of the Bible have already identified segments for readers. Segments are usually marked with extra spacing above and by giving a title to the segment. These designations are provided by the translators and offer a good place to begin identifying segments, but do not assume they are always correctly placed or titled. Different translations may mark segments as beginning and ending in different locations, and sometimes they agree on the boundaries of a segment but provide titles that suggest very different content within the segment. Occasionally, they just disagree on where a segment exists.

In doing your own work, you may differ with your translation's prescribed segments. As long as you have support for your designations, it is good to differ. Your study should also produce your own titles for each of the segments. Don't borrow from translations. In Appendix A, you will find a chart that reveals the differences between the segments of Ephesians as designated in the CSB, NRSV, and NET Bible. The segments with titles as developed by us are also given.

After you have determined the boundaries of a segment, and having already familiarized yourself with its basic content, give it a title. If you already gave the segment a title when dividing the book, ask yourself if there is a better title. If so, make the change.

Segment titles should follow the same guidelines as those for divisions and subdivisions. They should be brief (three to five words when possible). They should serve as a summative expression of the segment and to the degree possible indicate the unique message, or theme, of the segment. Minimally, the title should serve as a reminder of the unique contents of the segment. Be creative. Look for ways to use your titles as links to other segments in the book. However, make certain that each segment of the book has its own unique title.

Procedure for Studying a Segment

In RIBS the procedure for studying segments has five steps, with some subroutines: (1) survey and title the segment, (2) respace the segment, (3) make careful observations, (4) make interpretations of your observations in the segment and its components, and (5) list responses. We describe these steps in this chapter and the two following chapters.

For our purposes we will primarily be working with the segment found in Ephesians 3:14-21. However, when studying on the segment level, always start at the beginning of the book, and work your way to the end, segment by segment. Study in the order provided by the author. Also, keep in mind that it is in the study of segments that RIBS begins to place a heavy emphasis on interpretation and response.

Survey the Segment

You have already surveyed the book and its divisions. Now it is time to survey individual segments, which is much like the earlier surveys only with slight differences in emphasis. Read through the segment looking for (1) the primary purpose and function of the segment for the book as a whole and (2) answers to the six standard questions. When finished, give a title to the segment.

Identify the Primary Purpose
and Function of the Segment

Segments do not exist in isolation. All parts of a book relate to the whole as well as to other parts. They carry forth the narrative or further explain the major points of didactic prose (such as an epistle). When surveying a segment, take note of the unit's purpose within the whole of the book. Ask yourself why is it placed after the segment that goes before it? Why is it placed before the one following it? What does it contribute to the subdivision/division in which it is placed?

You may need to read the segment several times to determine its primary purpose and function. As you read, take time to notice the main events and ideas, and the progression of those events and ideas. After several readings, you should have a good idea of the main theme or purpose of the passage and the role it plays in the book. Pause now to look for the purpose and function of Ephesians 3:14-21.

Welcome Back. Based solely on the text of the segment, compare your conclusions with ours. We concluded that the primary purpose of the segment is to communicate Paul's desire for the Ephesian believers to know experientially the fullness of God with an emphasis on the love of God as the means of that knowledge. After comparing yours with ours, try to write an improved version of yours. You do not have to agree with us.

In function, Ephesians 3:14-21 serves as a conclusion to the first major division of Ephesians. As such, it serves as a summation and climax of the main themes of this division: the blessings found in the triune life, the power at work in Christ, and the fullness of God. Furthermore, this segment functions in its own right as an immediate blessing upon the believers and as a springboard into the second division.

Ask the Six Standard Questions

As in the study of the book as a whole and in the major divisions and subdivisions, ask the six standard questions: Who? What? When? Where? Why? How? In poetry and non-narrative prose, there may be little that you can add at this level of study but ask the questions anyway. New insights at this stage can prove significant.

Again, pause to search the segment for answers to the six questions.

Welcome Back. Now, compare your findings with ours.

Who? We found no additional insights to the question of authorship or recipients. The main characters mentioned here are the Father, Jesus Christ, and the Spirit. Paul is the principal actor (praying), and the (Gentile) believers are the ones for whom he is praying.

What? The main theme of this segment is the desire and prayer of Paul for the believers in Ephesus to experience the fullness of the blessings of God that come through Christ by the power of the Spirit. This segment portrays the power and glory of God.

When? No additional findings.

Where? No additional findings.

Why? This segment serves as a powerful summation (not summary) of Paul's doctrinal emphasis upon the blessings of God found in Jesus Christ. As a summation, it prepares the reader for the second half of the book.

How? This segment is written in prose but has poetic overtones. As a benedictory prayer, it uses powerful descriptive and illustrative images. The repeated imagery of abundance creates a sense of expectation. In style and content, the segment is both a prayer to God and an address to the Ephesians. Paul is speaking directly to the believers even as he is interceding for them.

Give a Title to the Segment

Following your close readings of the segment, you will have an idea of its main theme or teaching. With consideration of this theme, give a title to the segment. The title should be short and concise and should uniquely sum up the segment. Remember: titles should be personal, creative expressions of your interpretation of a segment. The title you give should serve as a summative expression of the segment. Minimally, the title should serve as a reminder of the unique contents of the segment.

We have decided to keep the title of Ephesians 3:14-21 as "Paul's Trinitarian Prayer." We had considered trying to capture the imagery of abundance by adding a reference to it: "Paul's Trinitarian Prayer for God's Abundance," but we concluded that would make it too long. Other possible titles we considered are "Prayer for Abundance," or "A Trinitarian Prayer for Abundance." We settled on "Paul's Trinitarian Prayer" to indicate the trinitarian focus of the passage that extends the emphasis on the Trinity found in earlier segments. Also, it is written in the form of a prayer.

Chapter 15

The Analytical Method
--Respacing the Text

"… the division of the New Testament into chapters … [was] made
in the dark ages, and very incorrectly; often separating things
that are closely joined, and joining those that are
entirely distinct from each other."

—John Wesley

The next major step in the study of the segment is to apply a method
for analyzing the text, one known as respacing the text. Respacing
the text is also known as the "analytical method" because it involves
analyzing the grammatical structure of the text. When you respace a
text, you do not change or alter the text. Rather, you merely observe
closely how the author's meanings are developed through the
grammatical structure of the passage. In short, it is a method for
visually keeping the main ideas the main ideas.

Grammar Provides Clarity

In language there are rules that govern how the elements of language
are brought together to communicate a message. We call those rules
grammar. Grammar exists to provide more precision and clarity to
what is being communicated. It helps us come closer to sharing
concrete meanings behind units of thought. The distance between
the meaning expressed and the meaning received is narrowed.

In some languages the rules of grammar focus on the forms of the
individual words; prefixes and suffixes indicate whether a word is a
subject or an object, past tense or present tense, etc. The order in

which the words appear are of little significance. In the English language, and in some other languages, it is the location of a word within a sentence that largely provides precision in meaning, i.e., typically the subject that is acting appears first, followed by a verb identifying the action, followed by an object (if included) being acted upon.

Translators pay close attention to grammar and punctuation, and we should also. Consider the NRSV translation of Ephesians 4:11: "The gifts he gave were that some would be apostles, some prophets, some evangelists, some pastors and teachers....". It is common to hear this text explained as a statement that when he ascended to heaven Christ gave the church five ministry gifts. But did He? Notice carefully the phrase, "some pastors and teachers." There is no comma after the word "pastors," and the descriptor "some" is also missing. This indicates that pastors and teachers are one unit. They are two functions of the same office; pastors are teachers. We often misread the text as if it states, "some pastors, and some teachers," but it does not. (Note: some scholars understand the original Greek text to support a view that pastors and teachers are separate offices. In that case there should be a comma after "pastors.")

Looking closely at the grammatical structure of a segment is an important part of understanding exactly what the author is saying. This method is especially helpful when trying to unravel a complex segment such as Ephesians 1:3-14, and there are plenty of complex segments in the Bible. While our focus is on respacing individual segments, it is possible to apply the method sequentially, segment by segment. When all the segments in a division are completed, you may combine them to provide a view of the grammatical structure of the entire division of the book.

When you utilize the analytical method, you are carefully analyzing how the author builds the 'argument' of a segment, that is, how the author develops the thesis paragraph by paragraph. Respacing the text allows the main points of a segment to visually 'leap off' the page. To do this, you should first reread the segment carefully looking for the main clauses and how they are connected.

You may remember from school the quite technical process of diagramming sentences. Respacing the text is not so technical. Don't get stressed out; there is not one and only one right way to respace a text. What the final product looks like will depend on the level to which you choose to do your respacing and to some degree your personal preferences. The goal is for you to identify the main points of the segment, how those points are amplified, and how the points are connected. The results will be a clear picture of the author's main point within the segment.

Respacing requires writing the text down paragraph by paragraph in a pattern by which significant items, such as clauses and major phrases, are placed on different lines and indented to a degree that reflects their role in the paragraph. This visualizes the author's grammatical structure and highlights his or her flow of thought. In general, the method requires placing major clauses and phrases more to the left and indenting lesser material toward the right. Conjunctions are placed on a separate line between the items they connect; and their level of indention depends on the type of conjunction: coordinating, correlative, or subordinating.

Ephesians 1:3-14 offers a good opportunity to demonstrate the basic method. The respaced passage in its entirety may be found in Appendix B. The following chart is excerpted from that chart. Notice how the main ideas are visually highlighted by being on the left, with items indented to the right being more descriptive/supportive in nature.

3Blessed is the God and Father of our Lord Jesus Christ,
who has blessed us with every spiritual blessing
in the heavens in Christ.
4For he chose us in him...
5He predestined us to be adopted as sons...
9He made known to us the mystery of his will, ...
that he purposed in Christ...

> [11]*In him we have also received an inheritance, …*
> [13]*In him you also were sealed*
> *with the promised Holy Spirit …*
> [14]*The Holy Spirit is the down payment*
> *of our inheritance, …*
> *to the praise of his glory.*

Observe that the thesis statement, "Blessed is the God and Father of our Lord Jesus Christ…" is farthest to the left. Indented one tab is the statement on why He should be blessed: "who has blessed us with every spiritual blessing." Now observe that there are three statements of equal weight on how God the Father has blessed us: "he chose us," "he predestined us," and "he made known to us." Notice further how the "mystery of his will" is amplified by appending Christ as the agent of the mystery, i.e., the mystery is the gift and Christ is the means.

The complex paragraph then makes two statements about Christ; "in him we have also received an inheritance," and "in him you also were sealed." The Holy Spirit is then presented as the agent of the sealing and as "the down payment" of "our" inheritance.

Flowing backwards, the statements about the Holy Spirit serve to amplify a statement about Jesus. The two statements about Jesus amplify a statement on how God the Father has blessed us with the knowledge of a mystery—all of which calls for acknowledging the blessedness of the Father.

In sum, respacing this passage helps to clarify how the spiritual blessings that come to believers from the Father are gifts to those who are in Christ. One of those blessings, knowledge of the mystery of God's will, serves as the backdrop for blessings from Christ, one of which is an inheritance. The Holy Spirit is given as a seal and down payment on that inheritance.

Theologically, this is known as the "economy" of the Trinity as it relates to salvation. In other words, this text reveals how the grace of God flows from and through the persons of the Godhead to believers. It reveals how the blessings that come from God flow from the Father, through the Son, and then by the Spirit into the believer.

Do not jump to conclusions. Make careful observations. This is not a statement about the Trinity, i.e., their relationship with each other. It is a statement about the flow of God's blessings. The relationships of the Father, Son, and Holy Spirit with each other are not being addressed. In short, this text does not imply some form of subordination within the Godhead.

Some Guidelines for Respacing

Now, let's look more closely at the respacing method. More grammatical elements exist than just clauses and supporting phrases. When respacing, keep some basic concepts of grammar in mind, and use them to guide how you respace. Pay special attention to punctuation, prepositional phrases, interposed phrases, and conjunctions.

Punctuation

When using the respacing method, don't rush past the punctuation. The original manuscripts of the Bible did not include punctuation marks. Concepts of punctuation were made through other means within the grammar of those languages. In the English language, punctuation is needed to understand how words, phrases, and clauses relate to each other. Punctuation provides vital information about the author's meaning and flow of thought.

Therefore, punctuation serves as an important part of any translation. Just as translators use different words and sentence structures, they punctuate differently. Each is careful to use punctuation marks in the best way possible to represent the original meaning of the text as they understand it. When you come across an awkward use of punctuation, it is helpful to see how other translations structure and punctuate the sentences.

Punctuation serves as an important part
of any translation.

For the analytical method of Bible study, the more significant punctuation marks are those that identify beginnings, endings, and pauses in thought. Capital letters indicate the beginning of something, either a sentence or a proper name. Periods are the strongest indicator of the end of something, most often a sentence. Question marks and exclamation marks also indicate an end, but they convey additional meanings—that a question is being asked, or a statement contains emotional emphasis.

Commas and Colons

Attention needs to be given to punctuation marks that indicate a pause rather than a beginning or a full stop: these include commas, colons, dashes, and semicolons. Commas (,) supply the notion of a soft stop; they divide items in a list and provide needed clarification to sentence structure. Colons (:) are comparable to commas, only a little stronger; they can provide a pause between a clause and items such as an example, a list, an explanation, a direct quote, or a question.

Semicolon

The semicolon (;) is perhaps the most overlooked punctuation mark. It is a strong pause coming close to a full stop. It has two uses. One use is to connect two otherwise independent clauses—each of which could stand on its own as a complete sentence. The semicolon indicates that the two are especially related in the context in which they appear. They are two sentences linked as one.

The other use for a semicolon is to separate items in a list when those items have commas within themselves. Returning to a discussion we began in Chapter 6 about Ephesians 4:11, only this time using the

KJV for illustrative purposes: "and he gave some, apostles; and some, prophets; and some, evangelists; and some, pastors and teachers." The verse contains a list of ministry offices: apostles, prophets, evangelists, and pastors and teachers. Look closely at the punctuation. You will notice that the text makes use of commas and semicolons: "... some, apostles; and some..." Commas are used as soft pauses to clarify who the various "some" are: "and some, apostles..." A semicolon is then needed as a stronger pause to separate the categories of offices.

Now notice the punctuation for the last item in the list: "and some, pastors and teachers." There is no punctuation mark between pastors and teachers. Along with the absence of the word "some" before "teachers," this punctuation makes it clear that the translators understood "pastors and teachers" to be one office delineated from the others by a semicolon. In this list, there are only four offices separated from each other by semicolons. Punctuation can make a great difference in the meaning of a text.

Dash

Dashes (a hyphen [-], an "en" dash [–] and an "em" dash [—]) are stronger pauses than commas, colons, semicolons, and parentheses—although they serve the same general purpose and may replace any of them. "Em" dashes are sometimes used much like brackets to mark the insertion of helpful information that is non-essential to the writer's flow of thought, and they may be used to insert a thought outside the thesis of the paragraph.

Prepositional Phrases

Pay attention to prepositional phrases. A preposition is a word that pre-positions a noun or pronoun to show its relationship with another noun in a sentence. For a literal example, in the sentence "Jesus took Peter, James, and John and led them up a high mountain by themselves to be alone," the preposition "up" positions "them" on a "mountain" with Jesus. The preposition "by" positions them in relation to others; they were with Jesus, alone. Of course, prepositions are seldom so literally a pre-positioning. The concept is that prepositions descriptively connect one noun or pronoun with another noun of greater importance.

Often a prepositional phrase can be left out of a sentence, and the sentence will remain a complete and understandable thought. In our example above from Mark 9, the sentence makes sense if it includes none, any, or all the phrases: *up a high mountain, by themselves,* or *to be alone.* Also, the three prepositional phrases are functionally equal; they may appear in any order and the sentence have the same meaning. The main and indispensable idea is that "Jesus took Peter, James, and John, and led them."

Also, sometimes a prepositional phrase introduces a main clause. The Gospel of Mark frequently uses such phrases as locators and introductory descriptors. They locate the subject and the action in space and/or time. An example from the CSB translation can be seen near the end of the passage on the Syrophoenician woman in Mark 7: "When she went back to her home" introduces the main concept that "she found her child lying on the bed, and the demon was gone." As the following example shows, the introductory phrase should be indented more than the main clause when respacing. It appears first but is secondary to the meaning of the sentence.

> *When she went back to her home*
> *she found her child*
> > *lying on the bed,*
> > *and*
> > *the demon was gone* (Mark 7:30, CSB).

Dialogue

In sections with dialogue, it helps to further indent the dialogue. This type of indention does not strictly follow the clause/phrase format, but it helps to indicate who said what. Note the following respacing of Mark 7:26-29. It attempts to show the dynamics of the dialogue between Jesus and a Syrophoenician woman:

He said to her,
    "Let the children be fed first,
        because
        it isn't right
            to take the children's bread
            and
            throw it to the dogs."
But
she replied to him,
    "Lord, even the dogs
        under the table
    ... eat the children's crumbs."

Then he told her,
    "Because of this reply,
you may go.
The demon has left your daughter."

    When she went back to her home,
she found her child
    lying on the bed,
and
the demon was gone (Mark 7:24-30, CSB).

The last sentence in this passage illustrates one of the challenges for the analytical method: what two items does the conjunction "and" connect? As charted here, the demon being gone is more a statement about the demon's departure from their home than having departed from the girl. If we interpret it as a reference to the demon having departed from the girl, then the conjunction and phrase would be indented to the same depth as "lying on her bed" as was done in the previous section. It is a matter of interpretation which might be clarified if we read the text in the original language—but we didn't.

Interposed Phrases

Sometimes a supporting phrase is inserted within a clause between the subject and verb or between the main clause and the object in a way that, while adding meaning, interrupts the flow of thought. This is increasingly more likely the more a translation is based upon a more word-for-word approach. This situation requires special guidelines for respacing, and there are three options.

Two approaches differ only as to whether the interposed line is placed above or below the rest of the clause. In these approaches, the two sections of the main clause appear on the same line with an ellipsis mark connecting them. The interposed phrase is placed near the ellipsis, either above or below. A line may then be used to connect the interposed phrase with the main clause. In these approaches, a text such as, "I pray that he may grant you, according to the riches of his glory, to be strengthened with power" (Eph 3:16, CSB) appears as either

> *I pray that he may grant you…to be strengthened with power*
> *according to the riches of his glory*

or

> *according to the riches of his glory*
> *I pray that he may grant you… to be strengthened with power*

Notice that the interposed phrase is indented an amount sufficient to make it easy to follow the flow of thought, and the connecting straight line further indicates where the interrupting phrase belongs. If you choose one of these approaches, stay consistent with whether you place interposed phrases above or below the main concept.

Another approach to diagraming interposed phrases is one that keeps the text unfolding in its original sequence:

> *I pray that he may grant you*
> *according to the riches of his glory*
> *…to be strengthened with power*

Take note that (1) the first and third lines are indented equally, (2) an ellipsis appears at the beginning of the third line to indicate the flow of thought, "I pray that he may grant you … to be strengthened," (3) the interposed text appears in the order the text was translated, being placed in between the two primary elements of the clause, and (4) the interposed phrase is indented more than one additional tab in order to make it easy to follow the flow of the main thought. If desired, the third line containing the second half of the clause might be indented one half of a regular tab. Whichever approach you choose, stay consistent!

Conjunctions

When you analyze segments, pay careful attention to conjunctions such as *and, therefore, because, after, since, so that, although, as soon as,* and *but.* These little words and phrases serve to link concepts and to recognize their relationship with each other. They are used to link similar items: clause to clause, phrase to phrase, word to word. They may give notice that a change in a main thought is about to occur and may help identify coordinated ideas and subordinated ideas.

Coordinating Conjunctions

Coordinating conjunctions such as *for, and, nor, but, or, yet,* and *so* link concepts that grammatically are of equal importance. The conjunction and the clauses, phrases, or words it serves to connect should be indented to the same level. The conjunction appears in the middle on a line by itself.

Correlative Conjunctions

Correlative conjunctions like *both/and, either/or, neither/nor, not only/but also,* and *whether/or* are conjunctions that work together. For purposes of respacing, treat them and the items they connect like coordinating conjunctions. Both parts of the coordinating conjunction appear on lines by themselves just above the elements they serve to correlate.

Subordinating Conjunctions

Subordinating conjunctions such as *after, as, as if, as long as, as much as, as soon as, because, before, by the time, even though, if, in order that, lest, once, only, since, so that, than, though, until, when, where, whereas, wherever, whether or not,* and *while* link concepts not equal in importance; that is, one of the concepts serves to support the other one. The conjunction and the clauses, phrases, or words it introduces should be indented one tab more than the main clause or phrase to which it is subordinate.

Consider this example:

> *He said to her,*
> > *"Let the children be fed first,*
> > > *because*
> > > *it isn't right*
> > > > *to take the children's bread*
> > > > *and*
> > > > *throw it to the dogs"* (Mark 7:27, CSB).

"Because" is a subordinating conjunction that connects the main clause "let the children be fed first" with the supporting clause that follows: "it isn't right to take the children's bread." "Because" and the subordinate second clause of the quote are indented equally with one tab beyond the first clause.

Also, note that the last two clauses ("to take the children's bread" and "throw it to the dogs") are grammatically equal actions and are joined by the coordinating conjunction "and" and are therefore indented equally.

Sometimes a subordinating conjunction introduces a subordinated phrase, in which case the conjunction and phrase are double indented as in this example.

> *Then he told her,*
> > *"Because*
> > *of this reply,*
> > *you may go.*
> > *The demon has left your daughter"* (Mark 7:29-30, CSB).

While this discussion of conjunctions may seem overly technical, it is important. Due to our personal inclinations, we may lay hold of a phrase or clause and mistakenly give it more priority than the author intended. We sometimes misread a subordinating point as if it is the main point.

Lists

Even though it consumes a lot of space, it is helpful to respace lists of items especially when they are joined with conjunctions.

> *There is*
> > *one body*
> > *and*
> > *one Spirit*
> > > *— just as*
> > > *you were called to one hope*
> > > *at your calling —*
> > *one Lord,*
> > *one faith,*
> > *one baptism,*
> > *one God and Father of all,*
> > > *who is*
> > > > *above all*
> > > > *and*
> > > > *through all*
> > > > *and*
> > > > *in all* (Eph 4:4-5, CSB).

Again, there is no absolutely correct way to respace a text. Respacing is a tool for making careful observations but may require an element of interpretation. When observing how the words, phrases, and clauses fit together, reasoned opinion may prove necessary. Consulting a differing translation may help clarify the meaning, but that might also add more confusion.

A Special Note: Supporting
—Not Inferior

When respacing, stay focused on keeping the main ideas as the main ideas, and the supporting ideas as supporting ideas. In other words, good Bible study involves knowing the difference between those ideas that are emphasized by the writer, and those that are secondary or supportive of the writer's main points. Supporting material is there to amplify or clarify the main idea. Bad doctrine can be the result of making supporting ideas into main ideas so as to miss altogether the main point or to invert the importance of the two!

Good Bible study involves knowing the difference between those ideas that are emphasized by the writer, and those that are secondary or supportive of the writer's main points.

We are not saying that supporting points are less inspired than the main ones. Neither are we saying that "supporting" indicates a lesser truth. On the contrary, a lesser point in an author's message may be an extremely significant statement in the context of the Bible as a whole. Good Bible study, however, requires that we study the book as literature, which requires that we understand how the writer develops the main message. How is the main message developed using supportive material?

For example, there can be no greater truth than the following statement from the first chapter of Ephesians in which, speaking about Christ, Paul says: "In him we have redemption through his blood, the forgiveness of our trespasses, according to the riches of his grace that he richly poured out on us with all wisdom and understanding" (Eph 1:7-8, CSB).

In the development of Paul's argument in Ephesians, though, this statement about Christ and our redemption is but one sub-sub-point given in support of his main thesis that "Blessed is the God and Father of our Lord Jesus Christ, who has blessed us with every spiritual blessing in the heavens in Christ" (Eph 1:3, CSB). See Appendix B where this entire segment is respaced.

An Exercise

Let us now return to Ephesians 3:14-21 and, using the guidelines above, respace the text. You may find it helpful to copy and paste the text from a digitized version into your word processing software and respace it there. Also, you would benefit by first respacing all the segments in the first division of Ephesians. Just be certain to complete 3:14-21.

Welcome Back. Now compare your work with ours, asking yourself why we respaced the way we did.

> *[14]For this reason*
> *I kneel before the Father*
> > *[15]from whom every family*
> > > *in heaven*
> > > *and*
> > > *on earth*
> > *…is named.*
> *[16]I pray*
> > *that he may grant you,*
> > > *according to the riches of his glory,*
> > *…to be strengthened with power*
> > > *in your inner being*
> > > > *through*
> > > > *his Spirit,*
> *[17]and*
> *that Christ may dwell*
> > *in your hearts*
> > > *through*
> > > *faith.*
> *I pray that you,*
> > *being rooted and firmly established in love,*
> *…[18]may be able*
> > *to comprehend with all the saints*
> > > *what is the*
> > > > *length*

and
width,
height
and
depth of God's love,
¹⁹*and*
to know Christ's love
    that surpasses knowledge,
  so that
  you may be filled
    with all the fullness of God.
²⁰*Now*
to him who is able to do
  above and beyond
…all that we ask or think
  according to the power
    that works in us
²¹ — *to him be glory*
  in the church
  and
  in Christ Jesus
    to all generations,
      forever and ever.
      Amen (Eph 3:14-21, CSB).

Notice that this passage includes examples of interposed phrases and different types of conjunctions. Also, verse 19 required special spacing. The phrase "that surpasses knowledge" is double indented beneath "to know Christ's love." The reason for this is to properly place the subordinating conjunction "so that" between the two conjoined main clauses and to indicate that "that surpasses knowledge" is a phrase (and not a clause) describing "Christ's love." That is, the main thought is not "to know Christ's love that surpasses knowledge." The main thought is "to know Christ's love … so that you may be filled…"

By respacing we can easily see the main points of Paul's prayer. Paul kneels before the Father. He prays the Father will grant the Ephesians to be strengthened and that Christ may dwell in their hearts. He also prays that they may be able to comprehend the extent of God's love and know Christ's love. He ends with recognition of God who is abundantly able to do and that he should receive glory. All of the other phrases exist to support these main points.

A Final Note

Respacing the text is not an end in itself. It is a tool that assists in making good observations. Respacing the text helps clarify what the main points are and how those points are connected. Typically, a segment should be respaced before making focused observations and interpretations on the segment (the subject of our next chapter). However, while respacing the text of a segment, you may see things that seem important. Jot them down in your notebook as observations but quickly return to the respacing task.

You will no doubt revise your respaced chart several times as you reflect on the sentence structures. That's when working with a word processing program becomes a real gift; you can highlight, drag and drop words and phrases to rearrange the text without having to start all over again.

More focused observations on the segment will be made after you have respaced text. But you will you find that the process of making those observations will sometimes challenge the way you respaced the text. That is normal and may lead you to respace the text differently. Just keep in mind that you want to see the text the way the author intended you see it.

Don't get frustrated. You are creating a map to where many treasures are found, and you are collecting many gems in the process.

Chapter 16

Focused Study of the Segment

"And whatever light you then receive, should be used to the uttermost, and
that immediately. Let there be no delay. Whatever you resolve, begin to
execute the first moment you can. So shall you find this word to be indeed
the power of God unto present and eternal salvation."

—John Wesley

Up to this point you have gained a good knowledge of the book you
are studying. You know something about the author, the original
recipients, the reason the book was written, and the primary purpose
and theme of the book. You also have a good grasp on the structure
and content of the book. You have made many observations and not
a few interpretations. Because you approached the book as Spirit-
Word, you have also been drawn closer to God and recognized
things that God is saying to you personally. And surely you have
responded in faith.

Having done all the above, plus having surveyed and respaced the
segment of the text, we are ready to make focused observations on
the segment, and to make interpretations of the meaning of the
segment. We are also ready to give more attention to how we should
respond to the voice of God flowing out of the text.

For the sake of continuity, we will be working again with the segment
contained in Ephesians 3:14-21. However, if we were doing a RIBS
study of Ephesians, we would have already completed focused
segment studies of each of the segments preceding 3:14-21. Our
study here will reflect those earlier segments but only to a limited

degree. You should review the contents of Ephesians up to our passage before proceeding.

Always keep in mind that the study of a segment is focused both inwardly and outwardly. Inwardly, you aim to see what the segment actually says and means. Outwardly, you aim to see how the segment connects to the things you already know about the book, with emphasis on the segments that came before it.

Always keep in mind that the study of a segment is focused both inwardly and outwardly.

While doing a focused study of a segment, keep in mind the five steps RIBS:

- Spiritually Prepare
- Review your notes
- Observe
- Interpret
- Respond

Traditional inductive Bible study does not explicitly include spiritual preparation as one of the movements and the later three are seen as sequential. First observe, then interpret what you observed, and finally apply your new understanding to your life.

As noted earlier, we prefer the concept of "responding" to that of "applying." In the scientific method, observations are made, a theory (interpretation) is developed to explain that which has been observed, and then the theory is tested by conducting an experiment (an application of the theory). In inductive Bible study, interpretation is to application what a theory is to an experiment in science.

Inductively deduced applications are too easily impersonal processes that rest authority in the individual's powers of reasoning rather than in the active Word of God. In consequence, the observation and interpretation phases tend to fail to see study as an opportunity to actually hear the voice of God, and the application phase tends to lack a sense of God's real presence in and authority over life.

In RIBS, we recognize that the three-fold sequential pattern is logical; it is the pattern in which we have all been trained to think. However, openness to the Spirit may alter the sequence and even fuse the elements into a single event. We may come to observe, understand, and act all in the same moment. This is made possible when Bible study is done as worship; there may be times when the only appropriate response will be more spontaneous than a delayed, reasoned action. Certainly, not all Bible study will include these transforming moments, but we must be open to them.

Therefore, be flexible with the threefold pattern of study. With any given segment, or set of segments, you may quickly move through interpretation to an immediate response. At other times you will need to meditate on your discoveries before responding. Meditation is itself a response—one that leads to further response. The important thing is that you hear what God is saying and that you live in surrender to His Word. It is a process, sometimes slow, sometimes rapid.

The critical point is that your observations, interpretations, and responses must be harmonious and be faithful expressions of the Word of God. They must flow out of the Scriptures into and through your life. The Holy Spirit must govern the process. The three movements must remain consistent with all God is saying through the Bible. When it comes to truth, knowing, being and doing are to be intertwined expressions of the same reality.

Recording Observations, Interpretations, and Responses

You will need to adopt a system for recording observations, interpretations, and responses. Experiment with differing systems to find the one that works best for you. You may adjust your system to fit the book you are studying or the method you currently use. The goal is for you to record the results of your study in a manner that gives you quick access to your discoveries and helps you pull it all together.

One system you might follow is to create a chart that visually connects the three elements: observation, interpretation, and response. The simplest chart would be to create three columns on the same page. The first column would be for observations, the second for interpretations, and the third for responses. In the second column, place an interpretation adjacent to the observation or set of observations from which it arises. In the third column, place personal responses adjacent to the corresponding observation(s) and interpretation(s). There will not always be a response for every observation/interpretation.

Figure 16.1 -- "Observations, Interpretations, Responses"

Observations	Interpretations	Responses
1. *Means-End.* Being "rooted and firmly established" in love is the means of comprehending the expansiveness of God's love (3:17-18). And knowing Christ's love is the means of becoming "filled with the	1. Love is of/from God. Being grounded in and comprehending love is the key to achieving the kind of relationship with God that He desires for us.	1. At the heart of spiritual growth and discipleship is love. Yet, we seem to pay only lip service to it. How do we nurture people in God's love? How do we nurture love in our own lives? Father, draw me into your love. Reveal to me my inner obstacles to loving as I should and help me remove them.

fullness of God" (3:19).		
2. *Supportive Relationship.* The prayer relates the believers to each member of the Trinity in a manner that reveals the full Godhead to be actively involved in helping the believers move toward having the fullness of God within (Spirit in v. 16; Christ in vv. 17, 19; God the Father in v. 18).	2. It is God's desire for Christians to have an intimate relationship with the Father, Son, and Holy Spirit, one characterized by believers being, or moving toward being, filled with the fullness of God.	2. Being filled with the fullness of God is beyond my imagination, yet I must believe it is the destiny of all who are alive in Christ. It remains essential that I hunger to have the fullness of God dwelling in me. Father, increase my hunger for you. Cleanse me of any desires that keep me from knowing you as fully as possible.
3. *Quantitative Relationships.* The prayer conveys a strong sense of abundance. (a) "the riches of his glory" (v. 16); (b) "...the length and width, height and depth of God's love" (v. 18); (c) "love that surpasses knowledge" (v. 19); (d) "filled with all the fullness" (v. 19); (e) "do above and beyond" (v. 20).	3. It is God's provision and desire that His spiritual blessings be abundant in our lives.	3. Father, why am I not constantly aware of your abundant spiritual blessings? Why do I so often feel spiritually impoverished? Open my eyes. Increase my faith, I pray.

Charting can take many forms. A second form would be to place each column of the chart on separate sheets of paper. The three sheets could be laid out before you as one large chart having three columns. One strength of charting is that it makes it easy to add interpretations and responses at any time after observations have been made.

Another approach for recording observations, interpretations, and responses is to follow a "note-taking" pattern. On paper this pattern looks like an outline. Observations would all have a level-1 indention. Interpretations would all have a level-2 indention and be placed beneath the observation it is interpreting. Responses would have a level-3 indention and be placed beneath the interpretation to which it relates. The pattern would be as follows:

        Observation #1
                Interpretation #1
                        Response #1
        Observation #2
                Interpretation #2
                        Response #2

Regardless of system for recording, the process is most easily done when using a computer word processing program. As discussed above, interpretations and responses are not always made immediately following an observation. When using pencil and paper, the various systems require either leaving a lot of space between observations for later entries or starting over every time you see something new and writing it all down on a separate sheet of paper. Using a computer allows you to make insertions easily at any point in time is a blessing.

Stages of a Focused Study

Following the analytical study of a segment, there are three stages for completing a focused study of the segment. First, you should look at the literary structure of the segment. Second, you should identify any literary devices. Third, you should make summative observations, interpretations, and responses to the text of the segment. As always, take time to prepare spiritually to study and review the notes you have taken.

Look at the Literary Structure/Design

Observations on literary structure seldom lead one to interpretations and rarely call for response. Yet, they still need to be made because they remain important for discerning the message of the book and how the author develops the message.

The primary benefit of respacing the text is to observe how segments are structured paragraph by paragraph. The respaced text offers a visual representation of the structure of the segment. The process of respacing requires the learner to identify the major clauses in each paragraph and how the words and phrases in the paragraph contribute to the meaning of each sentence. What are the primary units of thought, and how do any secondary units of thought amplify those units?

When looking for the literary structure of a segment, look first for the internal structure. Then look for how the segment fits into the division where it is found. Finally, give some consideration to its place in the book as a whole.

Internal Structure

Let's look together at the internal structure of Ephesians 3:14-21. A review of the respaced text of Ephesians 3:14-21 in the previous chapter exposes the obvious structure. As translated, Paul begins with a brief paragraph on what one might call a postured invocation; that is, he assumes a posture of prayer, consciously kneeling before the Father. The second paragraph includes two petitions on behalf of the Ephesians. The final paragraph concludes the segment with a benediction of praise.

Alternate Parallelism

A closer look at the respaced text reveals that the body of the prayer contains the two petitions (vv. 16-19) and is structured as an alternating parallelism in the form of ABC – ABC.

A = **I pray that he** may grant you, *according to the riches of his glory,*

    B = to be strengthened with power in your inner being through his Spirit,

        C = **and that** Christ may dwell in your hearts through faith.

A = **I pray that you**, *being rooted and firmly established in love,*

    B = may be able to comprehend with all the saints what is the length and width, height, and depth of God's love,

        C = **and** to know Christ's love that surpasses knowledge, so **that** you may be filled with all the fullness of God.

"I pray that he" is paralleled with "I pray that you." "To be strengthened" is paralleled with "may be able to comprehend." "And that Christ" is paralleled with "And ... that you." Notice that both "A" lines have interposed phrases. Also, the "C" lines have additional parallels between "that Christ may dwell in your hearts" and "that you may be filled." This parallelism adds an emphasis to the text and thereby contributes to the sense that a climax is being reached.

The respaced text allows us to accurately pull out the main ideas that constitute the inner structure of the prayer. This allows us to affirm the theme we identified earlier in our survey. The abbreviated main points are:

I kneel before the Father.
I pray
  that he may grant you to be strengthened
  and
  that Christ may dwell
    in your hearts.
I pray
  that you may be able
    to comprehend (the fullness of) God's love,
    and
    to know Christ's love
      so that
        you may be filled with all the fullness of God.
Now to him who is able
  — to him be glory to all generations.
Amen."

Clearly, Paul's prayer for the Ephesians centers on his desires (1) that they be strong with Christ dwelling in their hearts and (2) that they might be able to (a) comprehend the full extent of God's love, and (b) know Christ's love so that they might be filled with the fullness of God.

Place of the Segment in the Division

The prayer is the last segment of the third subdivision of the first division of the book. As such, it comes at the end of the first division. Paul begins the prayer with the words, "For this reason" explicitly tying the segment to something that went before. The questions that arise are, "To what is Paul referring? What is the reason for the prayer? Is the reason that which came immediately before the prayer? Specifically, is it the previous sentence about his suffering? Or is it the entire previous paragraph? The entire previous segment about his ministry? Or is it everything in the epistle that came before the prayer? Why does Paul pause to pray?"

Our earlier study of the divisions led us to conclude that the reason for the prayer was multilayered. It was in response to elements of the previous segment about his calling to minister among the Gentiles, especially their concerns about the faith that may have arisen because of Paul's suffering. On the other hand, one can understand the prayer as motivated by all that came before it.

If we had completed a segmented study of Ephesians 3:1-13, then we would have noted that Paul begins that segment with the same phrase, "For this reason," and we would have observed that Paul began that segment with an incomplete sentence—as if he started his prayer at that point but interrupted himself to remind the Ephesians of his place in their lives. That observation lends support to the interpretation that "For this reason" in 3:14 referred to all that went before. That is, if the prayer in 3:14-21 picks up where 3:1 was interrupted, the "For this reason" must include something that came before 3:1. These observations about the reason for the prayer in 3:14-21 strengthen the position that the segment is indeed the climax of the first division.

Place in the Structure of the Book as a Whole

If 3:14-21 is the climax of the first division, then how does it fit in the structure of the whole book? It seems that 3:14-21 is both a climax and a transition. It both concludes the first division and serves as a springboard into how the Ephesians should live as described in the second division of the epistle.

The segment, Ephesians 3:14-21, thus holds a significant place in the epistle. We have already observed in our study of the divisions and subdivisions that the first division is more theological, and the second is a more practical look at how believers should live. This current segment immediately follows Paul's defense of his apostleship to the Gentiles, which solidified his destiny (as a Jew who followed Christ) with theirs (as Gentiles who followed Christ). This final segment of the first half of the book then serves as a motivational springboard both into the second half of the book and into their future destiny (with Paul and Jewish believers) in Christ.

Note the Literary Devices

The respaced text allows you to take notice of the main ideas and supporting relationships. This in turn proves helpful for identifying the literary devices in the segment. So, right now, go over the respaced text of Ephesians 3:14-21 again looking for figures of speech, structural patterns, and literary techniques. (We will look for relational connections later.) Observe closely the author's use of literary techniques within the segment. Are figures of speech used? Which ones and why? What literary techniques such as *flow of intensity* or *climax* are used? Are structural patterns such as *parallelism* evident? Look, and look again!

When you have finished, return to compare your findings with ours. Do not skip this exercise. Finding literary devices requires a skillful eye and skill requires practice.

Welcome Back! Below you will find the literary techniques, structural patterns, and relational connections we observed.

Figures of Speech

We did not find any figures of speech. Paul is very direct in his prose. The language is very spiritual, which might give it the feel of hyperbole, but the tone suggests that Paul is understating the extent of God's blessings for which he is praying.

Literary Techniques

Looking first for literary techniques internal to the segment, we then looked for any that connect the segment with other segments, especially that which went before. Several literary techniques emerge in Ephesians 3:14-21.

Summation/Climax. Paul's prayer serves as a summation of the blessed condition of the believers as described in Chapters 1 and 2. It is not a summary in that the blessings listed earlier are not restated here. It does bring the theme and tone of abundance of blessings to a climax. The blessings already received, as described in the first two chapters, are now projected as a foundational impetus for the ultimate goal: "so that you may be filled with all the fullness of God" (v. 19).

Recurrence. There is one reference to the Spirit in the segment (3:16) but multiple references to the Spirit in the first division (1:13, 14, 17; 2:18, 22; 3:5). Further study will reveal that this continues throughout the book (4:3, 30; 5:18-19; 6:17-18). Most of these references are in the context of a trinitarian formula; that is, the Spirit is directly connected with statements about the Father and the Son as distinct persons (1:17; 2:18, 19-22; 3:16-19; 4:3-4, 30-32; 5:18-20).

Recurrence. Prior to the reference in 3:14, there have been two previous specific references to God as "Father:" "Blessed is the God and Father of our Lord Jesus Christ" (1:3) and "I pray that the God of our Lord Jesus Christ, the glorious Father" (1:17).

Recurrence. In the prayer, Paul makes three references to God's "power" existing within the believers:

- "power through his Spirit" (3:16)

- "that you may have the power to comprehend" (3:18)

- "Now to him who by the power at work within us" (3:20)

Recurrence. The emphasis on power (3:16, 18, 20) connects the prayer with other parts of the epistle: the greatness of God's power, (1:19); the exercise His power (1:20); over all power (1:21); the ruler of the power of the air (2:2); working of His power (3:7); struggle against cosmic powers (6:12). Note: the references to God's power are all in the first division of the book.

Recurrence. The introductory phrase, "For this reason" in 3:14 already appears in 3:1. A similar phrase appears in 1:15, "This is why." [Other translations have "For this reason," but the original in 1:15 is different.]

Recurrence. The concept of believers receiving gifts internally occurs three times, "strengthened with power <u>in your inner being</u>" (v. 16), "Christ may <u>dwell in your hearts</u>" (v. 17), "that <u>you may be filled with</u> all the fullness of God" (v. 19). This concept of internal reception is new within the epistle. Up to this point the blessings of God have not been described as internal to the believer. Ephesians 2:22 makes a parallel comment: "In him you are also being built together for God's dwelling in the Spirit," but this statement is about God indwelling the corporate Church and not about individual believers receiving blessings from God.

Recurrence. Love is a recurring theme in the segment (three times in 3:17-19).

Recurrence. Paul uses the phrase, "I pray that" twice (3:16, 17). In the first case, the prayer is that God will act to grant things to the Ephesians. In the second case, the prayer is that the Ephesians "will be able." In the first, they are to be recipients while in the second they are to be active participants.

Flow of Intensity/Climax. This segment is the "climax" of Paul's rhetorical argument and of the intensity of his argument. His words reach a high point here. Note the praise, the wonder, and the power found in this section. That this segment ends with "Amen" underscores the crescendo that this segment of Ephesians serves.

Structural Patterns

Remember from an earlier chapter, the structure (or structural design) of a book or division of a book is a different concept than that of structural patterns as literary devises. The first has to do with how the more general structure of the book is developed. The second, a structural pattern, is an established literary device the author uses for emphasis, clarity, or purposes of memorization. As previously noted, structural patterns can be more challenging to recognize in prose literature but are often present.

Because of their smaller size, a segment may be entirely or predominantly written in the form of a structural pattern. In that case, the structural pattern is the structural design. This is the case for Ephesians 3:14-21. As noted above, this segment has at its heart an alternating parallelism in the form of ABC–ABC. That parallelism is a literary technique that constitutes much of the literary structure of the prayer. (See above)

Relational Connections

Now let us turn our attention to relational connections. Remember, do not just look for isolated facts. Look at the relational patterns of the segment. Ponder the passage, and ask: "What type of relationships are seen in this segment?" Go back over the list of structural relationships discussed in Chapter 7 and read over them as you look and look again at the segment. Examine both the relationships internal to the segment and relationships between the segment and other parts of the book—especially the prior segments you have already studied in depth.

Stop and make as many observations as you can about the relational connections you find in Ephesians 3:14-21. Remember, look for connections internal to the segment and those that connect the segment to the rest of the book.

Welcome Back! Now compare your observations with the ones we made.

Inclusive Relationship

The prayer begins with a reference to God as Father of all humanity, including those in heaven and on earth: "I kneel before the Father from whom every family in heaven and on earth is named" (v. 15). This connection between God and all of humanity has not been seen in the letter up to this point. The focus has been on the believers' relationships with God and with each other. This inclusion of all families as children of the Father includes Gentiles; this strengthens Paul's arguments for the inclusion of Gentiles in Christ.

Agency/Means-End

Paul makes use of several agency or means-end images:

- The Father is the agency of the whole human family (3:15).

- The Spirit is the agency of power that strengthens the inner being (3:16).

- Christ's love is the agency for being filled with all the fullness of God (3:19).

- God is the agency of power who can accomplish abundantly far more than we can ask or imagine (3:20).

Quantitative Relationship

The prayer conveys a strong sense of abundance: (a) "the riches of his glory" (v. 16); (b) "the length and width, height and depth of God's love" (v. 18); (c) "love that surpasses knowledge" (v. 19); (d) "filled with all the fullness" (v. 19); (e) "do above and beyond" (v. 20).

Supportive Relationship

Power is a significant supportive component of the prayer, i.e., that they might be strengthened with his power (3:16), and the power that works in us (3:20).

Supportive Relationship

The prayer relates the believers to each member of the Trinity in a manner that reveals the full Godhead as actively involved in helping believers come into their fullness (Spirit in v. 16, Christ in vv. 17 and 19, and God the Father in v. 18).

Cause-Effect Relationship

The segment begins with the phrase, "For this reason," which indicates that the segment responds to some aspect of the content that preceded it.

Relational Space

The prayer is multi-directional in scope with emphases on blessings within the believers, believers grounded in love, and believers comprehending the "length and width, height and depth of God's love."

Authority

The prayer acknowledges God the Father's authority by stating Paul's submissive posture (kneeling before) and his petition that God "grant" blessings to the believers (3:14, 16).

Comparative/Contrastive

Paul's prayer begins with two contrasting images of God. First, he portrays God in expansive terms as "the Father from whom every family in heaven and on earth is named" (3:14). Second, he portrays God as existing in the inner being of the Ephesian believers (3:16).

Summative Interpretations
and Responses

Throughout your RIBS study, you should have been making interpretations that led to some responses. When Bible study is prayer with an emphasis on listening for the voice of God, interpretation and response should be intentional but may also be almost automatic. Relational interactions are typically spontaneous, so there must be an openness to spontaneity in Bible study. That which springs from the heart is not restricted to logical conclusions as its source.

However, meaningful relationships do call for times of reflection on what has been written and observed. A focused encounter with a segment of the living Word requires that time be given to interpret and summarize the message of the segment and that there be personal response to it.

Outline the Segment

At any point after respacing the segment, you should be able to outline it, indicating the main points as well as the supporting ones. We recommend, however, that you reserve this exercise until you have completed a thorough study of the segment. Approaching outlining as the end point of your observations rather than the beginning point helps to make sure you keep the main points as main points and the supporting points as supporting ones. When we outline a passage at the beginning of a study, we often force upon the text our ideas of what it should say.

Our outline of Paul's prayer appears next. Flip back to page 270 to review how we respaced the prayer and you can easily see how the outline that follows is governed by the respaced text.

<u>Paul's Trinitarian Prayer</u>

I.   The Posture of Prayer
   A.   Kneel Before the Father
      a.   From whom every family is named
II. First Petition
   A.   That they might be strengthened with power
      a.   In their inner being through the Spirit
   B.   That Christ might dwell in their hearts

        a.   Through faith
III. Second Petition
    A. That they might comprehend …God's Love
        a.   Length and Width
        b.   Height and Breadth
    B. That they might know the love of Christ
        a.   That surpasses all knowledge
    C. That they might be filled with all the fullness of God
III. Concluding Adoration and Praise
    A. To Him who is able to do
        a.   All that we ask or think
    B. To him be glory
        a.   In the church
        b.   In Christ Jesus
        c.   Forever and Ever!

Notice that the outline is not symmetrical because the respaced text is not symmetrical. Paul was not as concerned with symmetry as we often are. It is important to follow closely the flow of the author's thought and not force of personal preferences as to how an author should think.

Observations and Interpretations

Using the note-taking approach to making observations, interpretations, and responses as we have done instead of charting requires that we pay special attention to the difference between observations and interpretations. Do not fall into the trap of thinking that because it seems clear to you, it must be a factual observation. You will find it helpful to use one of the methods of notetaking described above. Either create a chart that places your observations, interpretations, and responses in separate columns, or use the system of indenting interpretations beneath observations and double indenting responses beneath interpretations.

Also, you will find group inductive study a great atmosphere for honing these skills, provided the members of the group commit to helping each other see their blind spots.

List Themes and Teachings

Interpretations always follow observations or sets of observations. You may make your interpretations immediately following a written observation. Or you may prefer to make your interpretations after all your observations have been written, or you may find it helpful to write some as you progress and others afterwards.

Regardless of how you record them, on the segment level, interpretations exist to answer the central question, "What does this segment say to all generations?" "What does God want His people of every stripe to know?" Answers to these questions identify the themes and teachings of the segment.

Remember, no matter how confident you are, your statements are still your personal interpretations. They are at best your creative restatement of the meaning of the Biblical text. They are your words and not the Word of God. You should be confident without being arrogant.

Here is a list of some of our interpretations of the prayer.

1. In this prayer, Paul is saying that (a) there is more to know of God than you now know, that (b) love is the way to know all we can know of God, and that (c) because the fullness of what God desires for us to know will be within us, to "know" is to conform to all we can know of God.

2. God wants all believers to live in the reality that his triune self exists as a fountain of blessings already living within them.

3. Love is a gift from God through Jesus, and love is the means of receiving the greatest gift, i.e., the fullness of God within. Love is the "already" and the "not yet" of the Christian life, the beginning and the end.

4. What is the "fullness of God?" "Fullness" must in part be a reference to the persons of the Trinity, but it also implies

more than their personal presence. The fullness of God within must also refer to all the attributes of God that humans can share, with love being foremost.

5. Paul desires that the Ephesians experientially know their inherited blessings in God—that they abound in God's love by having intimate relationships with the triune God who abounds in grace, love, and power.

Interpret! Interpret! Interpret!

Respond!

It is at this point that wholistic and reasoned responses become very important. The interpretations you list should be the most certain of your entire study. You should now be confident you have a good grasp of what the Biblical text says and means. By the Holy Spirit, you are becoming more and more one with the Word of God. As we have noted in previous chapters, true knowledge of the Word of God results in conformity with the Word. Your questions should have moved more completely from desires to understand to questions of how to truly and completely be in this world an expression of the Word of God, to be one with God.

Write your responses in two forms. One form should be more general and give expression to what God desires of everyone. The other form should be more specific and state what God is calling you to be and/or do. To Paul's prayer we might respond:

1. We should measure our relationship with God by His known presence in our lives and we must measure His known presence in our lives by the presence of His character in our lives. Father, cause your love to abound in us that we might know you more fully.

2. I must become more conscious of the ebbs and flows of God's love within my life so that I might be more and more confident of my relationship with and

knowledge of my triune God. Father, help me to become a more faithful expression of your love.

Respond! Respond! Respond!

Chapter 17

Artistic Interpretation

"Have I the skill to draw the natural inferences deductible from each text?"

—John Wesley

The ultimate end of a RIBS study is the renewing and strengthening of one's personal relationship with God. The penultimate goal is to rightly hear and rightly respond to the Word of God. Each person is responsible for taking the journey that leads to conformity with the will of God as revealed in the Bible. Sometimes the will of God for us explodes forth from a single verse. When it does, rejoice and obey. But, as we have stated over and over, the Bible is primarily to be studied as books of divinely inspired literature. The great truths of the Bible must be garnered by looking at the individual books and rightly interpreting their primary messages. As a RIBS study comes to a climax, it is important to write down in your own words the big ideas you have discovered.

You should take the time needed to prayerfully reflect on the big picture of the book you have been studying and write some summative notes in your notebook. What is the main message of the book? State any sub-messages that stand out to you. Briefly describe the book as literature. Include the structure of the book and any literary techniques that seem significant. How has God spoken to you personally through your study? How has your study impacted your life (be specific)? What is God calling you to out of this study when viewed as a whole? Thoughtful answers to these questions should engage your creative mind and prepare you to paint an interpretive picture of the book.

Re-creating the Word

When done well, Bible study results in thinking the thoughts of God after Him. This is a process of absorbing and re-thinking what God is saying. But it is more than thinking; it is, by the Holy Spirit, to become a living extension of God's Word, a process of translating words on a page into the fullness of life that God desires for us. God desires for us to become creative expressions of His Word.

Earlier we wrote about the importance of imagination and creativity for RIBS. From childhood, we all progressively built our verbal skills at the expense of other forms of communication. In the process we became better and better at expressing ourselves with words. The unfortunate side effect was that we progressively limited our imaginations and stifled other forms of creative expression. We lost touch with the things we needed to fully communicate our inner realities.

Always remember that the Word of God is given to communicate more than ideas. It addresses the totality of our human existence and not merely our brains. Artistic expression is a means of relearning how to speak from the depths of who we really are. Artistic expression is therefore a powerful tool for a thorough interpretation of a book of the Bible.

Yes, we must guard against allowing our imaginations to add to or distort what the Bible is saying. But we must use our imaginations in order to truly see what God intends for us to see. Without imagination, we cannot even formulate thoughts into words or translate words into concepts of meaning. Imagination is required to close the gap between symbols and meaning.

We need imagination in order to make observations, in order to "connect the dots." Likewise, without imagination there can be no interpretation. Interpretation is a creative art as well as a disciplined science. To truly understand a passage of Scripture, we must filter it through our own perceptions of reality; we must make a personal connection with it and own it as our own. We must receive into ourselves the Word of God as Word of God. We must embrace it and allow it to embrace us.

Receiving the Word of God requires that we interpret its meaning. Interpretation of the Bible is a process of creatively putting into our own words, images, feelings and/or sounds what God is saying through the biblical text. Interpretation is thus an act of constructing within our hearts and minds the message that God is giving to us and to the world.

We have not truly heard the Word of God until we are faithful echoes of the Word of God.

Good interpretation then does not end with seeing what the Scriptures reveal; it must spring forth into doing what the Word of God is doing, participating with God in His new creation. We have not truly heard the Word of God until we are faithful echoes of the Word of God. Hearing with our ears, believing with our hearts, and doing with our hands must merge into what was meant by the Old English word "hearken." To hearken is to listen attentively with an expectation of compliance. It is in hearkening to God's voice that we become "living epistles" of the gospel of Jesus Christ.

The Holy Spirit is with us and in us to accomplish these things. The Spirit who brooded over the face of the deep and called forth life (Gen 1:2) is present to brood over the depths of our being and with the Word of life call forth understanding and meaning, and more. The Spirit desires to join with us in making our very existence a creative expression, i.e., a living epistle, of God's ongoing work in the world. In this we can truly "re-member," or make new in our world, the eternal Word of God by formulating words, images, affections, and behaviors that are faithful representations of the Word.

Chart the Book

Giving artistic interpretation to portions of the Bible can invigorate our reasoned thoughts by lifting us out of their limitations. It can peel back the layers of learned religious slogans to expose the depths of what we are coming to know of God through our encounters with Him in His Word. The Bible can be interpreted and expressed as paintings, sculptures, dioramas, musical scores, and any other expression of the truth that lies within the text. Poems and songs may serve this purpose if the artist can rise to the level of communicating the meaning of a text and avoid simply recounting the narrative or summarizing the prose.

A foundational task for giving artistic expression to a book is to create a chart that displays how the message of the book is developed within the structure of the book. Such a chart is simply a "worded" visual that creates an image of the book as a whole and provides a 'bird's eye view' of the content and structure of the book. This kind of chart connects all the titles you created for the various divisions, subdivisions, sub-subdivisions, and segments in a manner that reveals how they unfold. [In future studies, you will find it beneficial to prepare this chart as you work your way through the inductive methods.]

In this model, the titles for major divisions are distinct and set apart on horizontal lines. They stand alone on the chart, e.g., "Blessed by God" and "Walking (Living) in Christ." The beginning and ending Scripture references for the major divisions are placed under the line on which they appear, with the beginning reference and the ending reference framing this line.

Under each major division the subdivisions, sub-subdivisions and the segments appear. The subdivision titles are elevated above the sub-subdivision titles and are placed at the point where the subdivision begins, e.g., "Blessed by the Father." The sub-subdivision titles then appear sequentially on horizontal lines (e.g., "Every Spiritual Blessing," etc.). Between each of the sub-subdivision titles, there is a slanted vertical line (a forward slash). Beneath each of these lines, appears the Scripture reference that identifies the beginning of the segment.

Note that except for "Walk as Wise" the sub-subdivisions also serve as segments. The "Walk as Wise" sub-subdivision is further divided into four segments (e.g., "The Will of the Lord," etc.).

Figure 17.1 -- "Chart of Ephesians"

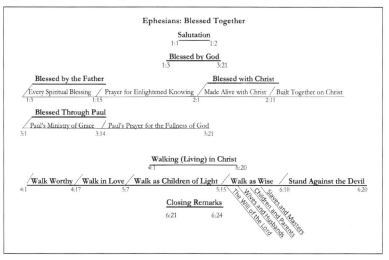

Use this kind of chart to gain a sense of the flow and intensity of the book. Refer to it often as a means of keeping your artistic interpretations firmly grounded in the written text.

Visual Artistic Interpretations

Visual artistic interpretations of a text are by their nature symbolic, in the whole and in each part. With them, elements of the book are symbolically represented. The larger goal, however, is to visually communicate the author's main message and not to provide all of the details the author included to support the message.

Don't worry about how good of an artist you are. The point of this exercise is not to create a great work of art but for you to see and re-create the Word of God in a new light, to 'speak' the Word in an alternative language. Let yourself become that little child who is entering the "kingdom of heaven" with no other desire than to draw a picture to share with their parent. While you might choose to show the artwork to others, you do not have to do that. It may exist only for your own benefit as a personal interpretation of a book of the Bible—one you hang on the private 'refrigerator' of your heart and mind.

The question is, how can I best visually communicate the essence of a book of the Bible? The image can be as simple as a stick-figure drawing or as complex as a three-dimensional, interlocking puzzle. Just keep in mind that the best artistic interpretations (1) give expression to the theme of the book; (2) are structured to represent the structure of the book, especially the major divisions; and (3) serve as a visual reminder of major elements of the contents of the book.

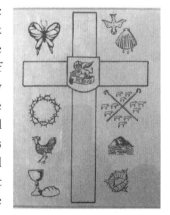

To the right, you will notice an artistic visualization of the Gospel of Mark created by one of our students quite some time ago.[1] On the reverse side of the picture the student provided a key explaining what each of the items in the painting represented. The central images in the painting are the Cross and the winged lion. The winged creature in the Cross is an ancient symbol for Mark. It represents how the

---

[1] The artist was Winfield Bevins who granted us permission to use it.

book begins with John the Baptist preaching like a lion in the wilderness.

The Cross in the picture serves two purposes. First, it represents how Mark's Gospel places a major emphasis on the Cross and Christ's movement toward it, making the crucifixion the climax of the story. Second, the Cross divides the picture into four sections representing the student's division of Mark into four sections (1:1-13; 1:14-8:33; 8:34-15:47; 16:1-20). The sections move clockwise from the upper right corner which represents the brief preface (1:1-13). The two sections beneath the cross represent the two major divisions of the book (1:14-8:33; 8:34-15:47). And the upper left-hand corner represents Mark's conclusion (16:1-20).

The symbols represent major events in the Gospel. The dove and shell with dripping water symbolize the Spirit descending on Jesus at His baptism. The shepherd's staffs and sheep represent the calling of the Twelve to follow Jesus as their shepherd. The mountain and lake represent the ministry of Christ in the region of Galilee. The three fish represent the feeding of the multitudes.

On the lower left-side of the Cross, the second major division (8:34-15:47) is depicted with symbols representing the Last Supper, Peter's denial, and the crucifixion. In the final division, the butterfly is a symbol of the resurrection.

To the right is another student artistic interpretation of Mark's Gospel. For this student, the major theme of Mark centers around the "Messianic Secret." Jesus repeatedly told people not to reveal who He was, yet His divinity kept breaking through. The montage depicts this by placing Christ behind broken glass that is falling away to let him be clearly seen. If you look closely, there are other symbolic elements within the image.

Written and Aural Interpretations

Musicians might choose to express their interpretations of a book of the Bible as original music. Music can capture the tone, intensity, and emotion of a book in ways that visual art cannot. Of course, lyrics would add another layer of interpretation. Much of the same effect might be achieved through scripted poetry designed to be read aloud.

Other forms of creative writing might be used to interpret the book. A parable or short story might be used. The story line should loosely follow the structure of the book. More importantly, the story should capture the themes of the book.

Song lyrics, poems and other creative writing should not attempt to summarize the book. They should offer a creative interpretation of the primary message of the book. To the degree possible, they should capture the ebb and flow of the book's structure and thematic emphasis. The objective is to use your artistic talents to present your interpretation of the book in a form to help people grasp the essential message of the author.

Don't get stressed out about this task! Just tap into your inner child and express what the book has come to mean to you.

Chapter 18

Other Inductive Methods

Seek Him in the written word,
Christ in every page they see,
See, and apprehend their Lord;
Every scripture makes Him known,
Testifies of Christ alone.
Here I cannot seek in vain;
Digging deep into the mine,
Hidden treasure I obtain
Pure, eternal Life Divine,
Find Him in his Spirit given,
Christ the Way, the Truth of heaven.

—Charles Wesley

Several focused methods for inductive study of the Bible exist: topical, doctrinal, character study, geographical, chronological, historical, rhetorical, and others. Aspects of each have already surfaced during the completion of a foundational inductive study, but focusing on one aspect of a book often surfaces things missed when studying segments.

We highly recommend that you only use these focused methods after completing the primary methods described in earlier chapters. It is possible to ignore this advice and apply a focused method to a book without completing the primary methods first. Any inductive study can bear fruit provided the inductive approach is followed: observe, observe, observe, before interpreting. However, a focused study is greatly benefited by first knowing the literary context in which the concept was developed.

The Topical and Doctrinal Methods

The topical method is a focused look at how the author uses the literary technique of recurrence to highlight a given topic. Topics can be anything that seems to have recurring presence in the book: fasting, prayer, temple worship, the role of women, healing, or anything else that seems to have some significance for the author. If the topic is doctrinal in nature, it could be labeled as the doctrinal method. This method should only be used to study topics (doctrines) significant for the development of the author's message—topics woven into the development of the theme.

Topics may be developed explicitly or implicitly. You can identify explicit topics through the recurrence of words, phrases, concepts, or happenings. Implicit topics may prove more difficult to identify, but they are no less important. Observing the explicit should trigger careful scanning for the implicit. For example, in John's Gospel, the word *believe* occurs about fifty times, which suggests it is a major theme for the book—one begging for a more focused study. That study must explore how John develops the theme using complex events and characters. The concept of believing is much more than a simple word study.

This topical method can prove very beneficial for spiritual growth and development. It provides heightened opportunity to be transformed in our thinking and behavior in that it allows us to present our beliefs and patterns of living to God for examination by the Scriptures.

Begin this method with a review of your notes (especially your observations) from earlier study with a focus on what you observed about the topic at hand. Give special attention to any notes that point toward connections between the topic and the main message of the book. In that way you will have a better understanding of the context in which the topic arises in the author's mind.

The topical method allows us to present our beliefs and patterns of living to God for examination by the Scriptures.

Following the review of notes, identify and list all the segments in which the topic is addressed, whether explicitly or implicitly (see Appendix D). This may require a quick re-read of the book. Revisit each segment in which the topic appears, and study what and how the topic contributes to the segment. Then, progressing from the beginning to the ending of the book, trace how the topic connects the segments in which it appears. Finally, make observations about how the topic contributes to the book as a whole.

Once you have completed these observations, interpret the meaning of the topic for the book as a whole and for your life. Begin by developing your interpretation of the author's definition of the topic, that is, what does the concept mean to the author? Then wrestle with why the topic is important for the author. What does it say that is important about Christian faith and life? Write a summative statement about the topic as used in the book.

As you complete these interpretations, allow them to critique you. What is God saying to you about you? Are there things for which you need to give thanks and praise? Are there areas of your life that need to change? If so, what must you do to make those changes? Be specific. Returning to Ephesians and the topic of grace as our example, we observed earlier that grace was a recurring term in the first half of the epistle. We observed that Paul used the word in his regular formula for salutations and conclusions (1:2; 6:24). We may now observe that in addition to the ones we observed in our earlier study of the first division, there are two instances early in the second division (see the fourth chapter) for a total of twelve verses in which the word appears (1:6, 7; 2:5, 7, 8; 3:2, 7, 8; 4:7, 29).

In addition to the opening and closing formulaic uses, the word "grace" appears in five of the eleven segments of the book: "Every Spiritual Blessing" (1:3-14), "Made Alive with Christ" (2:1-10), "Paul's Ministry of Grace" (3:1-13), "Walk Worthy" (4:1-16), and "Walk in Light" (5:7-14). This seems to imply that grace is a foundational element of all Paul is teaching, especially in the more doctrinal first division.

In the first division (Chapters 1-3), grace appears in the first segment of each subdivision but not in the second segment of any of them. It also appears in the first segment of the second division and the next-to-last segment. Furthermore, three of the twelve appearances (one-fourth of them) are in the same segment, the one where Paul describes his ministry (3:1-13). Paul seems especially aware of grace in his own life and ministry. Also, the uses of grace are weighted toward the beginning of the book and the beginning of divisions/subdivisions. This seems to imply that for Paul, grace is a central theme of his own relationship with God and a fountainhead of what he teaches, i.e., the gospel. All the blessings of God flow out of grace.

For the sake of time and space, we will only look closely at the first segment, where "grace" first appears. The remainder of our look at "grace" in Ephesians will be based on our having already studied grace in each of the segments in which it appears. Note that the following observations on the first segment rely on having respaced the text. We can observe that: This entire segment is extravagant in its description of the blessings that have come from God. Grace is not an exception. The Father's "glorious grace" has been "lavished on us" (v. 6). In the Beloved One (Christ) we have redemption "according to the riches of his grace that he richly poured out on us" (v. 7).

- Of the three primary blessings, grace is only associated with the middle one—our adoption—and not with being chosen or with having the mystery revealed to us. It should also be noted that "adoption" is parallel with "redemption." Grace brings both into being.

- Grace is attributed to the Father and the Son using parallel wording. While in grammatical structure the grace from Christ is "subordinate" to that which comes from the Father, they are comparable in nature, i.e., the Father's grace is "glorious" and "lavished on us," while the grace of the Son is "rich" and has been "richly poured out on us."

- God has predestined us to adoption not "by" His grace, but "to" the praise of His grace. God's blessings to us reveal His glorious grace as being praiseworthy. Grace is "of" God and not just "from" God.

We now skip to observations about how grace connects to other segments and to the book as a whole.

- First, there are four phrases containing the word "grace" that appear twice each in the book: "saved by grace" appears twice in the same segment (2:5, 8); the uses of "riches of his grace" do not appear together (1:7; 2:7); "God's grace" appears twice in the same segment (3:2, 7); and "grace was given" is split between two segments (3:8; 4:7). Interestingly, both appearances of "saved by grace" are in the same segment, and both appearances of "God's grace" are together in a segment, while the other two dyads are entirely separated. We might conclude (or interpret) from this that one emphasis of Ephesians is that grace is God's abundant gift by which Christians are saved.

- Second, multiple references exist in Ephesians to grace being a gift: "that he lavished on us" (1:6), "that he richly poured out on us" (1:8), "the immeasurable riches of his grace" (2:7), "it is God's gift" (2:8), the "gift of God's grace" (3:7), "grace was given to me" [Paul] (3:8), "grace was given to each one of us" (4:7), and it is "Christ's gift" (4:7). Grace is therefore understood in one sense as an object to be received. Paul does not say that God "graced us" or "gifted us" with salvation. He says rather that God gifted us with grace, which is then the agent of salvation (2:5, 2:8). This seems significant since the root meaning of grace is the idea of a gift.

- Grace is an object of praise in that it is spoken of with a sense of grandeur: "glorious grace," which He "lavished on us" (1:6), and "riches of his grace" (1:7; 2:7). Also, the grace given to each believer is according to the measure of Christ (4:7). This later statement appears to refer to the sufficiency of grace to bring believers into maturity and unto the full stature of Christ's fullness (4:13-14).

- We saw in Chapter 1 that grace is presented as coming from both the Father and Christ. Both attributions are repeated later in the book: the Father in 2:7 and 3:2, and Christ in 4:7. Grace is a gift from the triune Godhead.

- It is also of interest that a shift in tenses takes place between the chapters. In the first segment of the book (1: 3-14) the blessings are mostly described as having been given and received (past tense). This continues into the third segment (2:1-10) where Paul emphasizes that their transformation has (past tense) come by grace, that is, they once were dead in their offences, but they now are "alive together with Christ." Their present realities are highlighted by the repetition of the climatic phrase, "you are saved by grace" (2:6, 8).

- In the same segment, the future state of believers is introduced in terms of grace: "so that in the coming ages he might display the immeasurable riches of his grace" (2:7). Clearly, Paul attributes all the blessings given to those who are in Christ to grace: past, present, and future.

- On the other hand, there are agents (means) of grace: Paul is a means of grace (3:2), and Christian speech is a means of grace (4:29). Grace can be mediated through persons and their speech. Furthermore, the first segment of the second division (4:1-16) implies that as gifts come from the ascended Christ, the ministers of the church are also a means of grace.

From all this we can conclude (interpret) that (1) Paul understands grace to be a gift that God has provided as an abundant fountainhead of blessings for those called to be in Christ; (2) grace encompasses all of the blessings that come from God: past, present and future; (3) grace is more than sufficient to bring believers as one body into the fullness of Christ; (4) grace is communicable, that is, persons who have received grace can be the means of grace coming to others; (5) grace is almost, but not quite, personified; it is a central agent of our salvation; and (6) contrary to what some believe, in the book of Ephesians, Paul makes it clear that the grace of God is without limit.

In terms of response, we are left with many questions: (1) How might we better express thanksgiving for the grace we have received? (2) In what ways are we living (or not living) in the abundance of God's grace? (3) Where does our focus on grace rest: past, present, or future? (4) In an age of individualism, how can we expand our concept of grace to encompass unity with other Christians? (5) From whom are we receiving grace and to whom should we knowingly minister grace? (6) What must we do to be more effective in communicating the grace of God to those who need it?

We should remember that while the Bible is one book, and there is only one faith, that does not mean that the authors of the various books of the Bible held to a set of exact definitions for the vocabulary they used. Paul's concept of grace was not exactly the same as Peter's concept. As with us, the meanings of words and concepts shifted over time as people had new experiences and God refined their theologies. The apostles who wrote about growing in knowledge and faith were themselves continuing to grow in knowledge and faith as they wrote.

Beyond that, at any given time, within each book, each writer used his own vocabulary in slightly different ways depending on the context in which a word was used. Understanding a word or concept in the Bible should begin with trying to understand its meaning in its specific contexts. The combinations of those more specific meanings should guide our theology. Therefore, topical studies should always begin by focusing on the topic in a single book being inductively studied. After that, feel free to compare and contrast the topic within and between other books. That is, understand Paul's theology of grace in Ephesians before comparing it with his theology of grace in his other epistles, and study all of Paul's uses before comparing them with Peter's theology of grace in his epistles.

One of the strengths of the topical/doctrinal method is that the process involves looking at the text through a different set of lenses. This method is a tool for seeing things that may have been overlooked during the earlier basic inductive study of a book. Many of the things seen by using the method may not directly relate to the topic being studied. They will add to the list of observations previously made and may thereby strengthen, refine, or even correct interpretations made earlier. When a topical study is done well, it enriches the entire study of a book.

The Character-Study Method

The character-study method is another focused study that provides additional insights to the book as a whole. The character-study method is, as the name implies, the study of one or more characters within the book. The study may provide lessons based singularly on the character's life, that is, "Here is someone I want to be like, or not." But its greater purpose is to see what the character contributes to the main message of the book. In other words, character studies involve much more than studying the actions and personalities of individual characters in a book. Characters are literary tools used to build the author's message.

Character studies are closely associated with narratives such as the Gospels, but do not overlook their potential for use in other types of literature. Virtually all books have characters connected to them. Sometimes the character is largely "off stage" but well developed by the author through allusions.

In narratives, character development serves as the primary tool authors use to develop their themes. They have main characters and various levels of supporting characters, who may be loosely identified by the space given to the character. Exceptions to this rule of thumb exist, but the number of verses containing a reference to a character is a good place to begin when looking for how important they are to the plot.

Characters may also be grouped in terms of their relationships with the main characters. The main character is the protagonist. Typically, another leading character, the antagonist, has the role of opposing the main character. (This role may be filled by a group.) The struggle between these two main characters circumscribes the main message of the narrative.

Supporting characters usually align with one of the main characters, although they may switch sides before the story is over. Then there are characters who are little more than props, those who do not work toward or against either set of leading characters; they serve only as a support material for the character development of others.

Characters include more than individual persons. In narratives, groups of persons may function like a single character. For example, in the Gospels, groups such as the crowds, demons, scribes and Pharisees all function like single characters. Characters identified as being a member of a group may represent the group or be an exception to the group.

Character studies should follow the same pattern as topical studies given above. Choose one character to study at a time. Study the character in the context of individual segments in which they appear. Pay special attention to the relationships that character has and how the character contributes to the themes of the book. Study the character's development throughout the book from beginning to end. Pay attention to transforming crisis experiences.

In the Scriptures, authors commonly employ tandem characters to emphasize themes: Moses and Joshua, Elijah and Elisha, Saul and David, David and Solomon, Jesus and the Holy Spirit, Peter and Paul. These connected characters may appear in the same book or in a multi-volume series such as 1 and 2 Kings or Luke-Acts. These character relationships are a form of parallelism. The second character either repeats many of the experiences of the first with similar responses, or the second character provides a moral/spiritual contrast. Comparing parallel characters can prove helpful for honing in on the theme of a book and on the author's desired response to that theme.

In terms of response, character studies can serve as well-lit mirrors for us to look at ourselves. What is my "gut response" to this character? Why? How would I have related to this character if we had lived in the same time and place? Why? In what ways would I have acted the same as this character? What traits do I share with this character, both good and bad? What does God want me to learn from this character?

The Geographical Method

The geographical method can be a helpful focused look at a book after completing the foundational methods in the inductive approach. Because the "where" question has already been addressed at various points in an inductive study, some geographic references should already have been noted, if they exist. If there have been multiple references, it is good to take the extra time needed to ask why the author considered that information important. What purpose does it serve in the development of the author's message to note the places where events took place?

The geographical method requires the use of Bible maps and can be augmented with the use of Bible dictionaries and encyclopedias. Geography is one means of measuring the scope of a narrative. For example, readers often tend to see the ministry of Christ as limited to the region immediately around the Sea of Galilee and in Jerusalem.

A geographical study of Mark's Gospel reveals that Mark divides the ministry of Jesus differently than the other Gospels. He makes no reference to Christ making multiple trips to Jerusalem and teaching there. Instead, following Jesus's baptism by John (1:1-13) in the Jordan River near Jerusalem, Mark presents the ministry of Christ as predominantly in the region of Galilee (1:14-10:52) until He makes His journey to Jerusalem to be crucified (11:1-13:33). Once Jesus is in Jerusalem, Mark gives great details of the movements of Jesus in and around the city.

Mark also presents Jesus as having traveled outside of Judea and Galilee; the two regions most closely associated with Judaism. Christ went as far away as the ancient ports of Tyre and Sidon on the Mediterranean Sea to the northwest of Israel and traveled through the region of the Decapolis (7:24-37). Both these locations were Roman areas where Jews were in the minority. The geography takes on even more significance when connected to the accounts of Jesus casting demons out of Gentiles in both regions (5:1-20; 7:24-30).

In Mark 5, Jesus crosses the Sea of Galilee to the region of the Gerasenes. There Jesus casts a legion of demons out of a man. The demons enter a herd of swine that then rush into the sea and drown. The Decapolis was a region east of the Jordan River defined by the ten Roman cities that constituted the region. The man was no doubt a Gentile, for Mark is clear that after his deliverance he went throughout the Gentile region announcing what the Lord had done and that this was at the instruction of Jesus.

The story of the Syrophoenician woman whose daughter had a demon inside her (Mark 7:24-30) takes on different shades of meaning when one considers that Jesus was on her 'turf' in a Roman port city in the region of Phoenicia. The house Jesus enters is no doubt part of a Jewish community in the town, but unlike Galilee or Judea, Jews would have been the minority population there. In that setting, Christ's response to let the children be fed "first" seems to imply more strongly that the gospel was coming to the Gentiles than if he had spoken those words back in Galilee.

These geographical facts have strong implications for understanding the breadth of Christ's ministry in Mark and Mark's understanding of Christ's vision for His Kingdom. The Messiah went among the Gentiles and ministered to their needs. Perhaps the portability of the gospel was implied by the fact the two of the Gentile places He visited were port cities.

Chronological and Historical Methods

The chronological and historical methods for studying a book of the Bible are closely related. Both also gain help by the student's use of Bible dictionaries and encyclopedias.

For both methods, keep in mind that in biblical times, time was not measured the way it is in our time. For us, time is largely linear; we count the hours and check the days off the calendar one after the other. In biblical times, time referred more to cycles and events, to seasons more than years. For that reason, chronological time might be thought of as sequential time. The emphasis is more on the order of events than on the exact time of events. With that said, some references to time are intended to convey a more linear sense of duration. Mark's references to Jesus being crucified at "the third hour" (9:00 a.m.), the skies going dark at "the sixth hour" (noon), and Jesus dying at "the ninth hour" (3:00 p.m.) convey important information about how long Jesus suffered on the Cross.

As noted earlier, there were no clocks in biblical times, so references to time were made predominantly in terms of events. When doing a chronological study, you must look for symbolic representations of time, like time-bound events. For instance, Peter denied Christ when the rooster crowed, which is a reference to dawn. Events such as Passover take place on designated days of the year and may be used by an author to reference time as duration—that is, three Passovers equal three years. However, even in those situations, the reference to Passover is always more to the meaning of the Passover event than to the chronological passing of time.

Chronological studies may focus on the chronology within the book. In that case, it essentially focuses on the "when" question as it threads through the text as a whole. When the book references events that took place before the book was written, though, those events should be studied as well. In addition to that, chronology may look at significant events not mentioned in the book but known to be contemporary with the main event at hand. For example, it is helpful when studying one of Paul's epistles to place it within the chronology of his other epistles and his missionary journeys.

The historical method is like the chronological method except that it places more emphasis on events in history than a chronological study does. The historical method attempts to put the content of the book into historical perspective. It expands the "what" question to look at historical information that might lie behind the author's writings. Are there historical events that took place at the time the book was written that may have influenced the author? Are there historical events to which the author referred explicitly or implicitly? What was significant about those events as it relates to the author's mindset? In short, this method looks at the book as a historical document, written in a historical context, and influenced by historical events. When, why, and how do historical events shed light on the author's meaning?

Be Creative

Many different methodological lenses exist through which one might look at a book of the Bible. Be creative, but not too creative. You may think of a lens that is unique to the book you are studying. For example, you may be aware that Luke was a physician, and that fact could trigger a legitimate method of looking at Luke's writings through the lens of first-century medicine. Or, you might look through Peter's epistles with the lens of first-century fishing to see if there were any influences from his early livelihood.

Be careful to limit the lenses you use to those appropriate for the time in which the book was written. It is a major mistake to interpret biblical literature from the perspective of later realities. Looking at Luke's writings through the lens of twenty-first-century medicine may be fun, but it will tell us nothing of what was in Luke's mind when he wrote. It will more likely distort his message.

Modern science has much to tell us about how the universe works, but it has very little, if anything, to tell us about the meanings and intentions of biblical authors. Trying to prove that things recorded in the Bible are scientifically sound could strengthen a person's theology—depending on the person—but might also harm a person's faith. The process is contrary to the nature of the Bible as Word of God. Such examinations will not lead to hearing the voice of God in the Scriptures better; they reduce the Bible to a specimen to deconstruct using current scientific beliefs. Faith in the truthfulness of Scripture should not require modern scientific verification. Let the Bible speak on its own terms.

Chapter 19

Yielding to the Spirit: RIBS in Small Groups

"If any doubt still remains, I consult those who are experienced in the
things of God; and then the writings whereby, being dead,
they yet speak. And what I thus learn, that I teach."

—John Wesley

Each week small groups gather in homes or in churches for Bible study. The people who attend these groups do so because they love God, each other, and the Bible. However, often pastors and group leaders feel at a loss as to the right curriculum. Also, it seems that small groups tend to go toward one of two extremes. When they study the Bible, people either sit and listen to someone lecture, or they have a "free for all" with the discussion going in many directions—most of the time away from the text.

Inductive Bible study, when practiced in the context of a small group, has the same transformative power as when someone studies the Bible alone. It can help a group come to know and love the Word of God. It helps to keep the focus on the Bible and away from tangents. It allows people to participate in a shared exploration of God's Word instead of being passive receivers of a lecture.

Group leaders can learn not only how to study the Bible inductively, but they can also learn a method of inductively leading people into the Word of God so they encounter the sacred Scriptures as Living Word that transforms.

Below we describe a Relational Inductive model for leading small groups in Bible study. This teaching-learning process involves four movements, which we have named: "Sharing our Testimonies," "Searching the Scriptures," "Yielding to the Spirit" and "Responding to the Call." These four movements serve to take learners from life, into the Scriptures, and back into life.

In this model, the entire teaching-learning process is rooted in an inductive approach to study. Moreover, this model seeks to honor the Holy Spirit as the lead teacher and the one ever-present in the Word of God and active in the lives of all believers. Often, Bible study curriculum gives lip service to the work of the Holy Spirit but limits how the Spirit works in the teaching-learning process.

The model seeks to go beyond "the Holy Spirit will help you understand" into a more dynamic understanding that the Spirit desires to be active in all aspects of group Bible study. The Spirit who inhabits the Scriptures also inhabits the leader and the members of the group. Gathered around the Bible, they are by the Spirit gathered with Christ as their Lord. With that realization they should experience Bible study as a time when "the Holy Spirit brings them into the very presence of a living God." Get the difference? It is a life-changing one.

A Different Kind of Group Bible Study

Before preparing a lesson for Bible study, it will help to consider the general nature of both the group and of the leader of a group in Relational Inductive Bible Study. When we speak of groups in the context of the church, we are speaking of far more than a small gathering of individuals. Groups are persons-in-relationship. In groups, individuals soon get to know each other, really know about each other. They develop concern for each other and demonstrate that concern through acts of care and commitment. In that kind of environment, it is possible to shift the group away from thinking about existing for personal development to thinking about itself as existing for the life and development of the group and its members.

Group Bible study can become more than the sum of its parts. If we believe that Jesus gathers with two or three who come together in His name, and if we believe the Church is the body of Christ, then we should understand a small church group as a living expression of the body of Christ. As such, the Holy Spirit dwells there and gives gifts to the group through its members.

Relational Inductive Bible Study calls for the group members to adopt a mission-mindedness for Bible study. We study not just for ourselves and for understanding but to faithfully submit to the Word. While it is important to properly interpret the Scriptures, our goal must be to allow the Scriptures to interpret us and give direction to our lives. We must strive to be doers of the Word and not just hearers. Through ongoing obedience to God's Word we are empowered to live a joyous and fulfilling life.

> While it is important to properly interpret the Scriptures, our goal must be to allow the Scriptures to interpret us and give direction to our lives.

In this process, each individual must search the Scriptures and walk in the light of God's Word as He shines it upon his or her path. However, each must also recognize that no Scripture is of private interpretation. The search for truth in the Scriptures must serve as a function of the group as well as of the individual. Bible study should have as a goal finding agreement as to the meaning of and response to a text. When this is not forthcoming, though, the group should encourage each person to remain faithful to his or her own understanding and commitments. We learn from each other and draw strength from each other, but shared learning happens best when we honor each other as free-thinking individuals. Each member must be faithful to what he or she believes God is saying personally to them through the text. This kind of Bible study leads to unity without a demand for uniformity.

There is a place and time for teachers to be authority figures and dispensers of information, but this type of group Bible study is neither the time nor place for that. In Relational Inductive Bible Study, the leader is not so much an instructor as a guide and a co-learner. The role of the leader is to guide the group into an inductive study in which every member participates in an exploration of the Bible. As a guide, the leader must go ahead of the group and scout out the land in order to facilitate the shared journey into the Word. As a member of the group, the leader must desire to learn from all the members. Effective leading requires effective listening.

There are two other roles for the leader. First, the leader must develop the skills needed to lead a small group. For inductive Bible study, this includes establishing norms for how the group will work together in Bible study: each person must feel safe in the group, each should have equal opportunity to contribute as they desire, everyone's contribution should be respected, no one should dominate the discussion, and disagreements about the text should never be personal.

Second, the leader is a co-learner but must also ensure that the group has any needed resources. Specifically, the leader must ensure the group has access to essential extra-biblical information, e.g., important background information not contained in the text. This might include questions related to authorship, historical context, geographic context and maps, unfamiliar characters, definitions of terms, etc. If the information is in the text, the leader typically should not provide it. If it is not in the text, the leader should interject it at the point the information is needed, or the leader could prepare handouts with the information.

A Word about Selected Passages

You have been assigned as teacher of a young adult Bible study class. The church school director gives you a teacher's manual and perhaps a teacher's commentary. You notice that the lessons are on different topics for each session. Moreover, you observe that lessons may contain Scripture texts from different books of the Bible, all united around a common theme.

How do you apply direct-inductive Bible study to this situation? You do not have time to do a book study each week. Do you just go by the outline given in the teacher's manual and forget doing your own in-depth study? No! You do not have to abandon inductive Bible study in favor of the teacher's manual. You can incorporate good inductive study, glean from the teacher's manual, and create a powerful lesson plan.

While the material given in Sunday school manuals is helpful, it is never meant to replace your own direct study of God's Word. You should compare your work with others for support and modification, but each lesson should be your own.

You can apply RIBS to the study of selected passages. You just scale down or condense your book study. We recommend choosing one or two of the selected passages and focusing on those for your lesson. Break these down into segments, and follow the steps listed below. Teach the segment or a group of segments. The theme will arise from a good study of the segment. Remember, you are teaching the Bible, not the commentary, and not a theme. Don't let the commentary override the Scriptures, and do not let the text get lost in the themes. In other words, let the Word of God speak. Allow it to come alive before your students.

Steps to Follow in Studying Selected Passages

1. Survey the passage for the overall message. Read the entire passage in one sitting. Then, do several more readings.

2. Discover—Look for the main theme and how it is developed. Don't forget to ask the questions Who? What? When? Where? How? and Why? (You may want to consult other sources on how your passage fits into the overall picture of the book from which it is taken.)

3. Divide the passage into segments. Give titles to each segment.

4. Respace the segments, noting the independent and supporting phrases.

5. Observe—Write your observations from the text.

6. Outline—From your analysis of the text, write an outline of major and supporting points

7. Interpret—Write personal responses and implications of this text for life. From this section you would write the aim of your lesson.

8. Compare—At this point you should consult your teacher's manual, commentaries, and so forth to compare your analysis of the passage with others.

Remember! Your study should be unique to you, yet within the general range of the others you have consulted.

Developing a Lesson

Now we will turn to Psalm 73 and use it to illustrate how to develop a learning session and how to lead a group in Relational Inductive Bible Study. Before we proceed, put yourself in the role of the leader of a group Bible study. Stop and do your own inductive study of

Psalm 73. When you have finished, come back here, and we will proceed together to see how the Psalm might be studied in a group.

Determine a Learning Objective

As a leader you have already carefully studied the passage to be studied, and you know the main themes and divisions of the text. You have already made many observations on the literary structure and devices. You have interpreted much of the text, and you are aware of the time and effort this required. Not all members of your group will be willing to do that level of work.

You must become their guide to the essential truths of the text being considered, and you must do that in a way that preserves their joy of discovery. It is all too tempting to tell them what you discovered instead of leading them on a shared journey of discovery and response. You will need to map out the journey, draw them into the search, and help them stay on track. You must explore the text with them as if for the first time.

Mapping out the journey begins with the theme of the text being studied. As guide, your primary responsibility is to keep the main point the main point. Discovering and responding to the main theme is the primary objective of inductive Bible study. As leader, your goal, then, is to guide them into discovering for themselves the main theme of the text. Discovering the main theme through shared observations and interpretations should lead to the pinnacle of the journey, a sense of corporate response to the Scriptures.

Think in terms of developing a clear aim for the entire session, one that passes through the entire session. Keep it concise, focused, and achievable during the time limits of a group session. On the other hand, it should include an active, measurable, behavioral response that points to "real life" outside of the sessions. Additionally, you should write it from the standpoint of the learners. Look at the destination through eyes of group members.

Poor aims are broad and without specific action on the part of learners. For instance, a poor aim for Psalm 73 might read: For the students to appreciate the sovereignty of God over both good and evil. This is a poor aim because it stops short of life response. It does not even indicate how one will know when the students "appreciate the sovereignty of God." How does one measure "appreciation?" Too many Bible study sessions have these vague and general aims. As a result, learners rarely accept responsibility to do anything as a result of studying the text; they may gain insight, but they stop way short of transformed living.

It is better to ask, "As a result of a study of this passage, what specific action might be required to obey the Word?" The leader should bathe his or her study with prayer for God's Spirit to show him or her the cutting edge of the Word where lives are transformed. At this cutting edge is where the lesson aim must be birthed.

In leading a group of learners through a study of Psalm 73, one might have a learning objective that reads: For the learners to respond to the prosperity of evil persons by entering God's sustaining presence (His "sanctuary) to find His perspective. Or you might find it helpful to state the aim in the form of a question a student might ask: What should I do when I struggle spiritually because I see evil doers prospering over others?

In either form, the above aim is general enough to fit almost any student. Everyone struggles with evil and oppression that seems to go unpunished, and everyone struggles against bitterness in the face of oppression and evil. On the other hand, this aim is specific enough in that it asks each student to identify her or his own particular struggles with evil persons who are prospering.

Notice also that the above aim requires the students do something concrete as a result of the Bible study. As a leader, you must desire for learners to take their struggles with evil into the sanctuary (as did the writer of the psalm), and you must do this for yourself. This "sanctuary" is metaphorical as well as literal. It is any place of God's divine presence.

Recognize your limitations. You cannot cause the learners to be transformed, but you can prayerfully guide the group toward that end. The Holy Spirit will work through the group to offer insight as to meaning, to expose to persons their own spiritual condition, and to bring transformation to fruition.

Keep in mind that as the leader,
you are the "leading learner."

Setting the goal for this kind of group Bible study requires that the leader know the members well enough to know the kinds of issues with which they struggle. The stated goal must be something that connects with their lives. It should be as narrow as needed for members to easily connect with as relevant to their personal lives but also broad enough to ensure everyone in the group can relate to it.

Keep in mind that as the leader, you are the "leading learner." During your preparation work, ask yourself how the text connects with your own life. That is a good place to begin thinking about how it intersects with others. This means you must place yourself under the authority of the Word and open yourself for transformation both before and during the group study. You must take your own bitterness into the sanctuary. It has been our experience that God almost always has more for us to learn during the session.

Finally, just as you have an aim for the overall lesson, it is helpful to have an aim for each movement of the lesson. These aims should support and develop the larger aim. They should work together to move the group into completion of the larger aim of the session. The aims for the movements should follow the same guidelines as the session aims.

Movement One:
Sharing Our Testimony

When we gather as the people of God to study His Word, we come with many different backgrounds, experiences, and stories. For the most part, we agree on the important things in life, but we don't agree about everything. We have different thoughts, and even our processes for thinking differ. We bring what we know and what we think we know before the same passage of Scripture. We study one Word, who is the same yesterday, today, and forevermore, yet we come with many words of our own and many stories to tell.

If the group members are followers of Christ, they share in His life and in the life of the Holy Spirit. They should be trusted to search the Scriptures sincerely and honestly if given the opportunity. But we must all come to the Scriptures as "living sacrifices," willing to be judged and transformed by the Word of God. The best way to do this is to offer our testimonies to the group as we study. In this we surface the similarities and the differences in our Christian journeys. By this the group becomes a community with a common desire to know and do the will of God.

As the leader, you must help the learners focus their thoughts and their conversation on the task at hand. The easiest and best way to do that is to help them discover their need to hear the theme of the text. In other words, we don't start a lesson with the text. We begin with common experiences, similar stories, and deep questions that connect us with each other and with the Word of God.

We all live in the tension of knowing and not knowing, loving and not loving, obeying the Word and not obeying the Word. This first movement, *Sharing our Testimony*, ushers the group into that tension. In other words, in light of the passage at hand, you will lead them into the Scriptures by beginning at the place where they need the message of the text. Begin where they are, not where they want to be.

This first movement then is a confessional one. It describes the contours of our anxious hearts—our joys and our sorrows, areas of confidence and sources of fear, struggles we all face, and victories we've won.

As the leader, you know the outcome set before the group (worded in your aim). In light of this outcome, begin preparing for this movement by reflecting on how the text intersects with your own life and then how it intersects with the members of the group.

Sharing our testimony is not just about telling stories about our past. Testimony here refers to sharing with the group some portion of our self-awareness. It may involve a story from our past, but it may be just current reflections on a past event or stating an opinion about a contemporary issue. Simply stated, our testimony is an honest presentation of who we are, given in terms of stories, beliefs, or opinions, etc. It is a statement that connects our lived experiences with our beliefs and convictions. In offering our testimonies for examination by God and by the group, we prepare ourselves for a transforming encounter with God in His Word.

Write an Aim for the Movement

Just as you have developed an overall aim for the session, develop and write down an aim for the first movement. It needs to contribute to the aim for the lesson: "For the students to identify struggles they are having with God allowing evil to go unpunished and to take those struggles "into the sanctuary" for transformation." Or, worded from the student's perspective: "What struggles do I currently have with evil doers who God seems to allow to prosper and what must I do to take my struggles "into the sanctuary" for transformation?

<u>Aim of the First Movement:</u> For the learners to reflect upon a current, or recent, situation in which they struggled to grasp why God was allowing evildoers to flourish. Or, stated from the perspective of a student: When I see God allowing evildoers to prosper, how does it affect me spiritually?

Design a Method

After setting an aim for the movement, decide on a method through which you will attain the goal. Here are three possible methods for achieving our aim: (1) Lead the students in an open discussion of their experiences with evildoers prospering and how it affects them. (2) Prepare a realistic role play scenario in which a person experiences evildoers prospering and have some students role play, discussing their struggles with a friend who is experiencing the same. (3) Show a video clip from a movie that portrays injustice. For instance, a clip from the movie, *Invictus* that portrays the struggles of Nelson Mandela during the ending of the apartheid era would be appropriate. If you choose this method, make certain the clip is no longer than ten minutes. If possible, choose a clip from a movie with which the group would be familiar. Otherwise, be sure to set the clip up with a brief summary of the context of the clip.

<u>Key Questions</u>: Regardless of the method you choose, prepare a few discussion questions that will help the learners connect with the chosen text on a personal level—questions that if answered will lead the group to attain the goal for the first movement. For Psalm 73, they might be as follows: "What are some of the ways you have reacted to situations in which those who prosper are arrogant and prideful?" "How does that situation affect the way you feel about yourself?" "Why is it so difficult to see evildoers prosper when God seems to ignore the good things you are doing?"

You may use your prepared questions in a variety of ways, depending on the method you choose for the first movement. They may constitute the bulk of a guided discussion you will lead. You might use them to stimulate focused discussion following an interactive group exercise. They might be read as rhetorical questions at the opening or closing of the first movement.

Sharing our Testimonies is a movement
designed to open the windows
of our hearts.

Give people opportunity to reflect on their struggles with suffering, good, and evil. Let them know that it is OK to struggle, to have questions, and to doubt. Keep in mind that in this movement you are not to resolve anything or to bring closure. *Sharing our Testimonies* is a movement designed to open the windows of our hearts. It is not a time to talk about the text or to sermonize. It is a time to share, to confess, and to name the past and the present. It is a time for learners to bring to the surface questions that probably already exist deep down inside. As such, this movement is a hopeful one because it anticipates an answer and seeks a future in which there is transformation from "not seeing" to "seeing and obeying."

The *Sharing Our Testimony Movement* should be relatively brief, i.e., typically twelve to fifteen minutes. It serves to whet the appetite for *Searching the Scriptures* and must not become an end in itself. Steer the group away from getting lost in their own narratives. Our stories bind us together, but the answers we seek are found outside of us in the Word of God. This first movement serves to stimulate questions and not to formulate answers. It builds quickly to a shared desire: "Let's see what God's Word says about this."

Movement Two:
Searching the Scriptures

Once the critical question, or set of issues, has been surfaced, move into a search for biblical answers. Remember, *Searching the Scriptures* is the movement in which the group works together in an inductive study of the biblical text. Here, you guide them into making observations on the passage of Scripture. Do not let this movement become a time when you do most of the talking. Stay focused on getting the group to explore what the text says.

Nurture an atmosphere of worship, one in which each member listens for the voice of God speaking into his or her life. Keep the study a group endeavor to encounter God in the truths of His Word. Begin this movement with prayer for God to help the group and its members to see and hear what the text is saying. Don't hesitate to pause for prayer and/or praise at any point in the search.

Also remember, Relational Inductive Bible Study requires us to bring our whole selves into the Word of God. Do not let the group flip a switch and suddenly become a "heads only" gathering. Help them bring their shared testimonies into the text and keep the search connected with life. A simple, one sentence, reminder of something said in the *Sharing Our Testimony* movement given at an appropriate time is sufficient.

Avoid a spirit of debate about ideas. Work for a consensus of understanding, but don't force it. There is room for differing personal opinions but not for arguments about them. Keep the study a group endeavor to encounter God in the truths of His Word.

As leader, you must set the pace of the study, especially for this movement. You must keep the study moving while at the same time ensuring everyone has an opportunity to speak. You must also try to make certain that everyone is understood when speaking. When someone expresses an unclear statement, practice reflective listening, i.e., in your own words, repeat back to the person what you understood the meaning to be: "Sally, am I correct to understand you to be saying…?"

It is helpful to start this movement with the six standard questions: Who? What? When? Where? Why? and How? Then, look at the literary structure and the literary devices used by the author. As leader, you may need to gradually introduce these concepts to the group by pointing them out in the text, but don't become the "expert" with all the answers. Your goal is to help them gain the skills to see for themselves. Above all, teach them to "Observe; Observe; Observe" before they interpret!

A Format for Study

What follows is a recommended format for the second movement:

- Read the entire text being studied. Have one person read the text. Do not take turns reading verses. When you break up the reading of the text, the flow of the text is lost.

- Lead the group in a discussion of the six standard questions. Give opportunity for people to find the answers for themselves. Supplement with your own outside research when the answers are not to be found within the text. You may omit the discussion of the questions that have already been thoroughly addressed in a book study, just briefly restate what the group has previously discovered.

- After the six questions are studied, the group should have a sense of the following: authorship, recipients, dating, main characters, and the main theme(s). When doing a book study, the group should also be aware of how the given text supports the major theme of the book. A brief review of how the group has answered the questions is helpful.

- Next, guide the group in looking at the literary structure of the text. How does the author develop the flow of thought? If complex sentences are present, help the group analyze those sentences so that pronouns and verbs are connected to the correct subjects in the sentence.

- Then, look at the author's use of literary devices: figures of speech, illustrative stories, literary techniques, structural patterns, relational connections. Are metaphors used? Is there parallelism? Are contrasts made? Is there cause and effect? Is sequence present and important? Do you see symbols?

- Finally, move into questions of interpretation: What is the main message God is speaking through this text? What other teachings (themes) come out of this text?

Now let's look at an illustration of the second movement in a study of Psalm 73.

A Sample of Movement Two for Psalm 73

<u>Aim of This Movement</u>: For the students to discover how the writer of Psalm 73 moved from protest and doubt to trust and praise.

<u>Reading of the Text</u>: You may want to have a person read the Psalm dramatically. They could come to the group prepared to 'be' the author (Asaph). You can introduce their reading by saying, "Our guest tonight is the psalmist Asaph. He has a testimony for us of God's deliverance from some deep struggles of faith."

<u>Ask the Six Standard Questions</u>:

Who? Authorship is attributed to Asaph (see superscription placed over the psalm). Asaph was David's music director. He probably wrote much of the music for the psalms, and twelve psalms are attributed to him. *To Whom?* This psalm was written for the people of Israel.

Characters? God, the author/narrator, Israel (the nation), the wicked, "Your People" (CSB)— "the circle of your children" (NRSV), "most people," and the people who praise the wicked.

What? The main theme of the psalm addresses the question of suffering by the righteous in contrast to the prosperity of the wicked. It deals with the eternal destiny ("their end") of the wicked. Supporting themes include the trustworthiness of God and the judgment of God on the wicked.

When? No specific date is given in the text. It is apparent that this is a pre-exilic psalm because of reference to the "sanctuary" (temple). Asaph lived and wrote during the time of both King David and his son, Solomon.

Where? No specific reference is given in the text as to the location of the writing. Most likely, given Asaph's vocation, this psalm was penned in Jerusalem.

Why? This psalm serves as a testimony and witness of God's faithfulness to the righteous and His ultimate judgment of the wicked. It addresses an issue common to those who would be faithful to the Lord.

How? Psalm 73 is an example of Hebrew poetry and is full of Hebrew parallelism.

Make Observations on Literary Structure:

Literary Type and Structure. Psalm 73 is poetic in nature. Each stanza of this psalm uses parallelism. Notice the following:

- Synonymous parallelism:

> But as for me, my feet came close to stumbling (v. 2)
> My steps had almost slipped (v. 3)

- Antithetical parallelism (notice the synonymous parallelism found within the larger structure of antithetical parallelism in Ps 73:1-2):

> God is indeed good to Israel,
>   to the pure in heart.
> But as for me, my feet almost slipped;
>   my steps nearly went astray (CSB).

- *Inclusio*: The beginning and ending of the psalm include the phrase, "But as for me" and refer to God being good.

<u>Make Observations on Literary Devices:</u>

The author makes use of several literary devices.

- Metaphor: In describing the wicked the author uses metaphorical images:

  > Therefore, pride is their necklace,
  > and violence covers them like a garment (v. 6).

  > They set their mouths against heaven,
  > and their tongues strut across the earth (v. 9).

- Simile:

  > "Like one waking from a dream,"
  > "Lord, when arising, you will despise their image" (v. 20).
  > "I was like a brute beast before you" (v. 22, NRSV)

- Climax: There is a clear moment of climax in this psalm that marks the turning point in the author's crisis of faith. Before entering the sanctuary, the author is bitter and questioning God. After coming into the sanctuary of God, where he perceived the end of the wicked, he sees the wicked and himself very differently.

  > When I tried to understand all this,
  > it seemed hopeless
  > until I entered God's sanctuary.
  > Then I understood their destiny (vv. 16-17).

- Contrast: Note the contrast between the author (the pure in heart) and the wicked as found before he entered the sanctuary (73:1-16).

  - <u>Wicked</u>: prosperity, no pains, body is fat, not in trouble, pride, violence, mocking, speaking oppression, setting their mouth against the heavens, their tongue parades through the earth. They ask, "How does God know?" They are always at ease, and they have increased in wealth.

- <u>The author</u>: Envious, stricken all day long, chastened every morning.

And the contrast between the author (the pure in heart) and the wicked that comes after entering the sanctuary (vv. 17-28).

- <u>Wicked</u>: Set in slippery places, cast down to destruction, utterly swept away by sudden terrors, like a dream when one awakens. God will despise their form.
- <u>The author</u>: Sees that when his heart was embittered, he was "senseless and ignorant, like a beast before God." Yet, he knows that "I am continually with Thee. Thou hast taken hold of my right hand." God will guide and receive the author into glory. The nearness of God is his good.

Many more observations can be made on Psalm 73. You can guide students to look and then look again to see what they are looking at. Be careful to lead the group in observing without interpreting. You may have to guide them in the distinction over an extended period. It is hard not to jump into interpretation, but the more observations one can make, the better the interpretation!

The Primary Interpretation

After sufficient observations have been made, lead the group in identifying the primary teaching that comes from this psalm. Do this in light of your overall aim for the lesson. This process may surface other truths within the text. Let those truths be stated and allow the group to affirm or challenge those interpretations. Always seek consensus. Always affirm the person making the observation, even if it is a poor one with which you will have to disagree. Keep the focus on the primary teaching for which there should emerge consensus.

<u>The Perspective of the Sanctuary</u>: Looking again at our sample text, Psalm 73, it is clear that coming into the presence of God

transformed the writer's bitter heart into one of thanksgiving for God's presence in his life; it enabled him to see the present in light of the end. He saw the end of the wicked. He saw his own bitter heart in a new light and saw the goodness and faithfulness of God. In short, he came to understand what is important in his situation. The author concludes, "But as for me, the nearness of God is my good."

Movement Three:
Yielding to the Spirit

The third movement of the Bible study involves yielding to the searching light of the Holy Spirit. The text has been thoroughly studied, and now it is time to give our full attention to what the Lord may be saying to His people about their lives. *Yielding to the Spirit* is a movement of introspection, confession, repentance, and submission to the Word of God. It allows the Spirit to speak directly to the learners (and to the teacher).

This movement challenges the members of the group to receive the Word into their innermost being. This cannot be rushed or forced. Be careful not to get in the way of the Spirit's work. Allow the Holy Spirit to be the teacher. Do not get sermonic, and do not let any group members to become sermonic. The role of the group is to function as a discerning community, seeking to hear how the Spirit desires to apply the Scriptures to their lives.

This is an intentional "figure-ground reversal"—the Bible ceases altogether to be an object of study and becomes (by and with the Spirit) a subject studying the learners. The key questions then are, "What is the Spirit saying to us through this passage about our lives and the world in which we live?" And "In what ways does God desire us to change to more fully conform to the image and will of Christ?"

> "What is the Spirit saying to us through this passage about our lives … in what ways does God desire us to change to more fully conform to the image and will of Christ?"

As we attend to the Spirit's living presence, He will open before us the meaning of the Word for our lives today. The Spirit will reveal the truth of the Scriptures and the truth about us. The Word of God and the people of God are united. We stand together before a real and present God who is actively speaking.

The atmosphere should be one of expectation. The gifts of the Spirit might be manifested. The Lord may speak through words of knowledge, prophecy, or tongues and interpretation. It is critical that we stay open to such insertions. Be a wise elder in these things; encourage people to seek the gifts, taking care to never manufacture them. Lead the group is discerning when the Spirit is speaking. Most often the Spirit confirms the Word through a shared sense of awe the realization that God is speaking.

Do not let this movement degenerate into naming principles that everyone *should* apply to their lives. Principles are like New Year's resolutions; they are easy to make and easy to ignore. Group Bible study should not culminate with learners writing vague opinions on "how to do better." It should serve instead as a sacred event of renewing of our covenant with Christ to live under his lordship.

A Sample of Movement Three for Psalm 73

Aim of This Movement: For the students to reflect prayerfully on a recent struggle with discouragement that was grounded in seeing how the wicked seem to prosper and to interpret themselves in light of Psalm 73.

<u>Key Questions</u>: In what ways do I currently (or recently) find myself oppressed by evil? How is it affecting me to see my oppressors prospering? Looking deep inside, how is this situation impacting my relationship with God? When have I felt that "I have been stricken all day long, and chastened every morning" (Ps 73:14)? How does it affect me when I see the righteous suffer while the wicked to go unpunished?

<u>Method</u>: Have the students write a psalm of lament that would reflect their current or recent situations and the questions they have for God. Encourage them to remain as open and honest as they are comfortable being. The writer of Psalm 73 was honest regarding his feelings. Encourage them to do this as an act of prayer in which they are listening to God.

Depending on how well you know the members of the group, you may have them write a private psalm or work in smaller groups to write one psalm that synthesizes their different experiences. In the first case, the psalms may be shared and discussed with a partner (they should know this will be done before they begin to write). In the second case, the psalms could be shared and discussed with the group.

Movement Four:
Responding to the Call

The last movement of the lesson asks the key question, "How are we to respond to the Word of God?" In this movement, the key elements are action and accountability. As we yield to the Spirit and with honesty face the depths of our heart, we then are ready to respond in obedience to the Living Word.

This is a movement in which transformation takes the shape of behavioral change. In this movement, the underlying question is "Lord, what would you have us do in response to your Word?" The role of the teacher in this movement is to provide opportunity for response and to lead the group in processing the personal and corporate call of the Spirit. It is not the role of the teacher to dictate response.

Know that the power of the Word of God is both particular and general. In other words, the Holy Spirit will convict and transform individual lives, and at the same time, speak corporately to the whole body. This is a great mystery of the power of God's Word to be both personal and corporate.

Give opportunity for the students to name what God is calling them to do in response to the passage. Members should be challenged to support each other in living these things out. One means of encouragement is holding each other accountable for any commitments made. Accountability is not casting judgment on successes and failures but simply inquiring about progress being made.

From time to time, when appropriate, the group should be challenged to plan a group activity in response to the Word they received. It rests largely upon you to identify when a shared response is fitting. In time, ideas may arise from the group. In either case, the plan must be developed by the group. Be a member of the group who fully participates, but do not become responsible for making the event happen.

A Sample of Movement Four for Psalm 73

Aim of This Movement: For the students to identify a place (a sanctuary) where they can take their laments and complaints and for them to commit to take their lament into the presence of God in that place.

Responding: During the coming week, students are to enter their sanctuary and seek God's perspective on their challenges with evil. Afterward, each will write the second half of the psalm they wrote or participated in writing. This second half should reflect their encounter with God in the sanctuary. The following week, give opportunity for students to testify regarding their experiences.

Key Questions: If you do not already have one, where can you make a sanctuary to talk with God about these issues? When can you take your challenges and/or complaints into the sanctuary? What do you expect to happen when you take your complaint before God? What are you willing to happen?

Accountability: While *Responding to the Call* is most often fulfilled after the individual has left the group meeting, that does not make it a private activity. Mutual support must be the norm for small groups. Support requires a measure of accountability. Members should develop relationships in which they interact about their lessons and their responses to them. A limited amount of group time should also be given to follow through on previous lessons.

Closing

The pattern a group follows for concluding their time together is important. It can help solidify the lesson or contribute to devaluing the lesson. It should include prayer toward the sacredness of the group's study. It should also include elements of encouragement and anticipation for what is to come.

Punctuality in the dismissal is also important. Group Bible study can at times generate lively discussions that could last for hours if allowed. If long discussions are allowed, the excitement of the evening will facilitate future absences. Be punctual when you start and when you end. Our rule of thumb is that a group Bible study should have a set length of between one hour and one-and-a-half hours. If the group meets in a home, we advise that there be an agreement that the time between the first person arriving and the last person leaving should not exceed two hours.

Postscript

Father, when we come to you in your Word.

Give us eyes to see, ears to hear, a mind to understand,

and hands to obey.

Help us know your presence and hear your voice.

Accept our disciplined study as service to you.

In this garden of your Word reveal our sins to us

Reveal your righteousness, hear our pleas for mercy,

Forgive our failures,

Renew our faith, our hope, and our strength.

May we know your warm and loving embrace.

May we be more fully formed into the likeness of our Savior.

In His Name we pray.

Amen!

JDJ

APPENDICES

Appendix A

Samples of Segment Titles

The following chart demonstrates how translators and students might disagree about where to place divisions in a book and how to distinguish segments by their titles. The chart lists the segment divisions and titles for Ephesians as they appear in the NRSV (first column on the left), the CSB (second column) NET (third column) translations. The segment divisions and titles prepared by us (the Johns) are in the right-hand column.

Notice that where the three translations agree on how the text should be divided, they offer similar titles. While some disagreement exists on how to divide the ending of Chapter 1, there are several disagreements about where divisions should be placed in Chapters 4 and 5. Also, notice how disagreements over where to divide result in significant disagreements about titles in those chapters.

Points of division and titles are part of the interpretive task. In inductive study, titles should be summative representations of the content of a division. They should be creative summations or interpretations of the text, your summations and/or interpretations. They are an important part of your study.

In preparing our chart of divisions and titles, we (the Johns) attempted to closely follow some literary clues in the text of the book. For example, we observed the recurrence of "walk" (or "live") in the second division and concluded "walk" was an indicator for how the segments should be divided.

Also, in the second major division, notice that we attempted to be faithful to the grammatical mood of the text in the wording of our titles. The CSV and NRSV provide titles that convert Paul's imperative mood (commandments) of the text to declarative/descriptive statements. This overly softens the level of expectation within the Biblical text. Paul is not making suggestions; he is stating his expectations.

Let the translation you use be a starting point for identifying segments, but not the final word. Make your own observations and create your own titles based on your observations of what is actually said in the text.

Examples of Segment Titles

NRSV	CSB	NET	Johns & Johns
1:1-2 *Greeting*	**1:1-2** *Salutation*	**1:1-2** *Salutation*	**1:1-2** *Salutation*
1:3-14 *God's Rich Blessings*	**1:3-14** *Spiritual Blessings in Christ*	**1:3-14** *Spiritual Blessings in Christ*	**1:3-14** *Every Spiritual Blessing*
1:15-19 *Prayer for Spiritual Insight*	**1:15-23** *Paul's Prayer*	**1:15-23** *Prayer for Wisdom and Revelation*	**1:15-23** *Prayer for Enlightened Knowing*
1:20-23 *God's Power in Christ*			
2:1-10 *From Death to Life*	**2:1-10** *From Death to Life*	**2:1-10** *New Life Individually*	**2:1-10** *Made Alive with Christ*
2:11-22 *Unity in Christ*	**2:11-22** *One in Christ*	**2:11-22** *New Life Corporately*	**2:11-22** *Built Together on Christ*

3:1-13 Paul's Ministry to the Gentiles	3:1-13 Paul's Ministry to the Gentiles	3:1-13 Paul's Relationship to the Divine Mystery	3:1-13 Paul's Ministry of Grace
3:14-21 Prayer for Spiritual Power	3:14-21 Prayer for the Readers	3:14-21 Prayer for Strengthened Love	3:14-21 Paul's Prayer for the Fullness of God
4:1-16 Unity and Diversity in the Body of Christ	4:1-16 Unity in the Body of Christ	4:1-16 Live in Unity	4:1-16 Walk Worthy
4:17—5:5 Living the New Life	4:17-24 The Old Life and the New	4:17-32 Live in Holiness	4:17-32 Walk in Love
	4:25—5:2 Rules for the New Life	5:1-5 Live in Love	5:1-5 Walk as Children of Light
5:6-14 Light Versus Darkness	5:3-20 Renounce Pagan Ways	5:6-14 Live in the Light	5:6-14 Walk as Wise

5:15-21 Consistency in the Christian Life	**5:21-33** The Christian Household	**5:15-21** Live Wisely	**5:15-21** Stand Against the Devil
5:22-33 Wives and Husbands		**5:22—6:9** Exhortations to Households	**5:22-33** Husbands and Wives
6:1-4 Children and Parents	**6:1-4** Children and Parents		**6:1-4** Parents and Children
6:5-9 Slaves and Masters	**6:5-9** Slaves and Masters		**6:5-9** Slaves and Masters
6:10-20 Christian Warfare	**6:10-20** The Whole Armor of God	**6:10-20** Exhortations for Spiritual Warfare	**6:10-20** Stand Firm
6:21-24 Paul's Farewell	**6:21-24** Personal Matters and Benediction	**6:21-24** Farewell Comments	**6:21-24** Paul's Closing

Appendix B

Examples of Respaced Text

The following are two examples of respaced text using two translations of Ephesians 1:3-14. The Apostle Paul is especially known for his use of complex sentences, making it difficult to analyze his sentences with confidence. You might note that the CSB appears clearer for the purposes of respacing. It is slightly more "thought for thought" than the NRSV. The NRSV is more closely tied to the original Greek word order which makes the flow of the translation more difficult to read.

You will also notice that the highlighting method is applied to the two examples. The nouns and pronouns naming the members of the Trinity are italicized. References to God the Father are also in bold type. References to Jesus Christ are underlined. References to the Holy Spirit are italicized. This highlighting method helps to clarify the flow of thought by identifying the actions and traits Paul attributes to each member of the Trinity.

Ephesians 1:3-14 (CSB)

Blessed is the **God and Father** *of our Lord Jesus Christ*,
  who has blessed us with every spiritual blessing
    in the heavens in Christ.
For **he** chose us *in him*,
    before the foundation of the world,
    to be holy and blameless in love *before him*.
He predestined us to be adopted as sons
    through *Jesus Christ* for **himself**,
    according to the good pleasure of **his** will,
    to the praise of **his** glorious grace
      that **he** lavished on us in the *Beloved One*.
      In him we have redemption through **his** blood,
        the forgiveness of our trespasses,
        according to the riches of *his* grace
          that *he* richly poured out on us
            with all wisdom
            and
            understanding.
He made known to us the mystery of **his** will,
    according to **his** good pleasure
that **he** purposed in *Christ*
  as a plan for the right time —
    to bring everything together *in Christ*,
    both
    things in heaven
    and
    things on earth *in him*.
In him we have also received an inheritance,
  because
    we were predestined
      according to the plan
        of the **one** who works out everything
        in agreement with the purpose of **his** will,
    so that
    we
      who had already put our hope in *Christ*
      …might bring praise to **his** glory.
In him you also were sealed with the promised *Holy Spirit*
  when you heard the word of truth,
    the gospel of your salvation,
  and
  when you believed.
The *Holy Spirit* is the down payment of our inheritance,
    until the redemption of the possession,
    to the praise of **his** glory.

Ephesians 1:3-14 (NRSV)

Blessed be the **God and Father** of our *Lord Jesus Christ*,
  who has blessed us *in Christ*
    with every spiritual blessing in the heavenly places,
just as **he** chose us *in Christ*
    before the foundation of the world
    to be holy and blameless
    before **him** in love.
He destined us for adoption as **his** children *through Jesus Christ*,
    according to the good pleasure of **his** will,
    to the praise of **his** glorious grace
      that **he** freely bestowed on us *in the Beloved*.
      In *him* we have redemption through *his* blood,
        the forgiveness of our trespasses,
        according to the riches of *his* grace
          that *he* lavished on us.

With all wisdom and insight
he has made known to us the mystery of **his** will,
    according to **his** good pleasure that **he** set forth *in Christ*,
  as a plan for the fullness of time,
    to gather up all things *in him*,
    things in heaven
    and
    things on earth.
In Christ we have also obtained an inheritance,
    having been destined
      according to the purpose **of him**
      who accomplishes all things
        according to **his**
          counsel
          and
          will,
    so that
    we,
      who were the first to set our hope *on Christ*,
      …might live for the praise of **his** glory.
In him you also, …
    when you had heard the word of truth,
      the gospel of your salvation,
    and
    had believed *in him*,
…were marked with the seal of the promised *Holy Spirit*;
    this is the pledge of our inheritance
      toward redemption
      as **God's** own people,
  to the praise of **his** glory.

Appendix C

RIBS Sample Worksheets

The following worksheets should be used as templates. Line spacing and other issues of sizing should be adjusted as is appropriate for personal observations, interpretations, and responses.

RIBS Survey Worksheets

First Reading

Observation	Interpretation	Response

Second Reading

Observation	Interpretation	Response
Who:		
What:		
When:		

	Where:				Why:				How:			

Third Reading

Observation	Interpretation	Response
Expansion/Correction of Previous Observations/Interpretations:		
Literary Structure:		

Themes:

Other:

RIBS Segment Worksheet

Book Title: _____
Subdivision Title: _____
Segment Title: _____

Division Title: _____
Sub-subdivision Title: _____

Text	Observation	Interpretation	Response

Appendix D

Recurrence in Ephesians

Charting the repetition of words, phrases, concepts, events, locations, etc., is an excellent tool for identifying themes and structures in the books of the Bible. When preparing charts, always keep types of observations together. Place theological words and concepts on one chart, locations on another chart, event types on another chart.

A quick review of this chart reveals that the theological concepts are concentrated in the first division of Ephesians (Chapters 1-3). On the other hand, they are especially concentrated in the first subdivision/segment ("Unity in the Body of Christ," 4:1–16) of the second division (Chapters 4–5). This might suggest that this segment serves as a transition between the doctrinal emphasis of the first division and the behavioral emphasis of the second division.

Recurring Theological Terms in Ephesians
(Segment titles and divisions are from the CSB)

Concept / Segment	"grace"	"faith" "faithful"	"mystery"	"body" of Christ	Christ as "head"
Salutation 1:1-2	1:2	X			
Spiritual Blessings in Christ 1:3-14	X (2)		X		
Paul's Prayer 1:15-23		X		X	X
From Death to Life 2:1-10	X (3)	X			X
One in Christ 2:11-22				X	
Paul's Ministry to the Gentiles 3:1-13	X	X	X (3)	X	
Prayer for the Readers 3:14-21		X			
Unity in the Body of Christ 4:1-16	X	X (2)		X (3)	X
The Old Life and the New 4:17-24					
Rules for the New Life 4:25--5:2	X				
Renounce Pagan Ways 5:3-20					
The Christian Household 5:21-33			X	X	X
Children and Parents 6:1-4					
Slaves and Masters 6:5-9					
The Whole Armor of God 6:10-20		X	X		
Personal Matters and Benediction 6:21-24	X (2)	X			

Sources/Recommended Reading

Arthur, Kay Lee, David Arthur, and Pete De Lacy, *How to Study Your Bible: Discover the Life-Changing Approach to God's Word*, Eugene, OR: Harvest House Publishers, 2014 (first published in 1994).

> No one has done more to popularize and resource inductive Bible study than Kay Arthur and Precept Ministries International (PMI), a ministry she co-founded with her husband, Jack, in 1970. PMI has developed a global ministry of training persons in how to do inductive Bible study and how to lead Bible study groups based on the inductive method. PMI publishes an extensive collection of curricular material for Bible study based on the inductive approach.

> We offer one small criticism of their work. The ministry is devoutly Evangelical on the fundamentalist and Reformed side of theological commitments. This bias is subtle and appears most often in the kinds of questions raised in the curriculum.

Köstenberger, Andreas J. and Richard Alan Fuhr. *Inductive Bible Study: Observation, Interpretation, and Application through the Lenses of History, Literature, and Theology.* Nashville: B&H Academic, 2016

This book is one of the more recent texts on inductive study. It integrates current issues in biblical hermeneutics with inductive Bible study, making it a good textbook for Evangelical seminaries but not well suited for local congregations.

Leigh, Ronald. *Direct Bible Discovery: A Practical Guidebook for Personal Bible Study.* Nashville: Broadman Press, 1982.

Traina, Robert A. *Methodical Bible Study*, Zondervan Academic 2002 (First edition 1952).

Traina, Robert A. and David R. Bauer. *Inductive Bible Study: A Comprehensive Guide to the Practice of Hermeneutics.* [Baker Academic; Reprint edition (August 5, 2014 (First edition 2011.)

Robert Traina might be considered the dean of inductive Bible study. His foundational book, *Methodical Bible Study*, was first published in 1952 and has since then been a standard textbook on Bible study methods in Evangelical Bible colleges and seminaries.

Traina was a professor of biblical studies at The Biblical Seminary (now New York Theological Seminary), the school founded by Wilbert White for the express purpose of training ministers using the inductive approach to Bible study. Traina later moved to Asbury Theological Seminary, where he served as academic dean and professor of biblical studies for several decades.

In 2011, a major revision of *Methodical Bible* Study was published posthumously with coauthor David R. Bauer under the title, *Inductive Bible Study: A Comprehensive Guide to the Practice of Hermeneutics.* While the original volume was readily accessible to lay persons, the revised version is aimed at graduate seminarians.

Traina's influence on Evangelical Bible study cannot easily be overstated.

About the Authors

Jackie David Johns (PhD – The Southern Baptist Theological Seminary) is Professor of Practical Theology at the Pentecostal Theological Seminary where he has been a faculty member since 1985. Prior to pursuing his doctoral degree, he served for 3 years as an instructor at Northwest Bible College in Minot, North Dakota (1976-79). Jackie is an Ordained Bishop in the Church of God (Cleveland). Always committed to the ministry of the local church, he has served as pastor to congregations in North Dakota, Kentucky, and Tennessee. Most recently, he was the pastor of a congregation he with his wife founded in Cleveland, Tennessee where he served for 27 years (1989-2016).

Cheryl Bridges Johns (PhD – The Southern Baptist Theological Seminary) serves in the role of Distinguished Visiting Professor at United Theological Seminary. Prior to that she served as Professor of Christian Formation and Spiritual Renewal for 35 years at the Pentecostal Theological Seminary (1986-2021). Cheryl is an Ordained Minister in the International Pentecostal Holiness Church. She is a noted Pentecostal theologian who has served as President of the Society of Pentecostal Studies. She is a sought-out conference speaker and convention preacher.

Jackie and Cheryl both grew up in the classical Pentecostal tradition and have sought to influence that movement to be faithful to the heart of its history while also being faithful to rising generations that need to hear and understand the gospel of Jesus Christ. They are the parents of two daughters: Alethea Allen, MD and Karisa Smith, PsyD. They have five grandchildren who Jackie refers to as "prototypes of perfection": Camdyn Allen, Charlie Allen, Carter Allen, Tegan Smith, and Harper Smith.

Made in the USA
Columbia, SC
09 March 2025

54817311R00213